RECORD

OF THE

FEDERAL DEAD

BURIED FROM
LIBBY, BELLE ISLE, DANVILLE
AND CAMP LAWTON

PRISONS

AND AT

CITY POINT, AND IN THE FIELD BEFORE
PETERSBURG AND RICHMOND

PUBLISHED BY THE
U.S. CHRISTIAN COMMISSION,
FROM REPORTS OF ITS AGENTS

HERITAGE BOOKS
2012

HERITAGE BOOKS

AN IMPRINT OF HERITAGE BOOKS, INC.

Books, CDs, and more—Worldwide

For our listing of thousands of titles see our website
at
www.HeritageBooks.com

A Facsimile Reprint
Published 2012 by
HERITAGE BOOKS, INC.
Publishing Division
100 Railroad Ave. #104
Westminster, Maryland 21157

Originally published
Philadelphia:
James B. Rodgers, Printer
52 & 54 North Sixth Street
1866

International Standard Book Numbers
Paperbound: 978-1-55613-344-2
Clothbound: 978-0-7884-9430-7

CONTENTS.

RICHMOND—BELLE ISLE, ... 5

RICHMOND—OAKLAND CEMETERY, ... 8

COLD HARBOR, ... 11

DANVILLE, ... 16

POINT OF ROCKS, ... 42

CITY POINT—DEPOT FIELD HOSPITAL, ... 69

CITY POINT—NEAR LEPSEY'S HOUSE, ... 90

CITY POINT—CAVALRY CORPS CEMETERY, ... 93

CITY POINT—ON LINE OF RAILROAD, ... 97

MEADE STATION—THE RUFFIN PLANTATION, &C. &C., ... 101

PETERSBURG—FAIR GROUNDS HOSPITAL, &C., ... 118

FIELDS BEFORE RICHMOND AND PETERSBURG, ... 142

SAILOR'S CREEK, ... 157

CAMP LAWTON, GA., ... 159

INDEX, ... A

PREFACE.

The work of examining and cataloguing the graves of the heroes of the Secession War, in and around Richmond, was undertaken in behalf of friends at home, to save them the weary task of groping among the dead for their loved and lost ones. The results of the work, which was carried on by the Agents of the Christian Commission, under the direction of HEN. C. HOUGHTON, Chief of the Individual Relief Department, are embodied in the following pamphlet, which can lay claim to only an approximate accuracy. Further search might furnish additional particulars, and we doubt not that such search will be made. But even in aid of this, the record here given will be valuable.

NOTE.

THE following statements will help give a correct impression of the condition of the graves in the different burial-places mentioned, and an estimate of the probability that there have been other soldiers buried, of whom no identification can now be made.

In all the lists, the graves are given in the order in which they lie.

The lists of Danville and Camp Lawton were copied from an official record; all the others were taken from the boards put up by comrades. In many cases the marks are in pencil, and will soon fade out. In others, the boards, which are often rude and small, will soon decay, and the possibility of identification cease, unless some friendly hand interpose with a more lasting memorial. Quartermaster-General Meigs is already giving attention to this important matter; and it is to be hoped that all our honored dead will be gathered out of all the battle-fields into permanent and beautiful cemeteries, where their names, cut in stone, will be read as long as their deeds are remembered and loved.

BELLE ISLE.—Nearly all of the graves marked with head boards. Names well cut in by the knives of comrade soldiers.

OAK WOOD CEMETERY, (page 8,) (not Oakland,) contains the bodies of soldiers buried from Libby Prison. Graves were in very bad condition; not one in twenty had any mark; many more had only sticks at each end. The colored sexton told us that the poor people had taken off the boards for fuel during the winter. All graves that could in any way be identified, have been marked, as stated on page 8.

POINT OF ROCKS CEMETERY.—Graves all neatly marked, and list complete. This was the cemetery for the base hospital of the Army of the James. ` Soldiers who died in their regimental camps during the winter, were brought here for burial.

CITY POINT—Depot Field Hospital.—Graves all well marked. List complete.

CITY POINT.—List complete.

CITY POINT, CAVALRY CORPS CEMETERY.—Graves well marked. List complete.

The lists from page 97 to 159, were taken from the head-boards. Ordinarily, the date of the death is marked on the boards, but is not given in these lists. There are a few graves, and but a few, scattered over these fields without a mark. For them no identification is possible, except by some one who witnessed the burial. Over the marked graves the rude lettering cut with a pocket knife in rough boards. Sometimes, on a hewn stick, or tree, or barrel stave, is found an eloquent token of reverent affection for a fallen comrade.

CAMP LAWTON.—A register of *deaths*, (not of graves,) probably complete. See page 159.

Philadelphia, Dec. 26th, 1865.

BELLE ISLE.

The Cemetery at Belle Isle has been fenced in by the Commission, but the head-boards remain as when the city was occupied, the
names being carved in, not painted.

R. Gillingham, B, 72d P. V., February 2, 1864.
T. Herkness, H, 154th N. Y., January 28th, 1864.
Edward Brisell, D, 5th Iowa, December 27, 1863.
B. Stephens, C, 45th N. Y., January 5, 1864.
I. Alts, A, January 2, 1864.
W. Ladon, G. } Both on one board.
I. Kent, D, January 3, 1864. }
H. T. Moss, 4th Me., January 3, 1864.
J. R. Kemple, B, I. V., January 4, 1864.
J. Oipper, F, 63d O., Jan 4, 1864.
A. G. Woodburn, H. 1st Va., January 4, 1864.
C. Schneider, E., 19th J. Cav., December 28, 1863.
F. Gregory, C, 18th P. V., June 5, 1864.
G. Hilber, I, 11th Ky., January 5, 1864.
W. Graham, D, 1st U. S. I., January 5, 1864.
H. Crow, E, 72d P. V., January 5, 1864.
J. Ashford, C, 5th Ind., January 9, 1864.
B. Sheneler, I, 16th Me., January 9, 1864.
S. B. Paul, A, 1st Ky., January 5, 1864.
George Hale, D, 120th N. Y., February 17, 1864.
F. Biggord, A, 45th O., February, 1864.
H. Whittim, D, 10th Wis., January 26, 1864.
G. W. Nudham, E, 2d Tenn., January 23, 1865.
R. Styes, G, Loudon Rang., January 26th, 1865.
John Lewis, G, 11th Ky., February 1, 1864.
W. Connoy, (citizen) February 19, 1864.
—— McConnanckel, L, 16th Ill., February 22, 1864
S. H. Miller, I, 12th Mass., February 22, 1864.
W. Welch, G, 14th Conn., February 25, 1864.
—— McGinnes, M, 14th P. V., February 18, 1864
O. Watherspoon, I, 75th O., December 23, 1863.
J. Sharp, F, 57th P. V., December 23, 1863.
T. Dihey, B, 151st N. Y., December 19, 1863.

Ollis Shindler, F, 31st Miss., December 13, 1863.
R. Reortburn, E, 2d Tenn., December 11, 1863.
Nathaniel Bartlett, C, 16th Me., December 10, 1863.
Er—— Pettijilu, A, 27th Minn., January 10, 1863.
Reuben Ladd, H, 4th Vt., December 8, 1863.
Henri Palmer, A, 123d Ohio, December 8, 1863.
M. Corcoran, A, 28th Mass., December 7, 1863.
Q. M. Taylor, E, 154th N. Y., December 3, 1863.
Claus West, A, 92d N. Y., November 29, 1863.
Dennis Ryan, (citizen) November 24, 1863.
N. Marsh, E, Ringold's Battery, November 22, 1863.
M. Kidd, H, 1st Ky., November 18, 1863.
W. Sledmond, H, 8th Tenn. Cav., November 17, 1863.
C. Tatter, B, 20th Ind., November 17, 1863.
G. Gabbits, C, 6th N. Y., November 17, 1863.
Wm. Kute, G, 1st Mich. Cav., November 14, 1863.
Ch. Martin, C, 18th Mass., Nov. 14, 1863.
Dan Gorton, B, 45th O., November 14, 1863.
Jesse Hill, C, 71st P. V., November 14, 1863.
C. Putts, Band of 14th U. S., January 29, 1864.
S. N. Grove, H, 45th Ohio, June 31, 1864
P. J. Mahoney (shot) D, 12th Mich.
Ed. R. Clark, September 14, 1863.
T. Myers, 8th Pa. Cav., A, September 22, 1864.
B. Willis, H, 30th Ind., October 6, 1863.
Nie Jentees, I, 2d Wis., October 8, 1863.
A. Clark, G, 6th Wis., October 4, 1863.
John Sprague, I, 12th P. V., December 10, 1863.
A. Lamoreau, D, 143d P. V., October 20th, 1863.
W. Limbarter, F, 4th Mich., (shot) October 25, 1863.
H. Slory, H, 4th Md., October 27, 1863.
John McKinsy, K, 75th O., October 31, 1863.
John Vansel, B, 1st Tenn. Cav., November 12, 1863.
Dav— Ridg——, I. 45th, November, 1863.
W. Risling, E, 76th P. V., November 2, 1863.
W. Fisthaner, B, 107th Ohio, October 27, 1863.
M. Oloden, A, 4th Mich., October 27, 1863.
Alf. Montrison, H, 154th N. Y., October 12, 1863.
Wil. Sanders, G, 2d W. Tenn., October 20, 1863.
W. Starkweather, D, 64th Rifles, N. Y., October 16, 1863.
A. D. Brotschi, G, 173d N. Y., October 8, 1863.
John Recom, K, 7th N. J., October 7, 1863.
G. W. Adeloser, L, 1st Md. Cav., September 25, 1863.
Wm. Meng, I, 28th Ill., September 15, 186—.
L. Butcher, M, 7th Ohio Cav., February 7, 1864.
A. Burns, D, 1st N. Y., February 5, 1864.
W. Hoffman, E, 11th N. Y., February 5, 1864.
P. Wolf, E, 1st Tenn., January 5, 1864.
W. W. Gracce, F, 46th P. V.
Chas. Tinkpunner, K, 73d N. Y., December 26, 1863.
H. Walters, G, 126th N. Y., December 26, 1863.

S. H. Spees, G, 45th Ohio, December 25, 1863
P. Curran, K, 14th N. J., November 14, 1863.
Wilh. Detrow, D, 10th Ky., October 14, 1863.
John White, G, 150 N. Y., November 13, 1863.
W. Ricket, H, 97th N. Y., (shot) November 8, 1863
S. Weeber, F, 124th Ohio, November 1, 1863.
R. Richards, D, 4th Me., October 28, 1863.
J. Conray, I, 2d U. S., October 27, 1863.
James Tayler, B, 100th Ohio, October 20, 1863.
W. Clemment, E, 12th N. H., October 20, 1863.
Sam'l Vulso, F, 13th P. V. Cav., October 17, 1863.
Jos. Asher, B, 10th Wis., October 8, 1863.
Jos. Domer, B, 100th Ohio, October 7, 1863.
John Assar, E, 4th Me. Cav., September 28, 1863.
Dan'l Walker, A, 100th N. Y. S. V.
E. Maxfield, G, 122d O. V. I.
Wm. Allen, F, 2d Md., January 31, 1864.
J. Seller, I, 10th Va., January 31, 1864.
A. Washburn, I, 14th N. Y.
James North, K, 154th N. Y., September 18, 1863.
A. Beardsley, K, 10th N. Y. Cav., October 3, 1863.
D. Johnston, I, 125th N. Y., October 7, 1863.
W. F. Hendri, D, 11th N. Y. Cav., October 18, 1863
———— Hammacher, K, 88th Ill., October 17, 1863.
B. Bowman, F, 2d Pa. Cav., October 20, 1863.
A. Smith, A, 104th N. Y., October 25, 1863.
Jos. Graham, E, 105th P. V., October 27, 1863.
Francis Thorp, B, 40th N. Y., October 31, 1863.
J. Miller, A, 2d W. Tenn. Cav., November 1, 1863.
H. Seister, H. 52d N. Y., November 9, 1863.
Jas. Tibbit, H, 20th Ind., November 13, 1863.
H. Lockran, I, 2d Va., November 14, 1863.
W. E. O. Dyne, December 26, 1863.
W. Barnard, A, 2d Tenn., February 18, 1864.
J. Weber, K, 2d Me., February 18, 1864.
C. Wheeler, F, 14th Conn., February 17, 1864.
H. Lewis, E, 119th P. V., February 12, 1864.
T. Evans, A, 11th Tenn., February 9, 1864.
M. S. Leidsinger, C, 56th P. V., February 3, 1864
R. Cillengham, B, 73d P. V., February 6, 1864.
J. Hawsey, H, 95th N. Y., February 9, 1864.

OAKLAND CEMETERY.

The following are the graves of those who died in Libby Prison, and who were buried in a gravelly ravine just outside of the Oakland Cemetery, one and a half miles out of Richmond. The Commission, through its agents, Messrs. Clarke and A. Lawrence, provided new head-boards, with the names neatly painted, for every grave which could be identified, and procured an order to have the ground fenced in, which was done by the Quartermaster, under their inspection.

Asst. Surg. H. L. Pierce, 5th Md.
J. Selrick, 1st Md.
W. J. Jemmins.
Geo. Pyersin, 6th Mich.
Arthur Shill, (incomplete.)
Lewis O'Lury, G, 101st O. V.
J. Jinical, 13th Penna.
A. Davis, 131st.
W. Ward, 150th Pa.
J. S. Potter, 22d Mich.
H. G. Ling, D, 24th Mich.
James McDewell, 16th Pa.
J. Inhoff, H, 9th Mass.
Charles Shind, 103d Pa.
J. Trimpert.
H. Michell, B, 4th Me.
Anthony
D. Valentine,
A. Hart, 37th Wis.
William Robe.
Thos. Jones, 44th Ohio.
Woolcott, 1st Mass.
J. Pierce, G, 5th Mich.
F. Codrag—
F. Japl—(incomplete.)
J. Briggs, 7th A.
J. Kilear, E, 95th N. Y.
W. Waycox.
R. Frankl—
C. Peakring,

C. Hardien, H, 151st N. Y.
J. O, Bumin, K.
A. L. Vanlack, G, 126th Ohio.
Jno. E. Os——, 11th N. Y.
Rugles L——ll, 3d M.
R. R. Labdey, 4th Mich.
W. C. Bell—, G.
J. E. Crakl—
H. Goodrich, G, 44th Ill.
Fulton Linc—
Jno. Chick, 59th Ohio.
J. H. Tomsen.
Shelton, 3d Tenn.
O. B. Hin——
H. Venman, Mass.
J. Dilkson, H, 77th Pa.
William Dan—
F. Schlotman, 110.
F. Rabb, 16th Pa.
Jno. Cooly.
William Cass.
J. Cleamond, 92 Ohio.
Isaac Stiles.
H. E. Eagear, Penn.
Wm. Wright, 7th.
James Decker, 76th Pa.
Matly Leic—, 78.
G. Zimmerman, B. Granby, 95th N. Y.
J. Bu——, 64th Mich., O. Bryant.
H. Hach, 52 N. Y., J. Stock.
J. L. Buttran, 143d Pa.
E. Bellows, G, Wm. Howley.
G. Shult, B. Bates, C. Parker.
Henry Friday, 100.
H. Cobran, Samuel Alexander.
G. C. B. Bigdy, G, 76th.
J. Harman, 7th Me.
Wm. F. Dim——
Linsey, 59th Ohio.

The following list of names was obtained by Rev. J. B. Clark, from boards in Oakwood Cemetery. Lot on top of the hill:

Capt. H. J. Biddle, Maj. Gen. McCall's Div., U. S.
M. G. Baker, New York.
Chas. Jin——, Mich.
C. M. Walker, A, 7th U. S.
E. H. Smith, A, 7th Mich.
Corp'l W. M. Asnew, I, 140th Pa.
G. C. Mulky, F, 137th N. Y.
J. Kilenced, D, 27th Ct.
Wm. Thim—, 12.

P. Wittmer—
N. C. T.
2d Lt: J. B. King, G, 10th N. Y.
D. Thornton, 15th N. Y.
Lt. J. T. Jenkins, 154th N. Y.
A. W. Scott.
Corp'l Isaac I. Danenhower, M, 18th Pa. Cav.
Q. H. Rix.
Z. M. Patton.
Jno. Mason.
W. Bartholomew.
J. Summer, 7th Mich.
A. Harris, D, 48th N. Y.
H. L. Hayes, 110th Ohio.
F. Koering, 74th Pa.
J. Hunter, 2d N. Y.
B. Rowe, 16th Mich.
J. Foltz, Penn.
A. R. Greller.
Vuandeslin.
G. Iris.
Lt. J. T. Kitchem.
W. Body, K, 99th Pa.
Forbes.
M. Hogerson.
H. W. Tres—
B. Cossin.
B. Garrith.
A. Wise.
Joneles.
A. McCluney.
H. Frank.
C. G. Elliott.
Spencer Deaton.
Jno. Johnson.
H. Hensley.
Hugh Conner, 1st Engineers.
Jno. Huney.
——— Goodhue, 6th Maine.
P. Waltch.
M. Cross, 3d Mich.
J. P. Hutchins.
Nolenger.
H. Bell, 1st Engineers.

COLD HARBOR.

The following list of 141 graves, was prepared by Rev. E. F. Williams, Agent of the Commission, who, with Mr. Gilbert, of the American Bible Society, accompanied Gen. Ord's detail, sent May 1st, 1865, to bury the remains left on the field of battle. The bodies were securely buried, and the graves properly marked, and could now be easily obtained, if desired.

Names of persons killed at Cold Harbor, from June 1 to June 12, 1864, who were buried by comrades along our line of works, and their graves properly marked. Left of the road from New to Old Cold Harbor, just beyond common grave No. 1, in the valley, the following names appear:—

Chas. Saunders, F, 82d P. V. Killed June 1.
Jas. Farrell, H, 82d P. V., of Concord, Erie Co., Pa. Killed June 1.
Corp. Albert A. Jones, Co. A, 3d Conn. Killed June 1. Harrington, Litchfield Co.
Unknown. Envelope found, addressed "Surgeon Chas. H. Wilson, 49th P. V.,Washington, D. C."
1st Lieut. A. B. Blackman, G, 106th N. Y.
S. Hammond, C, 51st N. C. Right-hand side of the road.
Riley Jones, 82d P. V. Killed June 3.
Will Palmer, B, 82d P. V. Killed June 3. Grave violated; other graves undisturbed. Just in rear of main line of works.
Jas. E. Ross, D, 122d N. Y.
Sergt. H. McGlathray, F, 82d P. V. June 1.
Sergt. Benj. S. Young, G, 82d P. V. June 5.
Francis P. Lewis, G, 82d P. V. June 1.
H. L. Wells, K, 82d P. V.
Lewis C. Hang, B, 3d N. Y. June 1.
A. Eslich, K, 10th N. J.
Edward N. Bower or Bowen, G, 2d N. J.
Chas. Winckler, H, 10th N. J. Killed June 2.
E. M. M. Marchsess, Battery F, 1st Vt. Art'y. Killed by a shell.
Arthur Foster, C, 1st N. J.
George England.
N. F. Ball, A, 20th Mass. June 3
1st Lieut. J. B. Thompston, 19th Mass. June 3. Buried under an apple tree, near Gathwright's house.
Sergt. Stephenson. Could not be buried separate from others. Red stripe on pants indicated artillery.

O. E. Crommett, B, 19th Me. June 9.
H. C. Joice, I, 19th Me. June 9.
D. Chase, B, 20th Me.
Thos. Allen, B, 59th N. Y. Killed June 11.
John Wagenhauser, B, 59th N. Y. June 11.
Wm. Fee, B, 19th Mass.
E. D. Two cornelian rings on person, and one with badge of Q. A. C.
upon it. In possession of soldier who found them.
Unknown, bearing a medal marked Chas. F. May, A, 15th Mass. Badge
of 9th A. C. *Small Ambrotype.*

[A large number of bodies found in the water, near a fence, with nothing
to identify them, save a mark on one of the men, showing that they
belonged to the 3d N. Y. H. A. Now buried.]

Jas. Brown, G, 14th Conn. June 9.
B. Shay, I, 1st U. S. S. Shooters. June 4.
Wm. C. Brown, F, 14th Conn.
Enoch Smith, C, 12th N. J. June 5.
Jas. Ryan, 170th N. Y. June 12.
Saml. Maltson, 12th N. J. June 4.
Corp. Wm. McDaniels, 12th N. J.
C. C. Mead, H, 12th N. J.
Corp. W. W. Collins, G, 12th N. J. June 3.
Sergt. G. P. Chase, 10th N. Y. June 3. } On one board.
David A. Doremus, A, 10th N. Y.? }
H. Scarr, I, 1st Del.
Jos. R. Edwards, G, 12th N. J. June 3.
Edw'd Mills, D, 12th N. J. June 3.
Serg't Wm. W. Warren, A, 1st Del. June 3.
John W. Welsh, G, 69th P. V. Killed June 11.
David R. Snowden, A, 184th P. V. Killed June 3.
Wm. Beach, C, 184th P. V.
Wm. Hadsell or Radsell, G, 154th N. Y. June 5.
Patrick Farrell, 69th N. Y. Died June 3.
Daniel Ice, 7th W. Va. June 2.
R. R. Myers, C, 7th W. Va. June 5.
2d Lieut. D. F. Potter, A, W. Va. June 3. 2d A. C.

The foregoing names belong mostly to 6th A. C.
The graves from J. B. Thompson to this last, inclusive, are just in rear
of second line of our works, in a line just front of Gathwright's house,
to the right of the road going towards O. Cold Harbor, and in edge of
woods front and in rear of a ground line of works going towards Quaker Road, towards our left.

The following names probably belong to men in the 2d A. C.:
Corp. J. D. Martin, A, 7th W. Va. June 3.
J. Cupp, A, W. Va. June 3.
Albert W. Heudershott, B, 7th W. Va. June 3.
John H. Felty, E, 7th W. Va. June 7.

Patrick McMullen, B, 1st Mass. H A. June 5.
John W. King, I, 164th N. Y. Killed in action, June 5.
Marmaduke Hill. Near common grave.
T. Wood, F, 10th N. J.
Jos. Howell, F, 82d P. V.
Corp. E. H. Tarbox, A, 82d P V. Killed June 3.
Chas. Saunders, F, 82d P. V. June 1.
P. A. Fenn, D, 2d Conn. Killed June 12.
Casper Mongèe, B, 14 N. J. June 11.
A. S. Nethers, rebel.
J. E. Henderson, D, 42d N. C.
Gilson M. Berryman, F, 42d N. C.
J. F. Leach, F, 42d N. C.
Sergt. I. Kennedy, C, 8th Ala. Killed June 7.

N. J. Doris, B, 11th Ala. Right of Quaker road, and with other graves
previously mentioned, toward Holt's House.
Chas. E. Byus, E, 2d Md., rebel Inf'y. Killed June 3.
M. Leggite, H, Orris' Reg't, S. C.

There are several other graves marked, belonging to this Reg't, on the
right of the road, in the woods, just after you pass a little stream which
crosses the road a few rods from Steward's house.

South east of Peter McGee's house:—
M. W. Beddick, K, 53d P V.
J. Hosmer, K, 53d P. V.
C. E. Besom, K, 53d P. V

East of the house, in a little valley, under the garden:—
Lt. Thomas McClure, Batt'y F, 7th N. Y. H. A. Killed June 4.
"Peace to his ashes; we have lost a brave, faithful, good officer, beloved
by all of his company. His loss can never be replaced. Sacred be the
spot that holds his remains."

Geo. Adams, and Chas. Edgerton, B, 7th N. Y. H. A. June 3.
J. Koomtz, C, 148th P. V. June 3.
W. H. Humphreys, H, 64th N. Y. June 4.
J. Cary, A, 40th P. V.

Grave near cherry tree, not far from last grave mentioned, which is on
Martin's place, in woods, marked,   Miller, —— Vt. June 11.
Sergt. J. W. Hutchinson, Batt'y A, 1st Vt. Killed June 10. His grave
is on left of Old Cold Harbor road, opposite Gathwright's house.
Sgt. J. D. Cunningham, B, 49th P. V. June 7. Under a wild cherry,
directly opposite Gathwright's house.
Two graves at foot of hill, marking obliterated. Fine head-boards.

Lt. C. S. Shepherd, G, 106th N. Y. June 1.
Corp'l H. R. Putnam, D, 118th N. Y. Killed June 3.
W. Dougherty, A, 118th N. Y. Killed June 10.
Geo. Speer, C, 2d Conn.

C. C. Hall, 4th N. J.
G. W. Parmeter, B, 92d N. Y.
John H. Wilson, H, 2d R. I.
Anson G. Smith, K, 2d R. I.

Several detached head-boards, either pulled up ruthlessly, or more probably, left on the ground after the bodies had been removed, marked as follows:

Riley Jones, A, 82d P. V.　June 3.
Jas. Gallagher, G, 122d N. Y.
Found on a pair of drawers:—S. J. Grimes, D, 155th N. Y
Lucian, 164th N. Y.

　Edge of Pine Woods, opposite Gathwright's house:
First Lt. Chas. P. Glauphlin, Co. F. 138 P. V.
Franklin Putt, B, 55th P. V.
Charles M. Davis, H, 55th P. V.
Corporal Zeringer, A, 148th N. Y.
F. L. Hillgars, B, 148th N. Y.　June 3.
John Slater, F, 148th N Y
J. P. R., D, 148th N. Y.
C. White, C, 148th N. Y.
Henry Goodrich, D, 115th N.Y.　June 3d.
Edward Coules, K, 115—
Corporal H. B. Putnam, D, 118 N. Y.　June 3d.

William Dougherty, A, 118 N. Y.　June 10th.　Across, under a cherry tree, near front of Gathwright's house:

Sergeant George Bolton, B, 77th N. Y.　June 4th.
Wm. E. Cole, H, 77th N. Y.　June 3.　Common grave No. 7.
Adam Beltey, 138th P. V., 2d Div.
L. Logan, K, 8th Me.　June 4.
Ord. Sergt. S. M. McGlathing.
Sergt. Benj. S. Young, G, 82d P. V.　Killed June 5.
Lewis C. Hang, B, 3d N. Y.
Sergt. Finnegan, D, 7th N. Y. H. A.　June 3.
Hiram Froego, 7th N. Y. H. A.　June 3.
Edward Mills, 12th N. Y.　June 3.
Saml. Matthews, I, 12th N. Y.　June 1.
Corpl. C. C. Mead, 12th N. J.　June 3.
Jos. Rob't Edwards, I, 12th N. J.　June 3
Corpl. Wm. Collins, G, 12th N. J.　June 3.
Corpl. Wm. McDaniels, B, 12th N. J.　June 3.
Enoch H. Smith, C, 12th N. J.　June 5.
Wm. Harris, A, 71st P. V.　June 10.
Sergt. Wm. Warner, A, 1st Del.　Killed June 3
John ———, H, 69th P. V.　June 4.
A. G. Clark, F, 69th P. V.　June 4.

The above graves, from Sergt. McGlathing to this last, inclusive, are abou forty rods southeast of common grave No. 4, under locust trees, just be-just behind our breastworks.

15

Wm. Marston, H, 145th P. V., 1st Div. 2d A. C. Killed June 4. North of common grave No. 5.

West of Peter McGee's house :—

E. T. Barstow, B, 184th P. V.   June 3.
A. G. Ward, D, 84th P. V.   June 3.
A. Green, B, 184th P. V.   June 3.
J. Hellry, I, 53d P. V.
Dan'l Dow, H, 5th N. H.   Killed June 8.
C. F. Beem, K, 53d P. V.
J. Hosmer, K, 53d P. V.
M. W. Redlich, K, 53d P. V.
Sergt. W. S. Hazzard, H, —— P. V.
Corpl. D. H. Lewis, 152d N. Y.   June 3.
Three graves may be found on McGee's place.
C. C. Hall, E, 4th N. J.   June 2.
R. Coules, D, 27th Mass.

DANVILLE.

On the 15th of May, 1864, two U. S. C. C. Agents—Messrs. Houghton and Williams—visited Danville, and obtained the following list, which dates from November 24, 1864, to April 28, 1865. The prisoners had been confined in four large factories. The cemetery is about a mile and a half from the town, and is well arranged. The graves are marked by head-boards, with the names legibly painted, and more care is evident than in any other Confederate prison burial-place. The bodies of any of our soldiers can be obtained—through Mr. Hill, of that city, undertaker—by their friends, at any time during the Fall.

The initial letters, after the date, indicate the disease of which each died. D. C.— Chronic Diarrhœa; F. T.—Typhoid Fever; V.—Small-pox; R. C.—Chronic Rheumatism; Pn.—Pneumonia; F. A.—Fever and Ague; E.—Erisypelas; B. C.—Chronic Bronchitis; H.—Liver Disease; H. C.—Chronic Liver Disease; D. A.—Acute Diarrhœa; C.—Consumption; V. F.—Varioloid; Pl.—Pleurisy; C. C.—Heart Disease; N.—Neuralgia; S.—Scurvy; F. C.—Congestive Fever; D.— Diphtheria; P.—Paralysis; Cat.—Catarrh.

Names of Federal sick and wounded who have died at Danville, Va., during the war :

E. Dunn, B, 8th Mich., November, 24, 1863, D.
Fredelin Strectinwater, A, 19th U. S. I., November 26, 1863, D.
Nathaniel Fultz, K, 89th Ohio, November 27, 1863, D.
Elijah Terry, H, 42d Ill., November 27, 1863, F. T.
Aaron Cronk, K, 25th Mich., November 28, 1863, F. T.
A. Grinnels, K, 4th Ky. Cav., November 28, 1863, V.
A. P. Arnold, F, 4th Ky. Cav., November 28, 1864, V.
E. Case, C, 29th Ind., November 28, 1863, D. C.
J. A. Sidler, G, 87th Ind., November 29, 1863, V.
Joel Williams, H, 3d Ky., November 30, 1863, V.
Wm. Evans, I, 51st Ohio, November 30, 1863, D. C.
Corp. Wm. Brandt, I, 39th Ind., November 30, 1863, R. C.
Frank Gerstung, I, 112th Ill., December 1, 1863, F. T.
J. Askinburg, H., 16th U. S. I., December 2, 1863, D. C
James Connor, A, 79th Ohio, December 3, 1863, V.
Wm. Dinsmore, D, 51st Ill., December 4, 1863, V.

Frank Parker, F, 1st Tenn. Cav., December 4, 1863, V.
James Nally, H, 6th Ky. Cav., December 5, 1863, V.
John Johnson, C, 8th Mich., December 5, 1863, V.
Corp. W. A. Jones, C, 33d Ohio, December 5, 1863, D. C.
Sergt. Elihu Billings, I, 89th Ind., December 6, 1863, Pn.
Wm. Gambol, H, 18th U. S. I., December 6, 1863, Pn.
J. Newton, G, 73d Ohio, December 6, 1863, D. C
F. Leith, C, 68th Ind., December 6, 1863, D. C.
J. Cope, H., 21st Ill., December 6, 1863, F. A.
C. A. Brown, A, 19th Mass., December 7, 1863, Pn.
F. Brickford, D, 22d Mich., December 7, 1863, F. T.
W. Carroll, F, 8th Tenn. Cav., December 7, 1863, F. T.
R. Livingston, I, 82d Ind., December 7, 1863, V.
A. Allen, I, 14th Mich., December 8, 1863, Er.
M. Brannon, K, 8th Mich., December 10, 1863, D. C.
J. Coyfort, C, 11th Tenn., December 10, 1863, D. C.
J. L. Beath, H, 89th Ohio, December 10, 1863. D. C.
H. Knapp, A, 22d Mich., December 10, 1863, Pn.
A. Howlett, F, 18th Ky., December 10, 1863, D. C.
W. W. Smith, I, 14th Mich., December 11, 1863, Pn.
G. T. Jennings, C, 11th Ky. Cav., December 11, 1863, F. T.
Thos. Nolan, A, 16th U. S. I., December 12, 1863, D. C.
H. T. Layfield, B, 59th Ohio, December 12, 1863, F. T.
W. R. Ford, I, 112 Ill., December 12, 1863, V.
John Sweaney, A, 8th Tenn. Cav., December 12, 1863, V.
John Ferguson, F, 8th Tenn. Cav., December 12, 1863, V.
M. Wilson, A, 1st Cav., December 13, 1863, D. C.
Jno. M. Evans. E, 35th Ohio, December 14, 1863 V.
O. Fall, D, 22d Mich., December 14, 1863, V.
J. Carson, G, 36th Ill., December 14, 1863, V.
J. Close, G, 25th Iowa, December 14, 1863, Pn.
J. Reder, B, 1st Ohio, December 15, 1863, D. C.
D. C. Chase, D, 8th Mich., December 15, 1863, D. C.
C. McDonald, A, 1st Wis., December 15, 1863, V.
M. Dougherty, C, 8th Kansas, December 15, 1863, F. T
T. H. Hemry, G, 21st Ohio, December 15, 1863, Pn.
E. G. Browning, B, 3d Tenn. Cav., December 16, 1863, V.
C. Closson, C, 15th U. S. I., December 16, 1863, Pn.
W. Priest, A, 29th Ind., December 16, 1863, F. T.
J. Fryar, F, 8th Tenn. Cav., December 16, 1863, D. C.
H. H. Lee, B, 92d Ohio, December 16, 1863, V.
J. W. G bbs, K, 92d Ohio, December 16, 1863, V.
H. Wheeler, D, 65th Ohio, December 16, 1863, V.
S. R. Howard, D, 65th Ohio, December 17, 1863, D. C.
J. Alison, D, 64th U. S., December 17, 1863, Pn.
S. Garner, C, 30th Ind., December 17, 1863, D. C.
R. B. Cunningham. B, 3d Tenn. Cav., December 17, 1863, V.
T. W. Shepard, I, 115th Ill., December 17, 1863, V.
John Lester, F, 90th Ohio, December 17, 1863, V.
J. Marshall, A, 28th Mass., December 18, 1863, Pn.
Morgan Presley, A, 8th Tenn. Cav., December 18, 1863. V.

2

T M. Applegate, D, 81st Ind., December 18, 1863, **V.**
F. Moores, I, 29th Ind., December 19, 1863, V.
T. K. Monroe, E, 6th Ind., December 19, 1863, V.
Wm. Miller, A, 42d Ill., December 19, 1863, V.
J. B. Shafer, A, 89th Ohio, December 19, 1863, V.
G. H. Herrick, 79th Ill., December 20, 1863, V.
T. Morgan, K, 9th Tenn. Cav., December 21, 1863, D. C.
F. Collins, C, 1st Ohio, December 21, 1863, D. C.
A. Shultz, F, 22d Ill., December 21, 1863, D. C.
H. J. Brooks, E, 88th Ill., December 21, 1863, C. C.
H. Lewis, D, 32d Mich., December 21, 1863, F. T.
W. Higgins, G, 18th Ohio, December 21, 1863, V.
P. Kimbol, E, 4th Ky., December 21, 1863, V.
J. German, F, 22d Mich., December 21, 1863, V.
A. Bray, B, 3d Tenn. Cav., December 21, 1863, V.
Sergt. J. A. Howard, H, 9th Ky., December 21, 1863, **V.**
A. Snooke, B, 42d Ind., December 21, 1863, F. T.
S. Gates, F, 33d Ohio, December 21, 1863, F. T.
Isaac Mosier, B, 11th Mich., December 22, 1863, V.
John Gray, G, 8th Tenn. Cav., December 22, 1863, V.
G. Presley, A, 8th Tenn. Cav., December 22, 1863, V
John Morehead, C, 21st Ohio, December 22, 1863, Pn.
A. Wiley, F, 38th Ill., December 23, 1863, Pn.
Corp. J. Tinker, G, 8th Tenn., December 22, 1863, V.
J. H. Evans, A, 3d Tenn. Cav., December 24, 1863, V
A. Nickolson, F, 14th Ohio, December 24, 1863, V.
W. Ward, A, 8th Tenn. Cav., December 24, 1863, V.
D. Hahn, I, 44th Ill., December 24, 1863, V.
B. F. Leiby, K, 65th Ohio, December 25, 1863, V.
H. Webster, B, 1st Ohio Cav., December 25, 1863, V.
Samuel Cox, B, 1st Tenn., December 25, 1863, V.
W. Bothby, H, 96th Ill., December 25, 1863, D. C.
Frank Fry, A, 4th Ohio Cav., December 25, 1863, B. C.
J. Giles, K, 22d Mich., December 25, 1863, V.
Adam Wills, H, 89th Ohio, December 25, 1863, B. C.
M. Strange, D, 9th Tenn., December 26, 1863, B. C.
J. M. Lawson, A, 75th Ind., December 26, 1863, V.
Corp. S. Losaga, K, 8th Mich. Cav., December 26, 1865. **V.**
J. S. Deusemore, I, 10th Ind., December 27, 1863, V.
P. Rincheart, A, 13th Ohio, December 27, 1863, V.
E. Powell, H, 21st Ill., December 27, 1863, V.
John Glossuer, H, 8th Mich. Cav., December 28, 1863, V.
J. H. Tibbits, K, 21st Mich. Cav., December 28, 1863, V.
W. G. Jackson, B, 3d Tenn. Cav., December 28, 1863, V.
J. Frary, I, 101st Ohio, December 28, 1863, C. C.
C. W. Wood, D, 3d Tenn. Cav., December 29, 1863, V.
Arch'd Cook, K, 51st Ill., December 29, 1863, V.
John Thorn, E, 18th U. S. I., December 29, 1863, V.
J. Weddles, D, 73d Ill., December 30, 1863, V.
C. A. Barnes, C, 89th Ohio, December 30, 1863, D. C.
J. H. Pool, F, 22d Mich., December 30, 1863, V.

19

David Burr, F, 1st Wis., December 31, 1863, B. C.
J. Hale, F, 13th Ohio, December 31, 1863, V.
L. W. Oliver, B, 86th Ind., December 31, 1863, V.
J. McCay, H, 18th Penn. Cav., December 31, 1863, V.
H. Vacanborough, I, 22d Mich., December, 31, 1863, Pn.
A. Harper, A, 8th Tenn. Cav., January 1, 1864, B. C.
H. Stewart, I, 31st Ill., January 1, 1864, V.
Alfred Sevanders, H, 99th Ohio, January 1, 1864, Pn.
L. Wellington, A, 141st N. Y., January 1, 1864, D. C.
H. J. Williams, B, 16th U. S. I., January 2, 1864, D. C
H. Gillespie, C, 18th Pa., January 3, 1864, D. C.
Ira. Barber, D, 65th Ohio, January 3, 1864, F. T.
J. Tucker, G, 2d Mo., January 3, 1864, V.
A. Wade, A, 3d Tenn. Cav., January 3. 1864,. V.
H. Spencer, C, 21st Ohio, January 3, 1864, V.
R. Williamson, H, 4th Tenn., January 3, 1864, V.
J. Suffrige, H, 8th Tenn., January 4, 1864, V.
D. Chappell, K, 121st Ohio, January 4, 1864, V.
P. Kirwin, F, 5th Ky., January 4, 1864, D. C.
H. C. Payne, C, 96th Ohio, January 4, 1864, H. C.
C. Jacobson, K, 10th Wis., January 4, 1864, V.
M. Green, C, 21st Ill., January 4, 1864, V.
B. F. Turner, B, 89th Ill., January 4, 1864, V.
J. Thatcher, I, 99th Ohio, January 4, 1864, V.
Corp. Wm. Everly, F, 74th Ill., January 5, 1864, C. C
A. J. Smith, F, 36th Ind., January 5, 1864, V.
Sergeant F. M. Boston, B, 92d Ohio, January 5, 1864, V.
Corp. John Smith, D, 39th Ohio, January 5, 1864, V.
Saml. Robertson, H, 88th Ill., January 5, 1864, V.
Wm. George, A, 3d Tenn. Cav., January 5, 1864, V.
A. Cocraham, B, 8th Tenn., January 6, 1864, V.
W. McGee, D, 9th Tenn., January 6, 1864, V.
H. Adams, D, 3d Tenn. Cav., January 6, 1864, V.
M. E. Carpenter, H, 13th Mich., January 6, 1864, V.
A. Leitey, I, 99th Ohio, January 6, 1864, V.
Jno. Darrigh, D, 2d Ohio, January 6, 1864, V.
Corp. James Hunter, B, 11th Ohio, January 7, 1864, V
A. H. Burton, H, 79th Ill., January 7, 1864, E.
R. F. Babcock, H, 22d Mich., January 7, 1864, V.
Wm. Finchum, H, 79th Ind., January 7, 1864, V.
B. Phillips, B, 3d Tenn. Cav., January 7, 1864, V.
T. B. Chapin, 3d Wis. Bat., January 7, 1864, V.
David Clark, G, 35th Ohio, January 8, 1864, D. C.
Corp. E. H Neal, D, 21st Ill., January 8, 1864, Pn.
Thos. Vincenu, I, 22d Mich., January 9, 1864, V.
A. W. Kirby, C, 3d Tenn. Cav., January 9, 1864, V.
J. Laclaid, K, 1st Wis., January 9, 1864, V.
S. L. McNeal, I, 89th Ohio, January 9, 1864, V.
N. Griffin, H. 32d Ky., January 9, 1864, V.
Robt. Townsend, F, 74th Ohio, January 10, V.
Corp. G. S. Snider, F, 79th Ill., January 10, 1864, V.

J. M. Camp, B, 3d Tenn. Cav., January 10, 1864, **V.**
Corp. Danl. Plyly, K, 89th Ohio, January 10, 1864, **V.**
B. Rubley, G, 15th U. S. I., January 10, 1864, V.
W. Ladd, A, 36th Ohio, January 10, 1864, E.
W. Wilcox, I, 27th Ill., January 10, 1864, Pn.
B. F. Nealy, C, 3d Tenn., January 10, 1864, Pn.
A. J. Miller, K, 99th Ohio, January 11, 1864, .V.
M. Willard, H, 21st Mich., January 11, 1864, V.
B. Sympson K, 6th Ky., January 11, 1864, Pn.
A. J. Truelock, D, 87th Ind., January 11, 1864, V.
W. Collins, H, 8th Tenn. Cav., January 11, 1864, V.
W. R. Barnes, I, 21st Wis., January 11, 1864, V.
Sergeant G. W. Johnson, H, 21st Mich., January 11, 1864, **D. C.**
E. Sufferage H, 8th Tenn. Cav., January 12, 1864, V.
J. Montgomery, H, 6th Ky., January 12, 1864, V.
Wm. Albert, B, 51st Pa., January 12, 1864, Pn.
Wm. Combs, D, 35th Ind., January 12, 1864, D. C.
W. Keggs, H 2d Ky. Cav., January 13, 1864, V.
G. Cross, D, 9th Tenn., January 13, 1864, V.
W. Holcombe, C, 22d Mich., January 14, 1864, V.
J. W. McClintock, C, 33d Ohio, January 14, 1864, **Pn.**
F. Little, H, 40th Ohio, January 14, 1864, D. C.
M. Jones, G, 21st Wis., January 14, 1864, V.
J. Whitehuroe, K, 30th Ohio, January 14, 1864, B.
Wm. Cockerham, B, 8th Tenn. Cav., January 14, 1864, **V**
Saml. Ray, C, 33d Ohio, January 14, 1864, V.
M. Harmon, Teamster, January 15, 1864, V.
John Ocherlin, G, 2d Wis., January 15, 1864, D. C.
John Bowers, A, 16th U. S. I. January 15, 1864, D. C.
Sergeant H. C. Moore, K, 38th Ill., January 15, 1864, **A**
W. H. Theller, E, 9th Ind., January 15, 1864, V.
J. F. Didler, G, 22d Mich., January 16, 1864, V.
H. H. Hughnorline, D, 121st Ohio, January 16, 1864, **V.**
F. M. Krill, H, 21st Ohio, January 16, 1864, F. A.
D. P. Moore, H, 11th Tenn. Cav., January 16, 1864, **Pn.**
Thos. Bynum, A, 1st Ala. Arty., January 16, 1864, Pn.
Wm. Ingersall, H, 96th Ill., January 16, 1864, V.
L. J. Colbey, I, 112th Ill., January 17, 1864, Pn.
J. Ashbrook, G, 38th Ind., January 17, 1864, V.
J. R. Lamoreux D, 16th U. S. I. January 17, 1864, **V.**
James Sirgent, D, 3d Mich., January 17, 1864, V.
W. W. Dorrah, B, 10th Wis., January 18, 1864, **Pn.**
J. Dennis, G, 6th Ky., January 18, 1864, V.
D. T. Hill, D, 13th Mich., January 18, 1864, **V.**
E. H. Gubb, C, 16th U. S., January 18, 1864, **V.**
C. S. Scott, B, 30th Ind., January 18, 1864, V.
G. W. Edmister, D, 21st Mich., January 19, 1864, **Pn.**
T. Robertson, K, 51st Ill., January 19, 1864, V.
H. Oaks, F, 2d Minn., January 19, 1864, Pn.
Corpl. A. Wickert, I, 2d Minn., January 19, 1864, Pn.
W. Muckel. F., 79th Pa., January 19, 1864, V

Henry Copus, G, 21st Ohio, January 20, 1864, V.
Sergt. H. Wize, D, 88th Ind., January 20, 1864, V.
E. Darling, I, 99th Ohio, January 20, 1864, V.
H. Green, C, 96th Ill., January 20, 1864, V.
Peter Williams, F, 18th U. S. I., January 20, 1864, V.
J. T. Austin, A, 21st Wis., January 21, 1864, V.
P. Addison, H, 10th Wis., January 21, 1864, V.
T. Robertson, K, 51st Ill., January 21, 1864, V.
W. W. Allemange, C, 33d Ohio, January 21, 1864, V.
Wm. Anderson, B, 79th Ill., January 21, 1864, C.
R. Ireland, C, 21st Ohio, January 21, 1864, V.
W. J. Tarham, E, 65th Ohio, January 21, 1864, V.
Sergt. J. A. Jordan, B, 21st Wis., January 22, 1864, V.
N. Aldred, K, 79th Ill., January 23, 1864, V.
J. Cigin, A, 14th Ohio, January 23, 1864, V.
Wm. Skinner, I, 75th Ill., January 24, 1864, Pn.
T. Tankerly, G, 4th Ky., January 24, D. C.
H. Steward, A, 3d Va., January 24, 1864, V.
S. Holcombe, C, 33d Ohio, January 24, 1864, V.
A. Stiles, A, 79th Ill., January 25, 1864, V.
Thos. Hunston, C, 15th Wis., January 25, 1864, D. C.
A. Groffh, E, 15th U. S. I., January 25, 1864, D. C.
Corpl. J. Routt, D, 18th Ky., January 25, 1864, V.
R. W. Martin, I, 9th Ky., January 26, 1864, V.
W. P. Tatman, A, 87th Ind., January 26, 1864, V.
Sergt. O. Bartlett, C, 22d Mich., January 26, 1864, V.
T. Brown, U. S. Gun Boat, January 26, 1864, Pn.
D. Barnett, D, 21st Ill., January 26, 1864, D. C.
J. Johnson, E, 8th Ky., January 27, 1864, V.
W. H. Desern, K, 5th Ky. Cav., January 27, 1864, D. C.
J. E. Bradford, C, 30th Ind., January 27, 1864, D. C.
D. Hess, K, 3d Ohio, January 28, 1864, Pn.
G. Middleton, I, 4th Ky., January 28, D. C.
A. H. Lawless, G, 73d Ill., January 29, 1864, Pn.
A. Wallace, C, 3d Tenn., January 29, 1864, Pn.
P. Harris, I, 21st Wis., January 29, 1864, V.
Wm. Thomas, 18th U. S. I., January 29, 1864, V.
Corp. S. Morrison, I, 33d Ohio, January 30, 1864, D. C.
Corp. J. W. Neely, F, 26th Ohio, January 30, 1864, F. T
B. F. Smith, A, 19th U. S. I., January 30, 1864, F. A.
D. Dusenberry, F, 38th Ill., January 30, 1864, Pn.
J. McFerrin, K, 21st Ohio, January 31, 1864, V.
Wm. Looker, F, 17th Ohio, February 1, 1864, V.
A. S. Oaks, B, 101st Ind., February 2, 1864, D. C.
H. Harmon, C, 41st Ohio, February 2, 1864, D. C.
D. L. Lawrence, B, 89th Ill., February 2, 1865, D. C.
S. Curry, E, 9th Ky., February 2, 1864, V.
J. Strickland, F, 42d Ind., February 3, 1864, V.
Corp. C. Benner, C, 79th Ill., February 3, 1864, V.
Wm. Cowden, D, 31st Ind., February 4, 1864, F. T.
C. D. Pierson. G, 21st Ill., February 4, 1864, V.

F. Reed, H, 15th U. S. I , February 4, 1864, V.
Wm. Cox, I, 6th Ky., February 4, 1864, V.
Corp. H. H. Hines, K, 3d Ky., February 5, 1864, D. C.
Corp. D. Brett, I, 21st Ohio, February 5, 1864, V.
W. J. Dougherty, H, 15th U. S. I., February 5, 1864, V.
J. Richards, F, 26th Ohio, February 6, 1864, D. C.
J. Taylor, F, 24th Wis., February 6, 1864, D. C.
W. R. Jones, I, 100th Ill., February 6, 1864, V.
H. H. Freeman, H, 21st Ill., February 6, 1864, V.
J. S. Hatter, A, 5th Ky. Cav., February 6, 1864, V.
Wm. McDaniel, D, 9th Tenn., February 7, 1864, D. C.
H. P. Miller, H, 33d Ohio, February 7, 1864, V.
J. Hollensworth, K, 8th Ky., February 8, 1864, V.
Wm. Martin, I, 89th Ohio, February 9, 1864, D. C.
J. Sherwood, D, 33d Ohio, February 9, 1864, V.
C. Blimmer, K, 8th Kansas, February 10, 1864, D. C.
E. W. Dudden, E, 3d Ky., February 10, 1864, V.
George Lucas, K, 22d Mich., February 10, 1864, V.
L. Y. Decker, D, 79th Pa., February 11, 1864, F. T.
Sergt. A. O. Bennett, F, 89th Ohio, February 11, 1864, D. C.
L. R. Mabene, D, 18th Pa., February 12, 1864, D. C.
J. Carr, H, 40th Ohio, February 12, 1864, V.
A. M. Read, F, 51st Ill., February 13, 1864, D. C.
A. Sailor, H, 125th Ohio, February 13, 1864, A.
J. A. Willis, B, 89th Ohio, February 13, 1864, D. C.
J. Michels, I, 38th Ill., February 13, 1864, D. C.
A. J. Booker, A, 3d Tenn. Cav., February 14, 1864, Pn.
J. F. Brown, F, 89th Ohio, February 14, 1864, Pn.
B. Bumgardener, F, 9th Ohio, February 14, 1864, D. C.
H. Cowan, E, 2d Ohio, February 14, 1864, V.
D. Brooks, I, 44th Ind., February 14, 1864, V.
E. Jacobson, K, 15th Wis., February 15, 1864, F. T.
Nelson Eagle, C, 30th Ind., February 15, 1864, D. C.
James Horney, I, 3d Ind. Cav., February 15, 1864, Pn.
Sergt. Isaac Laman, K, 1st Tenn., February 15, 1864, V.
Frank Holmes, B, 3d Tenn., February 15, 1864, V.
H. Miller, H, 10th U. S. I., February 17, 1864, D. C.
L. Stackhouse, D., 89th Ohio, February 17, 1864, Pn.
A. Peterson, F, 89th Ill., February 17, 1864, D. C.
A. F. Woods, I, 84th Ind., February 17, 1864. D. C.
T. J. Ewing, B, 36th Ill., February 17, 1864, V. F.
G. F. Pibbles, B, 13th Mich., February 17, 1864, V. F.
J. W. Rancliff, A, 1st R. I., February 18, 1864, D. C.
Harier Plum, I, 15th Me., February 18, 1864, D. C.
C. H. Rowe, G, 6th Ind., February 18, 1864, V.
J. A. Maynader, K, 6th Ky., February 20, 1864, Pn.
C. Bartha, G, 40th Ohio, February 20, 1864, Pn.
Corp. C. Hess, G, 65th Ohio, February 20, 1864, V.
E. Slasher, E, 67th Ohio, February 21st, 1864, V.
E. Blivins, E, 8th Ky., February 21, 1864, V.
T. Gwin, B, 5th Ky., February 21, 1864, V.

23

H. C. Harmell, I, 25th Ili., February 22, 1864, Pn.
W. A. Martin, F, 11th Ohio, February 22, 1864, D. C.
S. C. Shellingsburg, teamster, February 22, 1864, D. C.
G. Goiner, C, 1st Tenn., February 22, 1864, V.
C. N. Wallis, C, 11th Tenn., February 23, 1864, D. C.
G. Plunket, G, 13th Ky., February 23, 1864, V.
E. Hitch, K, 89th Ohio, February 24, 1864, Pn.
P. St. Clair, C, 89th Ill., February 24, 1864, C.
J. T. Douglas, B, 3d Tenn. Cav., February 25, 1864, D. C.
W. C. Welsh, B, 105th Ohio, February 25, 1864, B. C.
Thomas Hobson, G, 92d Ohio, February 26, 1864, D. C.
T. M. Hale, F, 33d Ohio, February 26, 1864, B, C.
C. Hammond, F, 21st Wis., February 26, 1864, B. C.
T. M., Mullican, K, 88th Ill., February 26, 1864, B. C.
J. Burns, G, 18th U. S. I., February 26, 1864, V. S.
J. Barnesley, E, 17th Pa , February 27, 1864, V. F.
Sergt. H. Huntington, C, 96th Ill., February 27, 1864, V.
J. W. Bruce, E, 89th Ohio, February 28, 1864, D. C.
M. Loop, F, 8th Mich., February 28, 1864, D. C.
J. Williams, F, 5th Ky., February 28, 1864, D. C.
M. Fanton, H, 18th Ky., February 28, 1864, D. C.
T. H. Hixon, K, 1st Ohio, February 29, 1864, Pn.
A. B Gamill, A, 3d Tenn., February 29, 1864, D. C.
G. Fuller, A, 89th Ill., March 2, 1864, Pn.
D. Desmold, D, 35th Ind., March 2, 1864, D. C.
A. Shock, I, 11th Mich., March 2, 1864, Anasarca.
R. Hooper, G, 13th Mich., March 2, 1864, E.
D. Park, G, 19th Ohio, March 3, 1864, F. T.
A. Sanders, 8th Ind. Batt'y, March 3, 1864, Grangrene fr. V.
R. Yodd, B, 10th Wis., March 4, 1864, D. C.
B. McFarland, F, 2d Ohio, March 4, 1864, D. A.
E. Denson, I, 58th Ind., March 4, 1864, D. C.
E. T. Burk, G, 15th U. S. I., March 4, 1864, Gangrene, fr. V.
H. Wood, K, 79th Ill., March 5, 1864, D. C.
M. Lane, C, 15th Ohio, March 5, 1864, Pn.
E. Herron, I, 6th Ky., March 6, 1864, Pl.
G. Runion, A, 89th Ohio, March 6, 1864, Pu.
E. Hoard, D, 22d Mich., March 6, 1864, Pn.
Corp. W. Cummings, G, 21st Ohio, March 7, 1864, D. C.
G. W. Holloway, E, 44th Ind., March 7, 1864, D. C.
J. W. Shriver, I, 89th Ohio, March 7, 1864, D. C.
A. Hines, M, 6th Ky., March 9, 1864, D. C.
A. Osterman, C, 38th Ohio, March 9, 1864, D. C.
E. Cramer, E, 15th U. S. I., March 9, 1864, D. C.
J. Dohl, K, 15th Wis., March 10, 1864, D. C.
J. C. Sutherlin, A, 3d Ky., March 10, 1864, E.
J. Cunningham, G, 18th U. S. I., March 10, 1863, F. T
J. Willhoit, H, 79th Ill., March 11, 1864, D. C.
S. Carter, D, 22d Mich., March 12, 1864, D. C.
A. McGrew, H, 4th Ohio, March 12. 1864, D. C.
J. Snider, I, 112th Ill., March 13, 1864, F. T.

O. Grout, K, 22d Mich., March 13, 1864, Rheum. fr. **V.**
R. Meghan, A, 15th U. S. I., March 14, 1864, D. C.
W. Lansey, B, 18th U. S. I., March 14, 1864, Ascites.
B. H. Phillips, B, 3d Tenn., March 14, 1864, D. C.
P. Christinger, D, 9th Mich., March 14, 1864, D. C.
D. Harlow, C, 3d Ky., March 14, 1864, E.
W. Cramer, C, 26th Ohio, March 15, 1864, D. A.
J. Craycroft, H, 15th U. S. I., March 15, 1864, D. fr. **V.**
T. J. Debrick, I, 89th Ohio, March 16, 1864, D. A.
J. B. David, D, 68th Ind., March 16, 1864, Pn.
Corp'l W. Pettebone, C, 22d Mich. March 16th, 1864. **D. C.**
D. D. W. Bush, C, 13th Mich., March 16th, 1864, C. fr. **V.**
W. B. Williams, D, 11th Ohio, March 17th, 1864, D. C.
J. L. Cunningham, B, 1st Ohio Cav., March, 16th 1864, Pn.
L. M. Lowe, I, 89th Ohio, March 17th, 1864, D. C.
William Rittenhouse, D, 16th U. S. I., March 17th, 1864, D. C.
W. S. Prestly, B, 3d Tenn. Cav., March 17th, 1864, D. C.
James Gooch, A, 38th Ill., March 17th, 1864, D. C.
J. McCarthy, K, 64th Ohio, March 17th, 1864, Neuralgia.
A. Minor, B, 19th Ohio, March 17th, 1864, V.
L. Carrol, F, 4th Ky. Cav., March 18th, 1864, D. C.
J. Sentance, I, 38th Ill., March 18th, 1864, D. C.
P. McCarthy, F, 4th Ky. Cav., March 18th, 1864, E.
J. Ogden, K, 89th Ohio, March 18th, 1864, D. C.
J. Hodges, B, 87th Ind., March 18th, 1864, D. C.
A. Moat, B, 100th Ill., March 19th, 1864, D. C.
J. Jessup, I, 84th Ind., March 20th, 1864, Œdema fr Diarrhœa.
J. Robinson, E, 112th Ill., March 21st, 1864, D. C.
J. Pierce, B, 25th Ill., March 22d, 1864, D. C.
P. Mullins, H, 30th Ind., March 22d, 1864, D. C.
C. D. Scott, K, 21st Ohio, March 23d, 1864, D. C.
W. H. Wright, D, 5th Ky. Cav., March 23d, 1864, **D. C.**
J. H. Jamerson, D, 30th Ind., March 23d, 1864, D. C.
F. Plump, U. S. Gun Boat, March 23d, 1864, D. C.
Sergt. W. W. Billis, I, 19th Ohio, March 23d, 1864, **D. C.**
W. Tuskin, F, 89th Ohio, March 23d, 1864, D. C.
V. B. Swan, K, 10th Wis., March 23d, 1864, D. C.
H. Hamner, D, 9th Ky., March 23d, 1864, D. C.
M. Crow, G, 79th Ill., March 23d, 1864, D. C.
J. Surface, F, 35th Ohio, March 23d, 1864, D. C.
P. Cartney, E, 19th Ohio, March 23d, 1864, D. C.
H. Bustin, A, 77th Pa., March 25th, 1864, D. C.
Corp'l C. Chilly, H, 40th Ohio, March 25th, 1864, D. fr **V.**
J. Casey, C, 18th U. S. I., March 25th, 1864, D. C.
P. Coil, I, 112th Ill., March 26th, 1864, D. C.
William Ramer, H, 11th Ohio, March 26th, 1864, D. C.
G. Derrickson, G, 73d Ill., March 26th 1864, D. C.
C. Chapman, B, 18th Ohio, March 26th, 1864, Colitis Chron.
M. Pratcliff, D, 89th Ohio, March 27th, 1864, D. C.
E. Hainist, E, 77th Pa., March 27th, 1864, D. C.
W. H. Spankey, H, 2d U. S., March 27th, 1864, R. C.

Corp'l W. Shell, K, 22d Mich., March 27th, 1864, D. C.
A. K. Smith, I, 33d Ohio, March 27th, 1864, D. C.
E. E. Willit, A, 1st Wis., March 28th, 1864, Ascites.
J. W. McElfresh, G, 89th Ohio, March 28th, 1864, D. C.
S. Neal, D, 5th Ky., March 28th, 1864, H.
J. Carn, K, 22d Mich., March 28th, 1864, D. C.
S. A. Boush, C, 33d Ohio, March 28th, 1864, D. A.
M. McFaller, H, 5th U. S., March 29th, 1864. E.
Corp'l J. R. Buckle, I, 89th Ohio, March 30th, 1864, D. C.
J. Clark, E, 21st Wis., March 30th, 1864, Ascites.
E. J. Allen, C, 9th Iowa, March 30th, 1864, D. C.
H. Hess, 3d Wis. Battery, March 30th, 1864, D. C.
J. Reid, H. 4th Wis., March 30th, 1864, D. C.
J. Cline, I, 13th Ind., March 31st, 1864, Gastritis.
J. W. Page, D, 27th Ill., March 31st, 1864, D. C.
J. Gailey, F, 15th U. S., March 31st, 1864, D. C.
J. Travis, F, 21st Ohio, April 1st, 1864, B. C.
J. Hand, C, 33d Ill., April 2d, 1864, D. C.
William Smith, B, 9th Tenn., April 2d, 1864, V.
G. Main, F, 21st Ohio, April 3d, 1864, D. C.
S. Starkson, H, 13th Wis., April 3d, 1864, D. fr. V.
J. H. Martin, F, 42d Ind., April 5th, 1864, D. C.
J McD. Havis, E, 18th U. S. I., April 5th, 1864, D. C.
F Waggle, K, 29th Ind., April 5, 1864, D. C.
F. Logan, C, 38th Ill., April 5, 1864, D. C.
Corp. W. Chaplin, F, 13th Ill., April 6, 1864, F. and A.
F. Patrick, C, 10th Wis., April 6, 1864, D. C.
J. Donnally, F, 33d Ohio, April 7, 1864, D. C.
W. Anderson, C, 93d Ohio, April 7, 1864, D. C.
W. T. White, D. 25th Ill., April 7, 1864, D. C.
W. Jacobs, D, 11th Tenn., April 7, 1864, D. C.
G. Paulson, F, 15th Wis., April 7, 1864, D. C.
O. Williams, D, 18th Ky., April 8, 1864, D. C.
J. Waters, E, 8th Ky., April 9, 1864, Pn.
J. McManey, C, 22d Mich., April 9, 1864, Pn.
J. C. Wheeler, E, 15th U. S., April 9, 1864, D. C.
R. Gow, A, 33d Ohio, April 9, 1864, Colitis Chronica.
F. M. Stevens, H, 35th Ind., April 9, 1864, D. fr. V.
W. Bumgardner, K, 115th Ill., April 10, 1864, D. C.
J. Rhyne, F, 94th Ohio, April 10, 1864, D. C.
John McGill, B, 44th Ill., April 11, 1864, D. C.
S. Ferguson, H, 94th Ohio, April 11, 1864, D. C.
J. Reynolds, B, 2d Mich. Cav., April 11, 1864, D. A.
H. Gilbert, D, 8th Ky., April 13, 1864, D. C.
Corp. A. Murphy, C, 93d Ohio, April 13, 1864, D. C.
Corp. G. R. Deabolt, K, 49th Ohio, April 14, 1864, Colitis Acuta
Sergt. G. Mays, I, 2d Iowa, April 14, 1864, Colitis Acuta.
Citizen J. G. Strutts, of Va., April 15, 1864, D. C.
G. Mayhan, H, 21st Mich., April 15, 1864, R. A.
J. McDowell, E, 113th Ohio, April 16, 1864, D. C.
J. Byerts, G, 18th U. S., April 16, 1864, D. A.

W. G. Taylor, 16th U. S., April 16, 1864, D. fr. V.
J. E. Tate, H, 42d Ill., April 17, 1864, D. C.
J. Foster, I, 88th Ill., April 17, 1864, D. C.
J. Bainhart, E, 18th U. S., April 17, 1864, D. A.
J. C. Hardy, K, 6th Ky., April 18, 1864, C.
J. M. Gordon, K, 4th U. S. Cav., April 18, 1864, Asthma.
Corp. L. Nolan, I, 79th Ill., April 18, 1864, D. fr. V.
E. Marshall, I, 18th Ky., April 19, 1864, D. C.
E. Sperry, A, 15th U. S., April 19, 1864, C.
E. Quillian, E, 1st Ohio, April 19, 1864, D. A.
E. Vanarsdale, D, 42d Ill., April 21, 1864, D. A.
G. A. Bryant, B, 33d Ohio, April 21, 1864, D. A.
R. R. Russell, D, 6th Ky., April 22, 1864, D. C.
F. Kremer, K, 22d Mich., April 22d, 1864, D. A.
F. Shiltz, K, 24th Ill., April 22d, 1864, D. A.
J. B. Davis, I, 89th Ohio, April 22, 1864. D. A.
J. Healy, A, 16th U. S., April 23, 1864, E.
Corp. A. Reynolds, K, 22d Mich., April 23, 1864, Epilepsy.
H. Smith, K, 79th Pa., April 25, 1864, D. C.
O. Anderson, B, 15th Wis., April 25, 1864, D. C.
J. L. Sharp, C, 8th Kansas, April 25, 1864, Debility.
Sergt. J. Kathan, F, 22d Ill., April 25, 1864, D. C.
E. Pursell, K, 21st Ohio, April 26, 1864, D. C.
A. Elexson, B, 15th Wis., April 26, 1864, D. A.
J. Arcry, B, 11th Ohio, April 26, 1864, D. C.
J. D. Fagian, F, 89th Ohio, April 26, 1864, D. A.
M. Fredgil, B, 3d Tenn., April 26, 1864, V.
N. R. Ashbrook, C, 15th U. S., April 27, 1864, R. fr V.
L. J. Allen, B, 5th Ky., April 27, 1864, Pn.
Corp, W. A. Menger, C, 94th Ohio, April 28, 1864, D. C.
E. Mangus, F, 29th Ind., April 29, 1864, D. A.
H. Negley, F, 81st Ind., April 29, 1864, Pn. fr. V.
John Davis, D, 89th Ohio, May 2, 1864, D. C.
L. Washburn, C, 2d Ky., May 4, 1864, D. C.
P. Weaver, F, 1st Ohio, May 7, 1864, bad wound.
J. Hastings, A, 15th U. S., May 8, 1864, Anasarca.
J. Mooney, I, 13th Mich, May 15, 1864, D. C.
H. H. Bartlett, H, 5th U. S., May 16th, 1864, Pn.
John Louis, D, 18th Ohio, May 17th. 1864, D. C.
T. Vanfleet, A, 22d Mich., May 19th, 1864, D. C.
W. P. White, H, 21st Ill., May 19th, 1864, Pn.
S. Thomas, D, 37th Ind., May 21st, 1864, D. C.
A. Bosher, B, 27th Mich., May 21, 1864, D. C.
C. H. Stone, D, 9th Tenn., May 22d, 1864, B. C.
C. F. English, H, 20th Ohio, May 24, 1864, D. C.
D. Crall, C, 101st Ohio, May 24, 1864, D. C.
T. Donneyhue, K, 15th N. Y., May 24, 1864, B. C.
M. Pearson, B, 11th Conn., May 30, 1864, F. & A.
W. Griffith, F, 18th U. S., May 30, 1864, D. C.
O. Nelson, G. B. Battal'n, May 30, 1864, Catarrhus.
W. A. Gibson, H, 40th Ohio, May 31, 1864, D. C.

A. G. Patterson, H, 19th Ohio, May 31, 1864, D. C.
A. Westle, teamster, U. S. A., June 1, 1864, Anasarca.
H. P. Collins, D, 29th Ind., June 3, 1864, Pn.
Corpl. J. H. Campbell, H, 5th U. S. A., June 3, 1864, Pn.
Corpl. H. Broadrup, I, 2d Ohio, June 4, 1864, D. C.
D. F. Terrill, B, 1st Ohio, June 4, 1864, D. C.
M. Lowry, D, 19th U. S., June 4, 1864, Pn.
J. Farley, I, 18th U. S., June 10, 1864, D. C.
T. Brown, H, 2d Ohio, June 10, 1864, R. C.
J. H. Martin, D, 26th Ohio, June 11, 1864, D. C.
Sergt. P. Kenney, C, 38th Ill., June 18, 1864, D. C.
J. Hartman, I, 9th Ohio, June 19, 1864, D. C.
M. Dickerson, H, 73d Ill., June 22, 1864, S.
Corpl. D. Daubenmarkle, F, 9th Ohio, June 24, 1864, D. C.
G. Hopwood, E, 7th Wis., June 25, 1864, F. C.
H. Nay, H, 79th Ill., June 26, 1864, Scorbutus.
D. Waldren, H, 89th Ohio, June 30, 1864, Ascites.
C. Dale, I, 1st N. C., July 2, 1864, D. C.
Corp'l M. Wills, A, 81st Ind., July 8, 1864, S.
J. Knight, B, 38th Ind., July 8, 1864, D. C.
E. Rickey, B, 13th Ohio, July 9, 1864, D. C.
A. J. Shoper, K, 21st Wis., June 12, 1864, D. C.
Corp'l W. C. Hurd, B, 141st N. Y., July 14, 1864, D. C.
D. Murphy, D, 88th N. Y., July 18, 1864, D. C.
Corp'l J. W. Dougherty, D, 10th Wis., July 20, 1864, D. C.
P. Smith, A, 16th U. S. I., July 26, 1864, D. C.
J. B. Hill, E, 17th Ky, July 26, 1864, D. C.
J. E. Daniel, H, 56th Mass., July 30, 1864, D. C.
J. Comfort, C, 38th Ill., August 3, 1864, D. C.
J. Robinson, D, 106th N. Y., August 5, 1864, Pn.
J. R. Willfong, G, 21st Ohio, August 5, 1864, D. C.
J. Bowers, I, 32d Ind., August 6, 1864, D. C.
S. H. Phelps, K, 57th Mass., August 6, 1864, D. C.
E. C. Varney, K, 9th N. H., August 9, 1864, D. C.
Y. Sloan, C, 81st Ind., August 10, 1864, D. C.
J. Bottom, A, 11th Conn., August 10, 1864, D. C.
D. Cortis, G, 57th Mass., August 11, 1864, F. T.
W. Barden, E, 10th Wis., August 12, 1864, S.
F. Lumazett, G, 21st Mass., August 12, 1864, bad wound.
B. E. Wheater, K, 9th N. Y., August 13, 1864, D. C.
R. S. Briggs, E, 37th Wis., August 13, 1864, F. T.
R. B. Graham, K, 25th Ill., August 15, 1864, S.
T. Buckley, I, 33d Ohio, August 17, 1864, D. C.
J. Perkins, D, 9th N. Y., August 18, 1864, D. C.
D. Carncross, D, 9th N. Y., August 19, 1864, D. C.
F. Ham, A, 5th Me., August 21, 1864, F. T.
H. George, F, 59th Mass., August 21, 1864, D. C.
J. P. Henderson, D, 100th Pa., August 23, 1864, D C
S. H. Taber, E, 58th Mass., August 24, 1864, F. T
A. Strout, H, 32d Me., August 25, 1864, D. C.
C. Preble, G, 32d Me., August 25, 1864, D. C.

W. S. Hall, A, 2d Mich., Aug. 26, 1864, D. C.
T. Noble, I, 3d N. Y. Cav., August 28, 1864, D. C.
J. Shanklin, E, 2d Mich., August 28, 1864, D. C.
R. Williams, freedman, 23d U. S., August 29, 1864, D. C.
J. Johnson, C, 43d N. Y., August 29, 1864, D. C
—Favrke, 58th Mass., August 29, 1864, Pn.
A. Wales, A, 8th Pa., August 30, 1864, D. C.
B. Willis, H, 40th Ohio, September 1, 1864, F. T
L. Thomas, G, 14th N. Y., September 2, 1864, Pn.
P. Dean, A, 17th Vt., September 3, 1864, D. C.
J. Koil, E, 37th Wis., September 3, 1864, D. C.
G. Trent, B, 13th Tenn., September 4, 1864, D. C.
Corp'l J. Brewer, A, 38th Ill., September 7, 1864, D. C.
P. Lefler, I, 126th Ohio, September 8, 1864, D. C.
W. Vanleer, freedman, H, 31st N. Y., September 8, 1864, D. C.
J. Baldwin, G, 144th Ohio, September 8, 1864, D. C.
C. Menedill, E, 32d Me., September 8, 1864, F. & A.
G. Hacy, E, 37th Wis., September 8, 1864, F. T.
Corp'l J. Stickert, I, 37th Wis., September 8, 1864, D. C.
W. Gothan, K, 106th N. Y., September 9, 1864, D. C.,
D. Leonard, H, 57th Mass., September 9, 1864, D.
A. Huston, C, 179th N. Y., September 11, 1864, D. C.
Serg't F. Quinby, C, 11th N. H., September 11, 1864, D. C.
W. Haynesworth, B, 122d Ohio, September 11, 1864, D. C.
S. Merrick, K, 138th Pa., September 13, 1864, D. C.
T. Person, I, 1st Mich., September 14, 1864, D. C.
J. Stanley, I, 9th Va., September 14, 1864, D. C.
J. Simpson, C, 2d Pa., September 15, 1864, D.
E. Blockman, M, 37th Mich., September 15, 1864, D. C.
E. Smith, freedman, A, 31st U. S., September 16, 1864, D. C.
G. Robertson, A, 100th Pa., September 16, 1864, D. C.
J. Ritchey, C, 122d Ohio, September 18, 1864, P.
T. Crow, H, 87th Pa., September 18, 1864, Pn.
T. Wilson, A, 14th N. J., September 18, 1864, D. C.
J. Graves, A, 179th N. Y., September 19, 1864, D. C.
R. Mills, B. 149th Ohio, September 19, 1864, F. & A.
F. Raap, C, 67th N. Y., September 20, 1864, D. C.
A. Jacobs, I, 11th Vt., September 20, 1864, D. C.
Geo. M. Lattin, B, 179th N. Y., September 21, 1864, D. C.
A. Baldwin, G, 144th Ohio, September 22, 1864, D. A.
J. Porter, K, 100th Ohio, September 22, 1864, D. A.
Thos. Taylor, G, 126th Ohio, September 22, 1864, F. T.
M. Undershover, I, 39th N. Y., September 23, 1864, D. C.
G. Zelhart, K, 122d Ohio, September 23, 1864, D. C.
S. Leithon, D, 1 Cav. D. C., September 23, 1864, D. C.
J. Kinaman, E, 149th Ohio, September 24, 1864, D. C
J. McGee, C, 2d Pa., September 25, 1864, D. C.
M. Welsh, B, 59th Mass., September 25, 1864, C.
J. Shepherd, B, 122d Ohio, September 25, 1864, B. C.
L. Spivney, G, 32d Me., September 25, 1864, D. C.
A. Hinsinger, E, 2d Pa., September 26, 1864, D. C

A. Allen, C, 9th Art'y N. Y., September 27, 1864, D. C.
J. Howlett, C, 2d Ind., September 29, 1864, D. C.
J. Knight, H, 32d Me., September 29, 1864, D. C.
C. Carpenter, B, 58th Mass., September 29, 1864, D. C.
N. Moore, C, 58th Mass., September 29, 1864, D. C.
B. M. McCaully, C, 119th Pa., September 30, 1864, D. C.
W. Wilson, H, 15th U. S., September 30, 1864, Ascites.
H. Warren, A, 57th Mass., October 1, 1864, D. C.
J. Skinner, E, 32d Me., October 1, 1864, D. C.
P. Frank, I, 149th Ohio, October 2, 1864, D. C.
H. Poleman, A, 87th Pa., October 2, 1864, D. C.
A. Haunson, D, 56th N. Y., October 2, 1864, D. C.
F. Trun, H, 59th Mass., October 3, 1864, D. C.
J. Grey, B, 106th N. Y., October 3, 1864, D. C.
D. Harvy, D, 2d Pa. Art., October 3, 1864, D. C.
J. Rumble, E, 14th Va., October 3, 1864, D. C.
B. Austin, F, 109th N. Y., October 3, 1864, D. C.
E. Christy, D, 28th Ind., October 3, 1864, D. C.
P. Neiw, K, 37th Wis., October 5, 1864, D. C.
E Stonifer, G, 1st Md., October 6, 1864, D. C.
H. Michals, D, 45th Pa., October 6, 1864, D. C.
H. Martin A, 32d Maine, October 6, 1864, D. C.
A. Wants, D, 45th Pa., October 7, 1864, Pn.
J. Boyle, E, 37th Wis., October 8, 1864, Pn.
E. Smith, K, 1st Vt., October 8, 1864, D. C.
G. Gaunt, I, 2nd Mich., October 8, 1864, D. C.
Sergeant J. Ballieu, F, 20th Pa., October 9, 1864, D. C.
H. Kimberlain, K, 110th Ohio, October 10, 1864, D. C.
E. Sheets, I, 11th Vt., October 11, 1864, Debility.
J. Jarvis, E, 3d Va., October 11, 1864, Colitis Chron.
R. Bennett, H, 106th N. Y., October 12, 1864, Colitis Chron.
W. Thurlow, 1st D. C., October 13, 1864, D. C.
B. F. Hiscott, F, 1st Regulars, October 13, 1864, D. C.
J. Tascoe, D, 31st N. Y., October 14, 1864, D. C.
S. Gruin, F, 14th N. Y., October 14, 1864, D. C.
P. Moriarty, G, 56th Mass., October 14, 1864, D. C.
C. Hastings, A, 1st N. H., October 15, 1864, D. C.
W. Lorman, D, 3d Md., October 15, 1864, D. C.
A. Cook, D, Freedman, 31st U. S., October 17, 1864, D. C.
—Wright, not known, October 17, 1864, D. C.
R. Williams, not known, October 18, 1864, D. C.
G. Sprague, F, 128th N. Y., October 18, 1864, D. C.
H. Phillips L, 8th N. Y., October 19, 1864, D. C.
G. West, G, 149th Ohio, October 20, 1864, D. C.
R. Parker, G, Freedman, 23d U. S., October 21, 1864, D. C.
J. Johns, A, Freedman, 27th Ohio, October 21, 1864, D. C.
C. Sidnor, D, Freedman, 29th Ill., October 21, 1864, D. C.
—Charles,.B, Freedman, 23d U. S., October 21, 1864, D. C.
J. Kilgore, K, 198th Tenn., October 21, 1864, Fract. of Skull
W. Mack, E, 106th N. Y., October 23, 1864, D. C.
Milton Burnsworth, E, 122d Ohio, October 23, 1864, D. C.

30

C. Edwards, D, 25th Wis., October 24, 1864, D. C.
M. B. Todd, D, 28th U. S. C., October 24, 1864, D. C.
J. Hall, F, 14th N. J., October 24, 1864, D. C.
Sergeant L. Rinhart, C, 2d Pa., October 24, 1864, Colitis Chron.
J. Welsh, E, 57th Mass., October 24, 1864, D. C.
J. Warden, C, 126th Ohio, October 24, 1864, D. A.
W. S. Burton, I, 126th Ohio, October 24, 1864, Colitis Chron.
T. Allen, K, 126th Ohio, October 25, 1864, D. C.
J. Anderson, D, 28th U. S. C. T., October 26, 1864, D. C.
J. Fisher, A, 25th N. Y., October 26, 1864, D. C.
D. Wilson, L, 9th N. Y., October 26, 1864, Pn.
D. Havens, D, 9th N. Y., October 26, 1864, Colitis Chron.
T. Higgins, K, 3d Va., October, 26, 1864, D. C.
R. Gibson, D, 9th U. S. C. T., October 27, 1864, D. C.
D. C. Brown, A, 17th Vt., October 27, 1864, Pn.
H. Fresboure, E, 38th Wis., October 27, 1864, D. C.
C. Attick, K, 1st Md., October 27, 1864, D, C.
G. Goodlow, E, 23d U. S. C. T., October 28, 1864, D. C.
T. Clary, C, 2d Pa., October 29, 1864, D. C.
J. Wesley, K, 28th U. S. I, October 31, 1864, D. C.
J. K. Hammond, D, 5th U. S. Cav., October 31, 1864, D. C.
F. Robinson, I, 1st D. C., October 31, 1864, Pn.
M. Sharp, F, 100th Pa., October 31, 1864, C.
F. Speet, D, 37th Wis., November 1, 1864, D. C.
B. F. Haven, H, 9th N. Y., November 1, 1864, D. C.
F. Lawrence, D, 12th Pa., November 2, 1864, D. C.
S. Lathrope M, 9th N. Y., November 2, 1864, D. C.
L. LaMotte, F, 11th N. H. November 2, 1864, Pharyngitis.
J. McGowan, H, 91st Ohio, November 2, 1864, D. C.
Henry Pateman, E, 164th N. Y., November 3, 1864, D. C.
L. Olsien, F, 37th Wis., November 3, 1864, Hemorrhage of lungs.
P. Casey, G, 109th N. Y., November 4, 1864, Pn.
P. Talley, G, 58th Mass., November 4, 1864, D. C.
J. Blair, E, 3d N. Y., November 4, 1864, Pn.
Captain E. S. Turner, B, 170th N. Y., November 4, 1864, Colitis Acuta.
Sergeant J. W. Phillips, H, 27th U. S., November 5, 1864, D. C.
Sergeant R. Thomas, E, 28th U. S., November 5, 1864, D. C.
L. H. Newcomb, H, 18th Conn., November 6, 1864, D. C.
James Smith, I, 56th Mass., November 6, 1864, Colitis Chron.
B. Smith, H, 58th Mass., November 6, 1864, D. C.
Corporal A. Dougherty, D, 10th Vt., November 6, 1864, D. C.
J. Brenner, G, 54th Ohio, November 6, 1864, D. C.
L. Woodbury, G, 10th Vt., November 6, 1864, D. C.
W. Morcy, D, 109th N. Y., November 6, 1864, D. C.
C. Dewes, I, 144th Ohio, November 6, 1864, D. C.
J. White, K, 14th N. J., November 6, 1864, F. T.
J. Garnes, G, 3d Va., November 6, 1864, D. C.
G. Jackson, A, 31st U. S. I., November 6, 1864, D. C.
W. Wallace, F, 32d Maine, November 6, 1864, Pn.
G. K. Mitchell, D, 28th U. S. I., November 7, 1864, D. C.
J. R. Prout, K, 23d U. S. I., November 7, 1864, D. C.

Corpl. Z. Westbrook, D, 37th Wis., November 7, 1864, D. C.
J. Amie, D, 27th U. S. I., November 8, 1864, D. C.
J. Hand, E, 14th N. Y., November 8, 1864, D. C.
C. W. Corry, L, Ist Cav. N. H., November 8, 1864, D. C.
C. Jones, Conscript, November 9, 1864, Pn.
Corpl. N. Darrow, I, 151st N. Y., November 9, 1864, Carditis.
S. Wasson, E, 20th Pa., November 9, 1864, D. C.
L. Vincent, F. 10th Va., November 9, 1864, D. C.
M. Cornell, F, 10th N. Y., November 10, 1864, D. C.
Wm. Brown, I, 1st Mich., November 10, 1864, D. C.
B. Smith, G, 31st Maine, November 10, 1864, D. C.
Corpl. T. Fisher, D, 59th Mass., November 10, 1864, D. C.
F. Kile, G, 149th Pa., November 11, 1864, D. C.
T. Blanpied, B, 122d Ohio, November 11, 1864, D. C.
F. Straud, E, 2d Maryland, November 11, 1864, Pn.
Corpl. Samuel Ellis, D, 1st Mich., November 11, 1864, Pn.
A. F. Riggs, D, 1st Cav. Va., November 12, 1864, D. C.
Sergt. S. P. Wells, C, 21st Maine, November 12, 1864, D. C.
W. S. Harlow, D, 58th Mass., November 12, 1864, D. C.
A. Lipe, G, 2d Art., Pa., November 12, 1864, Pl.
H. Christ, C, 58th Mass., November 12, 1864, Pn.
H. Southard, U. S. Navy, November 12, 1864, Parotitis.
F. N. Peack, H, 9th N. Y., November 12, 1864, D. C.
R. Martin, B, 43d Cav. U. S., November 13, 1864, D. C.
A. C. Morris, I, 109th N. Y., November 13, 1864, D. C.
A. Savage, B, 23d U. S. I., November 13, 1864, D. C.
H. Raymond, I, 2d Mich., November 13, 1864, Pn.
H. Hagoith, A, 2d Mich., November 13, 1864, D. C.
Corpl. J. P. Richardson, F, 9th N. H., November 13, 1864, Pn.
J. Miller, K, 16th Pa., November 14, 1864, Pn.
W. Akins, B, 106th N. Y., November 14, 1864, Pn.
U. Hunt, K, 12th Va., November 14, 1864, D. A.
W. Steele, K, 9th N. Y., November 14, 1864, Anasarca.
J. Goodall, G, 106th N. Y., November 14, 1864, D. C.
Corpl. J. Griffith, C, 110th Ohio, November 14, 1864, D. C.
W. Gifford, E, 58th Mass., November 14, 1864, D. C.
B. Allender, G, 54th Pa., November 14, 1864, D. C.
J. N. Ray, D, 149th Ohio, November 15, 1864, Pn.
M. Slimm, I, 10th N. J., November 15, 1864, D. C.
T. Lilly, G, 31st Maine, November 14, 1864, D. C.
C. Crandall, E, 43d N. Y., November 15, 1864, Pn.
W. White, B, 67th N. Y., November 16, 1864, D. C.
J. Fiery, E, 2d Md., November 16, 1864, Anasarca.
C. Ehenger, B, 99th Pa., November 16, 1864, D. C.
B. Holden, D, 31st U. S., November 17, 1864, D. C.
Corp'l C. Bronswell, B, 2d Md., November 17, 1864, D. C.
S. Bier, D, 16th Pa., November 18, 1864, D. C.
P. O'Donnel, A, 10th N. J., November 18, 1864, F. T.
J. King, C, 1st Cav. Ky., November 18, 1864, D. C.
H. Feathergill, G, 2d Art., Pa., November 18, 1864, Hydrothorax.
S. Hammond, E, 29th Mass., November 18, 1864, D. C.

R. Green, A, 29th U. S., November 18, 1864, D. C.
W. Wilson, C, 28th Cav. U. S., November 19, 1864, D. C.
S. Kirkpatrick, K, 3d Va., November 19, 1864, D. C.
A. Harrington, D, 144th Ohio, November 19, 1864, Pn.
Serg't J. A. Bixby, H, 9th N. Y., November 19, 1864, D. C.
J. Wheeler, L, 1st N. J., November 19, 1864, D. C.
T. Roe, C, 9th N. Y., November 19, 1864, D. C.
Serg't G. W. Abbott, F, 9th Maine, November 20, 1864, D A.
O. Cudworth, E, 106th N. Y., November 20, 1864, D. C
T. Martin, G, 2d Mass., November 20, 1864, F. T.
Joseph Martin, A, 1st Va., November 20, 1864, D. C.
J. S. Ryan, G, 149th Ohio, November 20, 1864, D. A.
Joseph Greenwood, M, 20th Cav. Pa., November 20, 1864, D. C.
J. Asay, A, 10th N. J., November 20, 1864, Pn.
Corp'l M. Smith, C, 57th Mass., November 21, 1864, D. C.
Serg't H. A. Hunt, B, 59th Mass., November 22, 1864, D. C.
L. F. Hull, A, 57th Mass., November 22, 1864, D. C.
W. Johnson, C, 27th Ohio, November 22, 1864, D. C.
A. Parker, K, 23d U. S., November 23, 1864, D. C.
A. Burns, G, 149th Ohio, November 23, 1864, D. C.
H. Hill, K, 9th N. Y., November 23, 1864, S.
G. W. Kepner, I, 17th Pa., November 23, 1864, D. C.
M. Powers, C, 57th Mass., November 23, 1864, D. A.
J. Townsend, K, 9th Art., N. Y., November 23, 1864, D. C.
R. Kimball, E, 9th Art., N. Y., November 24, 1864, B. C.
J. Tate, F, 2d Art., Pa., November 24, 1864, D. C.
A. Schoppe, C, 12th Cav., Pa., November 24, 1864, R. C.
W. Mannie, D, 11th N. H., November 24, 1864, D. A.
E. Rawden, B, 23d Ohio, November 24, 1864, Pn.
G. Baker, G, 109th N. Y., November 24, 1864, C.
Sergt. W. T. Gamble, B, 170th Ohio, November 24, 1864, B. C.
J. F. Haligan, F, 2d Cav., Mass., November 25, 1864, Cat.
John Hunter, G, 14th Art., N. Y., November 25, 1864, R. C.
S. Sepper, G, 120th Ohio, November 25, 1864, D. C.
E. Barnes, B, 44th Mass., November 25, 1864, D. C.
O. Mitcham, B, 38th Wis., November 25, 1864, D. C.
J. Morton, H, 109th N. Y., November 25, 1864, D. C.
R. Winkworth, F, 6th Mich., November 25, 1864, D. C.
B. S. Trail, C, 28th U. S. I., November 25, 1864, D. C.
Corpl. F. Snow, E, 59th Mass., November 25, 1864, D. C.
J. Dunivan, I, 65th N. Y., November 26, 1864, D. C.
J. Garrett, G, 126th Ohio, November 26, 1864, Anasarca.
Sergt. N. Bishop, C, 23d U. S. C. T., November 26, 1864, D. C.
Corp'l F. Snow, E, 59th Miss., November 26, 1864, D. C.
G. James, 32d U. S. C. T., November 26, 1864, D. C.
J. Miller, A, 23d U. S., November 26, 1864, D. C.
J. Downs, G, 1st Penna. Art., November 26, 1864, D. A.
J. Hays, H, 9th N. H., November 27, 1864, Pn.
John Lever, F, 58th Mass., November 27, 1864, D. C.
J. Murphy D, 58th Mass., November 27, 1864, D. C.
Corp'l J. Krantz, I, 16th N. Y., November 27, 1864, D. C.

J. Maloney, K, 1st Md., November 27, 1864, D. C.
P. Lawrence, G, 54th Pa., November 27, 1864, D. C
J. Wrenn, A, 31st Maine, November 27, 1864, D. C.
O. K. Nickols, A, 14th N. Y. Art., November 27, 1864, D. C.
A. Updike, G, 109th N. Y., November 28, 1864, D. C.
P. Wilcox, B, 58th Mass., November 28, 1864, Pn.
Serg't J. Bailey, C, 23d U. S. C. T., November 28, 1864, D. C
H. G. Harlow, C, 58th Mass., November 28, 1864, Anasarca.
W. H. Thomas, A, 13th Ind., November 29, 1864, B. C.
A. Motshler, D, 14th N. Y. Art., November 29, 1864, D. C.
W. Heard, D, 144th Ohio, November 29, 1864, D. C.
M. B. Todd, B, 28th U. S., November 29, 1864, D. C.
J. Jones, D, 28th U. S., November 29, 1864, D. C.
H. Bates, E, 106th N. Y., November 30, 1864, D. C.
H. Ponstler, K, 13th Va., November 30, 1864, D. C.
J. Mitchell, K, 1st Conn., November 30, 1864, D. C.
H. Sprague, G, 37th Wis., November 30, 1864, D. C.
Serg't E. O. Conklin, F, 1st Mich., November 30, 1864, D. C.
W. H. Grath, H, 23d Ill., November 30, 1864, Pn.
L. L. Church, A, 23d Ohio, November 30, 1864, Pn.
J. Lawrence, B, 5th N. Y. Art., December 2, 1864, F. & A.
D. Gray, G, 3d Mass., December 2d, 1864, D. C.
Corp'l A. F. Homer, G, 138th Pa., December 2, 1864, D. C.
George Creek, K, 1st Md., December 2, 1864, D. C.
James Davis, G, 1st Md., December 2d, 1864, D. C.
S. Jackson, D, 31st U. S., December 2, 1864, D. C.
H. Benjamin, D, 31st U. S., December 2d, 1864, D. C.
G. A. Glem, K, 3d Pa. Cav., December 3, 1864, D. C.
C. Phile, E, 151st N. Y., December 3, 1864, D. C.
M. O'Connor, B, 13th Ohio, December 3, 1864, Pn.
D. Jenkins, G, 1st Md. Cav., December 4, 1864, D. C.
H. Hendrick, G, 34th Ohio, December 4, 1864, Pn.
W. Howard, G, 17th Vt., December 4, 1864, D. C.
Crop'l J. Frinkham, H, 58th Mass., December 4, 1864, D. C.
Serg't G. Vinal, E, 1st D. C., December 4, 1864, D. C.
T. Pettis, B, 59th Mass., December 4, 1864, D. C.
C. Volk, M, 1st N. J. Cav., December 4, 1864, D. C.
J. C. Ringer, K, 3d Md., December 4, 1864, D. C.
Corp'l J. McLean, D, 54th Pa., December 4, 1864, Pn.
W. H. Warring, G, 109th N. Y., December 4, 1864, D. A.
A. Fromard, E, 31st U. S. C. T., December 5, 1864, D. C.
E. Rummell, A, 123d Ohio, December 5, 1864, D. A.
Thomas Wardman, D, 59th Mass., December 5, 1864, D. C.
J. W. Shumway, I, 151st N. Y., December 5, 1864, D, C.
W. P. Clegg, E, 12th Pa. Cav., December 5, 1864, D. C.
D. O'Brien, F, 23d Ill., December 5. 1864, Pn.
E. Edgard, M, 20th Pa., December 5, 1864, D. C.
G. Moore, E, 2d Md., December 6, 1864, D. C.
C. Vatang, F, 14th N. Y., December 6, 1864, D. C.
W. Williams, D, 33d U. S. C. T., December 6, 1864, D. C.
J. Brown, E, 12th Pa., December 6, 1864, E.

A. Butler, E, 22d N. Y., December 6, 1864, D. A.
Corp'l M. Foor, F, 138th Pa., December 6, 1864, Hydrethorax.
A. Kunkle, H, 4th N. Y. Cav., December 7, 1864, D. C.
J. Wolfe, D, 2d Pa. Art., December 7, 1864, D. C.
W. Zailagka, C, 12th Pa., December 7, 1864, D. C.
W. H. Cole, K, 37th Mich., December 8, 1864, D. A.
John O'Sulivan, F, 31st Maine, December 8, 1864, B. C.
W. Schafer, E, 5th Va., December 8, 1864, D. C.
G. B. Goud, I, 32d Maine, December 8, 1864, Pn.
Pat. Haffeman, K, 23d Ill., December 8, 1864, D. A.
J. Fox, I, 14th Pa., December 9, 1864, Pn.
F. Cain, A, 12th Va., December 9, 1864, Pn.
E. Gregory, G, 2d Ohio,December 9, 1864, D. C.
J. Brangle, F, 106th N. Y., December 9, 1864, D. C.
J. L. Cole, 4th N. Y. Cav., December 9, 1864, Pn.
E. Ayres, A, 10th N. J., December 10, 1864, D. C.
J. Meier, E, 16th N. Y. Cav., December 10, 1864, D. C.
A. Lecompt, F, 2d Md., December 11, 1864, Pn.
J. S. Colburn, H, 18th Conn., December 11, 1864, D. C.
D. J. Riggle, I, 14th Pa. Cav., December 11, 1864, D. A.
A. Castoe, H, 3d Va., December 11, 1864, D. C.
J. Miller, I, 2d Pa. Heavy Art., December 11, 1864, D. C.
L. Whitman, H, 14th N. Y., December 11, 1864, D. C.
R. Conver, E, 10th N. J., December 11, 1864, D. C.
G. W. Demerest, B, 3d N. J. Cav., December 11, 1864, Pn.
Tim. Tyree (Freedman, reg't unknown,) December 11, 1864, D. C.
S. Wright, A, 28th U. S. C. T., December 11, 1864, D. C.
D. Boyle, I, 34th Mass., December 11, 1864. B. C.
W. R. Salley, D, 10th N. J., December 12, 1864, Pn.
J. Glasscott, C, 2d Mass., December 12, 1864, Pn.
John Finley, E, 122d Ohio, December 12, 1864, R. C.
John Vanderburg, D, 1st Mich., December 12, 1864, Pn.
J. Graham, F, 37th Wis., December 13, 1864, Pn.
T. Conklin, H, 4th N. Y., December 13, 1864, D. C.
T. Parker, H, 2d Mass. Cav., December 13, 1864, D. C.
N. Allen, E, 31st Maine, December 14, 1864, Pn.
W. Shafer, G, 10th N. J., December 14, 1864, Pn.
J. Staples, C, 106th N. Y., December 14, 1864, D. C.
J. Sprague, G, 144th Ohio, December 14, 1864, Anasarca.
C. C. Barthick, D, 14th N. Y. Art., December 14, 1864, D. C.
V. Griggs, H, 14th N. J., December 15, 1864, D. C.
Corp'l D. Brann, C, 31st Maine, December 15, 1864, R. C.
W. Beaty, E, 133d N. Y., December 15, 1864, D. C.
C. Ormby, G, 2d Pa., December 15, 1864, D. C.
P. Maddron, I, 13th Tenn., December 16, 1864, Pn.
Colonel W. C. Rawlston, 24th N. Y. Cav., December 16, 1864, V. S. in
    abdomen.
Corp'l S. D. Kunkle, G, 15th N. J., December 16, 1864, Pn.
William Curl, K, 10th N. J., December 16, 1864, Pn.
Serg't J. A. Horner, C, 1st Mich., December 16, 1864, Pn.
H. C. Patton, E, 8th Ill., December 17, 1864, D.

A. Bainheart, B, 14th Pa. Cav., December 17, 1864, D. C.
J. Campfield, A, 9th N. Y., December 17, 1864, D. C.
H. Wilson, C, 57th Mass., December 17, 1864, D. C.
E. J. Whitman, L, 14th N. Y., December 17, 1864, B. C.
P. S. Reeves, D, 87th Pa., December 17, 1864, Pn.
C. Kirker, E, 2d Va. Cav., December 18, 1864, D. C.
John Shepley, F, 58th Mass., December 18, 1864, B. C.
Charles Henson, A, 2d Md., December 18, 1864, Pn.
Wm. Mastiden, L, 2d Ohio Art., December 19, 1864, Pn.
Sergt. D. Wolf, D, 20th Pa., December 19, 1864, D. C
J. Ford, H, 15th N. J., December 20, 1864, D. C.
C. L. Witters, C, 20th Mich., December 20, 1864, D, C.
John Loudon, C, 9th N. Y., December 20, 1864, D. C.
J. Williams, M, 27th Mich., B. C., December 20, 1864, B. C.
F. Cox, D, 170th Ohio, December 21, 1864, D. C.
M. McMara, C, 58th Mass., December 21, 1864, D. C.
Sergt. J. W. Tucker, 110th Ohio, December 21, 1864, Pn.
M. Buck, K, 6th Mich., December 21, 1864, Pn.
Captain John Digman, H, 183d Pa., December 22, 1864, R. C.
R. Brooks, B, 10th Vt., December 23, 1864, Pl.
Sergt. R. Blakely, A, 28th U. S., December 23, 1864, Colitis Acute.
P. Toole, K, 4th N. J., December 23, 1864, D. C.
J. Jackson, F, 23d U. S. C. T., December 24, 1864, D. C.
J. Gray, F, 23d U. S. C. T., December 24, 1864, D. C.
S. Thomas, H, 1st Md., December 25, 1864, D. C.
Sergt. A. G. York, D, 9th N. Y. Art., December 25, 1864, D. C.
E. Moore, A, 10th Vt., December 25, 1864, B. C.
J. T. Schiefer, B, 15th Va., December 25, 1864, D. C.
C. Withal, E, 31st Maine, December 25, 1864, D. C.
W. Daniel, E, 1st D. C., December 26, 1864, Pn.
L. Edwards, H, 6th N. Y. Cav., December 26, 1864, D. C.
J. Robinson, D, 45th Pa., December 27, 1864, D. C.
W. Johnson, C, 1st Pa. Art., December 27, 1864, D. C.
C. Parsons, D, 109th N. Y., December 27, 1864, D. C.
J. C. Whaley, B, 13th Tenn. Cav., December 27, 1864, F. T.
A. Porney, E, 23d Ohio, December 27, 1864, D. C.
C. Gibbs, C, 39th U. S. C. T., December 27, 1864, D. C.
A. Myers, E, 62d N. Y., December 27, 1864, D. C.
Corp. T. Morriarey, G, 151st N. Y., December 28, 1864, D. C.
C. F. Adkins, E, 1st Ky. Cav., December 28, 1864, D. C.
John Campans, G, 179th N. Y., December 28, 1864, D. C.
S. B. Rogers, A, 2d Mich., December 28, 1864, D. C.
L. Lachard, B, 151st N. Y., December 28, 1864, D. C.
D. Heltzel, I, 87th Pa., December 28, 1864, B. C.
E. Jackson, 31st U. S. C. T., December 28, 1864, D. C.
J. Bean, I, 37th Mass., December 29, 1864, D. C.
W. Fletcher, A, 3d Tenn., December 29, 1864, Pn.
Corp. E. J. Nickerson, A, 58th Mass., December 29, 1864, D. C.
J. Kunkle, K, 4th N. Y., December 29, 1864, D. C.
Sergt. John Stowell, F, 5th Mass., December 29, 1864, Pn.
John Conway, B, 58th Wis., December 29, 1864, B. C.

Sergt. J. W. Taylor, G, 23d Ohio, December 29, 1864, D. C.
C. Young, C, 16th N. Y., December 29, 1864, D. C.
L. D. Moore, (reg't and comp'y unknown,) December 29, 1864, D. C
J. S. Seley, C, 10th N. J., December 30, 1864, D. C.
Sergt. John Trusler, C, 9th N. Y. Cav., December 30, 1864, Pn.
J. B. Norris, B, 122d Ohio, December 31, 1864, B. C.
Corp. J. Welling, A, 1st Mich. Cav., December 31, 1864, D. C.
Corp. W. F. Brackett, A, 14th Pa. Art , December 31, 1864, Pn.
W. H. L. Gee, H, 45th Pa., December 31, 1864, Pn.
A. Copeland, A, 6th Vt., January 1, 1865, Colitis Acuta.
A. Newman, D, 1st Vt. Cav., January 1, 1865, Pn.
O. Sheldon, C, 106th N. Y., January 1, 1865, D. C.
Corp. W. Bolton, D, 112th Pa., January 2, 1865, D. C.
E. D. Muchman, C, 14th N. Y., January 2, 1864, Pn.
H. D. Blatchley, I, 10th Vt., January 2, 1865, D. A.
R. F. Fowell, D, 31st Maine, January 2, 1865, Pn.
J. F. Stedding, G, 3d Md., January 2, 1865, D. C.
Corp. S. B. French, I, 1st Tenn. Art., January 2, 1865, D. C.
Corp. H. K. Sudler, E, 2d Md., January 3, 1864, D. C.
John Elrah, A, 4th N. Y., January 3, 1865, D. C.
B. F. Starkey, G, 5th Wis., January 3, 1865, F. T.
J. Bolton, I, 9th Tenn. Cav., January 3, 1865, B. C.
George Matson, G, 87th Pa., January 4, 1865, Pn.
H. Somers, E, 12th Pa., January 4, 1865, D. C.
Corp. C. Aklee, B, 32d Maine, January 4, 1865, D. C.
A. S. Jolly, I, 144th Ohio, January 4, 1865, Pn.
W. Lambert, C, 126th Ohio, January 4, 1865, Anasarca.
C. Danley, D, 32d Maine, January 4, 1865, D. C.
J. Dewberry, C, 23d Ohio, January 4, 1865, D. C.
John Thomas, A, 54th Pa., January 5, 1865, Pn.
J. Russ, E, 22d N. Y., January 5, 1865, D. C.
Corp. W. H. Folks, E, 5th Va. Cav., January 6, 1865, Pn.
J. Coleman, K, 18th Pa., January 6, 1865, D. C.
M. Keily, B, 57th Mass., January 6, 1865, Pn.
P. Smith, E, 1st Va. Cav , January 6, 1865, Pn.
Sergt. W. C. Park, H, 57th Mass., January 6, 1865, F. T.
A. Grim, E, 10th Va., January 6, 1865, D. C.
Corp. J. Westcoat, E, 10th N. J., January 7, 1865, D. C.
N. W. Wesgate, I, 1st N. H. Cav., January 7. 1865, B. C.
A. Waxwood, A, 2d Md., January 10, 1865, R. C.
Lieut. M. Whitbeck, I, 51st N. Y., January 10, 1865, D. C.
D. Blanchard, C, 2d Mich., January 10, 1865, D. C.
W. Bassett, A, 58th Mass., January 10, 1865, Pn.
J. Bork, F, 106th N. Y., January 10, 1865, Anasarca.
A. Lipp, L, 1st Va., January 10, 1865, D. C.
D. Welch, A, 9th, N. H., January 10, 1865, D. C.
Sergt. C. Roe, C, 59th Mass., January 10, 1865, D. C.
D. Hoffman, E, 80th Ohio, January 10, 1865, D. C.
J. Clifford, B, 151st N. Y., January 10, 1865, D. C.
Corp. W. Adams, K, 10th N. J., January 10, 1865, Pn.
Corp. A. Babbet, E, 58th Mass., January 10, 1865, D. C

N. Mattis, A, 51st Pa., January 10, 1865, D. C.
John Hobson, L, 2d Ohio, January 10, 1865, D. C.
W. Drake, L, 22d N. Y., January 10, 1865, D. C.
Sergt. E. Andrew, D, 179th N. Y., January 10, 1865, C.
J. Davis, F, 9th N. H., January 10, 1865, D. C.
J. Wharton, M, 15th N. Y., January 10, 1865, D. C.
A. V. Tanner, H, 151st N. Y., January 12, 1865, F. T.
S. Hughes, F, 4th Mich. Cav., January 12, 1865, D. C.
Corp. E. Mahen, C, 58th Mass., January 12, 1865, D. C.
B. Blackburn, B, 110th Ohio, January 14, 1865, D. C.
W. Harris, B, 23d Pa., January 14, 1865, D. C.
F. Warren, D, 16th N. Y., January 14, 1865, D. C.
W. Winslow, I, 58th Mass., January 14, 1865, Pn.
J. Dyson, I, 13th Tenn., January 14, 1865, Rubeola.
J. Mead, C, 21st Mass., January 15, 1865, S.
N. Harris, (Freedman, reg't unknown,) January 15, 1865, D. C.
Corp. J. F. Evans, C, 9th N. H., January 15, 1865, D. C.
A. Woodmanset, B, 149th Ohio, January 15, 1865, Pn.
A. Hendershot, D, 15th N. J., January 15, 1865, D. C.
D. Cole, E, 13th Tenn., January 15, 1865, D. C.
Samuel Crane, I, 8th Ill. Cav., January 16, 1865, D. C.
L. Briner, E, 20th Pa., January 16, 1865, Pn.
H. W. Koothman, F, 12th Va., January 16, 1865, B. C.
E. Smallford, D, 1st Va. Cav., January 16, 1865, D. C.
E. Curry, B, 15th N. J., January 17, 1865, B. A.
A. C. Hickman, E, 37th Wis., January 17, 1865, D. C.
N. Newell, D, 31st Maine, January 17, 1865, D. C.
L. E. C. Hall, K, 11th Vt,, January 18, 1865, D. C.
W. Ransom, K, 87th Pa., January 18, 1865, D. C.
F. Gustin, E, 22d N. Y., January 18, 1865, D. C.
Corp. J. B. Creveling, G, 10th N. J., January 18, 1865, D. C.
O. C. Miller, D, 20th Mich., January 19, 1865, D. C.
R. Galfilland, D, 2d Md., January 19, 1865, Pn.
D. Misinger, K, 110th Ohio, January 20, 1865, D. C.
P. Conrad, A, 5th U. S., January 20, 1865, D. C.
J. Romey, F, 184th Pa., January 20, 1865, Pn.
S. Jones, H, 13th N. J., January 20, 1865, Anasarca.
Corp. H. Washburn, D, 179th N. Y., January 20, 1865, Anasarca.
H. Dean, H, 20th Mich., January 20, 1865, Anasarca.
T. Jones, C, 23d U. S. C. T., January 20, 1865, D. C.
Sergt. J. W. Korn, C, 3d N. J., January 21, 1865, Pn.
T. Rockford, B, 10th Mich. Cav., January 21, 1865, Pn.
Corp. J. Carr, I, 1st N. H., January 21, 1865, D. C.
J. Bodkin, F, 14th Pa., January 21, 1865, D. C.
John Carter, G, 3d Md., January 21, 1865, D. C.
R. Barnett, C, 9th N. Y. Art., January 21, 1865, D. C.
Corp. S. Terry, K, 13th N. Y., January 22, 1865, D. C
J. Hodson, G, 149th Ohio, January 22, 1865, D. C.
M. Whitnight, G, 2d Pa., January 22, 1865, Anasarca.
J. Houghton, B, 1st Tenn., January 22, 1865, D. C.
Corp. John Hyland, C, 5th N. Y. Art., January 22, 1865, D. C

D. Mickerson, D, 58th Mass., January 23, 1865, Anasarca.
H. Crampton, E, 8th Ohio Cav., January 23, 1865, Pn.
J. H. Monroe, K, 11th Vt., January 23d, 1865, Pn.
F. Hale, F, 23d Ohio, January 23, 1865, Pn.
W. A. Wright, F, 4th N. J., January 23, 1865, Pn.
J. Purdy, I, 2d Mass. Cav., January 24, 1865, B. C.
L. Costerlough, L, 23d Ill., January 24, 1865, D. C.
Corp. R. Akin, B, 9th N. H., January 25, 1865, D. C.
W. Modisett, C, 11th Va., January 27, 1865, D. C.
S. Bushhammer, G, 87th Pa., January 27, 1864, Pn.
W. Howser, I, 149th Ohio, January 27, 1865, D. C.
A. Cross, B, 32d Maine, January 27, 1865, Pn.
Thomas Lynch, I, 56th Mass., January 27, 1865, D. C.
A. Hood, K, 10th Va., January 27, 1865, D. C.
G. Deito, A, 28th U. S., January 27, 1865, D. C.
R. Smith, D, 23d U. S. C. T., January 28, 1865, D. C.
J. H. Martin, I, 87th Pa., January 28, 1865, D. C.
James Tucker, C, 9th N. Y., January 28, 1865, D. C.
M. White, H, 4th Pa., January 29, 1865, D. C.
W. Osborne, H, 8th Tenn., January 29, 1865, D. C.
Sergt. E. Hillery, D, 1st Md., January 29, 1865, D. C.
John Potter, F, 4th N. J., January 29, 1865, Pn.
Thomas E. Smith, C, 4th R. I., January 29, 1865, Pn.
J. Quinn, G, 1st Tenn. Art., January 29, 1865, Pn.
M. Crane, B, 10th Vt., January 29, 1865, D. C.
C. Goodfellow, G, 23d Ohio, January 30, 1865, D. C.
W. Butler, C, 9th N. H., January 30, 1865, Pl.
J. Miller, 39th U. S. C. T., January 30, 1865, D. C.
John Ditch, K, 1st N. Y., January 30, 1865, D. C.
G. McClosland, D, 12th Va., January 30, 1865, D. C.
G. Bishop, A, 15th N. J., January 31, 1865, Debility.
H. Washburne, G, 32d Maine, January 31, 1865, Mania.
E. Couch, D, 11th N. H., February 1, 1865, Scrofula.
F. E. Smith, F, 2d Mass. Cav., February 1, 1865, C.
Jacob Carr, H, 9th Tenn., February 2, 1865, E.
C. Foley, H, 59th Mass., February 2, 1865, D. C.
Daniel Dougherty, L, 59th Mass., February 2, 1865, D. C.
H. Jepperson, E, 8th Ill. Cav., February 2, 1865, D. C.
Corp. J. Bachman, E, 87th Pa., February 2, 1865, D. C.
H. Peck, D, 9th N. Y., February 2, 1865, Pn.
Corp. W. Davis, F, 34th Ohio, February 3, 1865, V. S. in left thigh.
G. Huffman, K, 2d Md., February 3, 1865, D. C.
C. G. Cook, A, 58th Mass., February 4, 1865, D. C.
A. Lear, A, 3d N. J. Cav., February 4, 1865, Pn.
Chas. H. Rogers, G, 45th Pa., February 4, 1865, D. C.
O. Brown, A, 9th N. Y. Art., February 4, 1865, D. C.
G. Babcock, G, 109th N. Y., February 4, 1865, D. C.
L. Stump, E, 20th Mich., February 4, 1865, D. C.
W. Dudley, E, 28th Ohio, February 5, 1865, Pn.
G. Messer, K, 8th Tenn., February 5, 1865, D. C.
S. Keyhill, K, 13th Tenn., February 5, 1865, Pn.

A. Hayes, I, 23d U. S., February 5, 1865, D. C.
R. Clayton, K, 4th N. H., February 5, 1865, D. C.
Corp. T. Small, H. 56th Mass., February 5, 1865, D. C.
P. Sigler, F, 1st Va., February 6, 1865, Pn.
R. Pigman, I, 9th Va., February 6, 1865, D. C.
Isaac Demas, A, 14th N. Y. Art., February 6, 1865, S.
S. Wagman, D, 2d Pa. Art., February 7, 1865, S.
Sergt. J. W. Poster, H, 1st Va. Cav., February 7, 1865, D. C.
J. Lippy, I, 10th N. J., February 7, 1865, Pn.
E. McKussick, A, 9th N. H., February 7, 1865, D. C.
Thomas Shipley, E, 1st Tenn. Bat., February 7, 1865, D. C.
J. Griffin, E, 1st Tenn., February 7, 1865, D. C.
J. Frazier, F, 122d Ohio, February 7, 1865, D. C.
J. Hilman, H, 98th Pa., February 8, 1865, D. C.
W. Dalrymple, B, 10th Mich., February 8, 1865, Pn.
Corp. J. Mead, A, 9th N. Y. Art., February 8, 1865, D. C.
Wm. Carter, D, 9th Tenn. Cav., February 8, 1865, Pn.
Pat Harnasay, K, 59th Mass., February 8, 1865, D. C.
John A. Miller, G, 10th Va., February 9, 1865, D. C.
D. C. Ruggles, Maj. and P. M. in U. S. A., February 10, 1865, F. R
U. T. Baker, F, 36th Ohio, February 10, 1865, D. C.
C. Manning, E, 59th Mass., February 10, 1865, D. C.
W. A. Foster, A, 1st Tenn., February 10, 1865, D. C.
W. Marks, E, 1st Tenn. Art., February 10, 1865, D. C.
L. Fauver, A, 23d Ohio, February 10, 1865, D. C.
W. Glasco, K, 13th Va., February 11, 1865, D. C.
Sergt. Vannostrand, A, 3d N. J., February 11, 1865, Pn.
Corp. A. P. Kratz, 2d Pa. Art., February 12, 1865, D. C.
G. R. Higgins, C, 23d Ohio, February 12, 1865, D. C.
W. Walker, G, 179th N. Y., February 12, 1865, D. C.
J. G. Pack, C, 2d Mass., February 12, 1865, Pn.
Chas. Major, B, 14th N. J., February 12, 1865, D. C.
J. M. Dewitt, C, 9th N. Y. Art., February 12, 1865, D. C.
P. Myers, F, 1st Md. Cav., February 13, 1865, D. C.
Wm. Crooks, F, 34th Ohio, February 13, 1865, D. C.
P. A. Haywood, H, 31st Maine, February 13, 1865, D. C.
Corp. J. Core, C, 10th N. J., February 14, 1865, D. C.
John Paul, D, 2d Pa. Art., February 14, 1865, D. C.
G. Martin, D, 2d Pa. Art., February 14, 1865, D. C.
J. Linton, B, 126th Ohio, February 15, 1865, D. C.
P. Butler, G, 10th N. J., February 15, 1865, Pn.
E. Cutts, A, 31st Maine, February 15, 1865, D. C.
M. Armstrong, A, 7th Ind., February 15, 1865, D. C.
R. Fleek, B, 2d Pa. Art., February 15, 1865, D. C.
J. B. Chase, D, 2d Pa. Art., February 15, 1865, D. C.
D. Gilmer, I, 14th N. Y. Art., February 16, 1865, D. C.
S. Brown, C, 3d Tenn., February 16, 1865, F. A.
J. Kelly, I, 144th Ohio, February 16, 1865, D. C.
P. Barnett, I, 59th Mass., February 16, 1865, D. C.
J. Hetzell, E, 3d Md., February 16, 1865, D. C.
Wm. Sumner, A, 106th N. Y., February 16, 1865, D. C.

L. Marcellers, A, 9th N. Y., February 16, 1865, D. C.
H. Grise, K, 2d Md., February 16, 1865, D. C.
G. W. Nalls, G, 3d Md., February 16, 1865, D. C.
T. W. Day, C, 29th Maine, February 16, 1865, Pn.
J. F. Thomas, H, 11th N. H., February 17, 1865, D. C.
W. Pentland, A, 3d N. J., February 17, 1865, D. C.
D. Sweeney, B, 13th Tenn., February 17, 1865, D. C.
J. K. Parker, B, 149th Ohio, February 17, 1865, D. C.
James Hill, B, 2d Maine, February 17, 1865, D. C.
D. G. Pattison, D, 116th Ohio, February 18, 1865, D. C.
Lieut. Joseph Willell, L, 8th N. Y. Art., February 18, 1865, D. C.
W. Mason, A, 23d Ohio, February 18, 1865, D. C.
G. Geary, D, 4th Pa., February 18, 1865, D. C.
J. Logan, H, 1st Pa. Cav., February 18, 1865, D. C.
D. Manderville, I, 15th N. J., February 19, 1865, D. C.
J. N. Marsh, E. 14th N. J., February 19, 1865, D. C.
M. Long, L, 9th Tenn. Cav., February 19, 1865, D. C.
Corp. W. S. Marsh, E, 14th N. J., February 19, 1865, D. C.
E. Gentry, E, 13th Tenn., February 20, 1865, Pn.
T. Stilton, D, 1st Va. Cav., February 20, 1865, D. C.
W. Wagner, K, 16th N. Y., February 21, 1865, D. C.
John Amob, K, 1st Mich., February 21, 1865, B. C.
W. Hall, F, 58th Mass., February 21, 1865, Pn.
W. Wilkerson, E, 10th N. J., February 21, 1865, D. C.
J. Farnsworth, G, 37th Wis., February 21, 1865, D. C.
J. Hester, C, 9th N. Y. Art., February 21, 1865, D. C.
J. Fisher, K, 1st Md., February 21, 1865, D. C.
S. Masher, B, 109th N. Y., February 23, 1865, D. C.
W. Murduff, C, 13th Pa., February 23, 1865, Anasarca.
Sergt. W. F. Howard, I, 59th Mass., February 23, 1865, D. C.
J. Ogburn, B, 4th N. Y., February 23, 1865, Anasarca.
J. Taylor, F, 21st N. Y., February 23, 1865, D. C.
G. Inman, A, 10th N. J., February 24, 1865, D. C.
J. Ackley, E, 12th Pa., February 25, 1865, D. C.
J. Taylor, C, 179th N. Y., February 25, 1865, D. C.
Sergt. J. Davis, C, 58th Mass., February 25, 1865, D. C.
John Roach, D, 34th Mass., February 25, 1865, D. C.
G. Presley, B, 122d Ohio, February 25, 1865, D. C.
G. Rhodes, I, 2d Mich., February 26, 1865, D. C.
Corp. W. E. Greer, H, 161st N. Y., February 26, 1865, D. C.
L. Show, E, 8th Tenn., February 26, 1865, D. C.
P. Hunt, A, 12th Va., February 26, 1865, B. C.
U. C. Tester, M, 13th Tenn., February 27, 1865, D. C.
E. Hills, K, 151st N. Y., February 27, 1865, D. C.
J. Adleshost, K, 2d Md., February 27, 1865, D. C.
J. Harmon, F, 1st Md., February 27, 1865, D. C.
E. Clayton, B, 2d Pa., March 1, 1865, D. C.
J. Britton, F, 14th N. J., March 2, 1865, E.
W. Green, G, 20th Mich., March 2, 1865, D. C.
A. Jasslyn, A, 122d Ohio. March 3, 1865, B. C.
W. Fletcher, G, 110th Ohio, March 2, 1865, D. C.

J. White, M, 8th Ill., March 3, 1865, D. C.
Corp. A. Bartlett, D, 45th Pa., March 3, 1865, D. C.
G. P. Fassett, F, 1st D. C. Cav., March 3, 1865, D. C.
C. Spraight, A, 2d Mass., March 4, 1865, D. C.
Sergt. J. Swaize, K, 15th N. J., March 4, 1865, D. C.
Sergt. E. M. Sutton, A, 1st Va. Cav., March 4, 1865, D. C.
C. P. Crowell, E, 151st N. Y., March 5, 1865, D. C.
J. Anderson, G, 14th N. J., March 6, 1865, Anasarca.
J. Thomas, I, 10th N. J., March 6, 1865, D. C.
S. Morgan, B, 32d Maine, March 6, 1865, D. C.
A. Bellfinger, B, 15th N. J., March 7, 1865, F. T.
P. Krizer, F, 125th Ohio, March 8, 1865, D. C.
J. Murphy, C, 18th Pa., March 8, 1865, D C.
J. K. Long, A, 45th Pa., March 8, 1865, D C.
F. Rollardson, F, 109th N. Y., March 8. 1865, D. C.
J. Rutter, K, 10th N. J., March 9, 1865, D. A
F. Elder, M, 8th Ohio Cav., March 10, 1865. D. C.
Corp. L. Clatter, I, 4th Ind., March 10, 1865, D. C.
A. J. Day, L, 11th Tenn., March 11, 1865, D. C.
G. Sutter, E, 2d Md., March 11, 1865, D. C.
C. E. Fanar, H, 58th Mass., March 12, 1865, D. C.
D. Doyle, H, 2d Mass , March 12, 1865, Anæmia.
W. Presley, K, 18th Ind., March 13, 1865. D. C.
J. Smith, G, 179th N. Y., March 16, 1865, D. C.
B. Writzland, C, 2d Mich., March 18. 1865, D. C.
Corp. J. Hess, F, 8th Tenn., March 19, 1865, Simple F. C.
G. W. Wescot, K, 38th Mass., March 19, 1865. Simple F. C.
E. A. Smith, B, 15th Conn., April 1, 1865. Tetanus Traum.
G. W. Docrathy, H, 25th Wis., April 4, 1865, Pn.
Major E. W. Osborne, 15th Conn., April 6, 1865, V. S. in left thigh.
A. Aspeler, 12th N. Y. Cav., April 11, 1865. Pn.
Corp. F. Phillips, I, 15th Conn., April 11, 1865, V. S. in right arm.
B. E. Taylor, A, 27th Mass., April 17, 1865, V. S. in left arm.
G. A. Martin, E, 27th Mass., April 24, 1865, F. T.
W. Proctor, 27th Mass., April 28, 1865, Pyæmia.

NOTE.—In addition to the above list, two (2) white soldiers died in prison, and one (1) on the cars, whose names I was unable to ascertain. Nine (9) Freedmen also died in prison, who could not be identified during my term of undertaking—extending from November 24, 1863, to October 21, 1864.

I will likewise inform the friends of the deceased, that there exists a statute in the State of Virginia, which forbids the exhuming of all persons who have died from variolous diseases.

Very respectfully,
Your obedient servant,
JOHN J. HILL, Danville, Va.

There were eleven Federal prisoners who died *in transitu*, and were taken from the cars, and buried here, during the period of time extending from October 23, 1864, to the surrender of General Lee's army.

Respectfully, yours,   D. H. STRICKLAND

List of Graves in Point of Rocks Cemetery.

This cemetery is beautifully laid out, and well cared for. The graves are arranged in concentric circles. The following list was made out by the agents of the Commission from the head-boards.

The following are buried at Point of Rocks Cemetery:

John H. Lent, D, 6th N. Y. A.
J. Handford, I, 6th N. Y. A.
F. Vanloon, 47th N. Y.
J. H. Soper, D, 6th N. Y. H. A.
R. Daggett, B, 6th N. Y. H. A.
J. W. Brooks, M, 6th N. Y. H. A.
A. Clark, D, 6th N. Y. H. A.
Wm. Kellum, L, 6th N. Y. H. A.
R. M. Jones, I, 148th N. Y.
Wm. Gloner, E, 16th N. Y. H. A.
W. H. Bass, B, 10th N. Y. A.
J. G. McClure, G, 148th N. Y.
J. Travers, D, 4th N. Y. H. A.
John Devolly, I, 158th N. Y.
J. E. Rees, C, 10th N. Y. A.
Jesse Harris, M, 10th N. Y. A.
B. Walker, B, 158th N. Y.
Wm. A. Atwater, F, 89th N. Y.
Charles Tully, F, 6th N. Y. A.
Wm. Johnson, 17th Inf., Bat. L.
M. Williamson, E, 1st N. Y. A.
T. M. Foster, F, 1st N. Y. Drag.
Henry Gould, L, 10th N. Y. A.
J. A. Miller, F, 10th N. Y. A.
H. H. Baker, G, 96th N. Y.
A. Elmer, F, 1st N. Y. Cav.
D. Vanivickle, F, 148th N. Y.
M. Devor, F, 17th S. C.
I. W. Bright, D, 35th N. C.
R. M. Brady, B, 2d N. C.
A. Schoofs, F, 8th Va.
J. V. Johnson, G, 56th W. C.
J. C. Ultz, C, 4th W. C.
J. Moore, F, 17th Va.
John Williamson, C, 48th P. V.

J. M. Burns, I, 55th P. V.
Daniel Foster, H, 2d Pa. H. A.
Amandis Yous, K, 54th P. V.
C. Wattenmyer, K, 199th P. V.
J. McLaughlin, H, 54th P. V.
Isaac Sapp, D, 97th P. V.
F. R. Spiller, H, 199th P. V.
Wm. Lander, E, 148th P. V.
Scott Hite, G, 188th P. V.
John Renklid, B, 199th P. V.
B. Kinsey, D, 53d P. V.
A. Stephens, A, 1st Pa. L. Art
D. Patterson, K, 58th P. V.
J. Love B, 54th P. V.
J. Barskey, A, 122d P. V.
C. I. Wood, A, 17th Me.
H. Tellman, B, 7th U. S. C. T.
Wm. Holliday, I, 43d U. S. C. T.
James Emery, K, 6th U. S. C. T.
George Queen, K, 107th U. S. C. T.
Charles Wright, A, 4th U. S. C. T.
Thomas Hall, I, 107th U. S. C. T.
J. Harden, K, 107th U. S. C. T.
W. Magruder, C, 107th U. S. C. T.
Alfred Merrick, D, 107th U. S. C. T.
John Bedford, D, 7th U. S. C. T.
James Vaughan, B, 107th U. S. C. T.
Barrell Avery, F, 117th U. S. C. T.
Samuel Finney, K, 107th U. S. C. T.
Joseph Garnett, B, 107th U. S. C. T.
S. Beasley, H, 109th U. S. C. T.
F. Green, D, 41st U. S. C. T.
Lewis Harris, E, 117th U. S. C. T.
Joseph Tanner, E, 117th U. S. C. T.
A. Robinson, I, 109th U. S. C. T.
J. Thomas, F, 23d U. S. C. T.
James Hall, K, 118th U. S. C. T.
Richard Taylor, C, 4th U. S. C. T.
Benjamin Cambell, H, 122d U. S. C. T.
Samuel Palmer, I, 31st U. S. C. T.
Charles Darsey, F, 4th U. S. C. T.
Alfred Steward, E, 117th U. S. C. T.
James Jago, C, 118th U. S. C. T.
John Sidney, B, 117th U. S. C. T.
H. Kendell, H, 8th U. S. C. T.
G. Thompson, D, 9th U. S. C. T.
H. Rogers, E, 115th U. S. C. T.
C. Welford, I, 9th U. S. C. T.
Stephen Dixon, F, 23d U. S. C. T.
F. Sanders, H, 22d U. S. C. T.
John Talmson, A, 117th U. S. C. T.

George Harman, G, 22d U. S. C T.
H. H. Davis.
Samuel Cooper, C, 29th U. S. C. T.
Mark Bishop, K, 45th U. S. C. T.
Wm. Tines.
James Dilley, A, 117th U. S. C. T.
William Joe, H, 45th U. S. C. T.
Charles Allen, I, 107th U. S. C. T
D. Atkinson, F, 107th U. S. C. T.
C. Edwards, F, 118th U. S. C. T.
J. Kellum, B, 9th U. S. C. T.
S. Elvers, A, 117th U. S. C. T.
Abram Myers, F, 114th U. S. C. T.
Wilson Evans, H, 118th U. S. C. T
I. Fortune, E, 109th U. S. C. T.
John Rigers, G, 116th U. S. C. T.
S. Vincent, G, 127th U. S. C. T.
A. Mitchell, K, 107th U. S. C. T
G. Hays, I, 116th U. S. C. T.
James Jones, H, 118th U. S. C. T.
J. McBride, C, 116th U. S. C. T.
William Roswell, K, 2d U. S. C. T.
Robert Wilson, B, 19th U. S. C. T
Levi Mayor, I, 114th U. S. C. T.
Samuel Coleman, T, 41st U. S. C. **T.**
Edmund Johnson, T, 45th U. S. C. **T.**
G. Beller, I, 107th U. S. C. T.
I. Alkinson, H, 118th U. S. C. T.
R. Parker, B, 36th U. S. C. T.
—— Anthony, H, 118th U. S. C. **T.**
Albert Bond, H, 117th U. S. C. T.
L. Anderson, H, 19th U. S. C. T.
John Cook, G, 114th U. S. C. T.
M. Burton, E, 10th U. S. C. T.
P. Vanison, F, 41st U. S. C. T.
C. Harrison, I, 36th U. S. C. T.
Ralph Jones, B, 115th U. S. C. T
E. Adams, E, 118th U. S. C. T.
G. Kright, E, 118th U. S. C. T.
Benjamin Stone, I, 123d U. S. C. T.
Wm. Williams, B, 116th U. S. C. **T.**
Isaac Tilley, K, 23d U. S. C. T.
Lewis Wortz, E, 117th U. S. C. T
Clark Witt, E, 116th U. S. C. T.
Jesse Taylor, F, 19th U. S. C. T.
H. Cullum, A, 10th U. S. C. T.
A. McCoy, A, 117th U. S. C. T
M. Thomas, B, 117th U. S. C. **T.**
Essex Mary, D, 9th U. S. C. T.
A. Bruce, E, 109th U. S. C. T.
T. Ingraham, K, 114th U. S. C. T.

I. Robinson, K, 29th U. S. C. T.
I. Hawkins, B, 19th U. S. C. T.
Edward Emery, D, 41st U. S. C. T.
G. H. Hartbrock, C, 43d U. S. C. T
Jacob Balkelt, K, 117th U. S. C. T.
John Smith, E, 116th U. S. C. T.
George Brown, H, 29th U. S. C. T.
Daniel Adams, D, 118th U. S. C. T.
Samuel Johnson, C, 29th U. S. C. T.
William Henry, E, 41st U. S. C. T
N. Courtney, D, 29th U. S. C. T.
Samuel Lewis, B, 29th U. S. C. T.
Charles Hubbard, E, 29th U. S. C. T
D. Webster B, 118th U. S. C. T.
John Brown, E, 29th U. S. C. T.
R. King, K, 118th U. S. C. T.
Samuel Dowdy, U. S. C. T.
J. Jackson, I, 117th U. S. C. T.
William Davis, I, 8th U. S. C. T.
William Cuffer, D, 36th U. S. C. T.
George Russels, I, 45th U. S. C. T
Jacob Barrett, C, 118th U. S. C. T.
James Lee. D, 29th U. S. C. T.
Thomas Hall, U. S. C. T.
A. Jones, E, 38th U. S. C. T.
B. Dickson, G, 118th U. S. C. T.
George Wright, E, 29th U. S. C. T.
J. H. Halman, A, 117th U. S. C. T.
W. H. Slade, H, 38th U. S. C. T.
C. Smith, K, 29th U. S. C. T.
J. Wheeler, U. S. C. T.
James Odum, U. S. C. T.
Lewis Wilson, B, 127th U. S. C. T.
D. Barney, U. S. C. T.
Robert Dalley, D, 98th U. S. C. T.
W. Breckerson, K, 117th U. S. C. T.
John Dandy, A, 16th U. S. C. T.
O. Anderson, I, 8th U. S. C. T.
W. Bowman, C, 107th U. S. C. T.
B. Wilson, D, 36th U. S. C. T.
I. Walker, E, 118th U. S. C. T.
Bill Green, A, 109th U. S. C. T.
S. Showell, K, 9th U. S. C. T.
I. Moore, U. S. C. T.
G. Crawford, C, 117th U. S. C. T
C. Hawes, I, 118th U. S. C. T.
J. Thomas, A, 19th U. S. C. T.
G. Cowell, G, 116th U. S. C. T.
J. Fields, K, 107th U. S. C. T.
Marcus Neal, G, 117th U. S. C. T
John Barnes, K, 19th U. S. C. T.

Richard Blunt, I, 37th U. S. C. T.
Oliver Swan, U. S. C. T.
John Cominger, G, 30th U. S. C. T.
John Adams, F, 118th U. S. C. T.
A. Clarke, F, 43d U. S. C. T.
Isaac Gibbs, G, 39th U. S. C. T.
Peter Reed, E, 9th U. S. C. T.
F. Marchall, G, 118th U. S. C. T.
A. McClain, G, 118th U. S. C. T.
G. Thompson, F, 117th U. S. C. T.
O. Hughes, 117th U. S. C. T.
Fred. Dorsey, G, 19th U. S. C. T.
Henry Burns, C, 117th U. S. C. T.
A. Letes, H, 118th U. S. C. T.
Chas. Johnson, E, 19th U. S. C. T.
H. Everett, H, 36th U. S. C. T.
Frank Onder, D, 115th U. S. C. T.
H. Camper, F, 29th U. S. C. T.
Luther Butler, A, 39th U. S. C. T.
Wm. Hays, H, 107th U. S. C. T.
M. Carson, B, 2d U. S. C. T.
M. Medley, F, 29th U. S. C. T.
Moses Bailey, C, 29th U. S. C. T.
S. Conway, U. S. C. T.
Thos. Speays, F, 114th U. S. C. T.
B. Ballett, H, 2d U. S. C. T.
L. Jenkins, H, 117th U. S. C. T.
Geo. Kelley, A, 117th U. S. C. T.
H. Carrell, D, 117th U. S. C. T.
Clemt. Brown, E, 23d U. S. C. T.
David Allen, H, 31st U. S. C. T.
I. Roberts, F, 29th U. S. C. T.
Geo. Parter, B, 117th U. S. C. T.
H. Furguson, G, 107th U. S. C. T.
H. Dowell, D, 107th U. S. C. T.
S. Johnson, A, 5th U. S. C. T.
Wm. Williams, D, 29th U. S. C. T.
W. Todd, F, 116th U. S. C. T.
I. Harrison, I, 107th U. S. C. T.
Jacob Lewis, G, 38th U. S. C. T.
Benj. Hall, G, 107th U. S. C. T.
Chas. Weather, I, 107th U. S. C. T.
Andrew Bailey, G, 29th U. S. C. T.
F. Boston, G, 107th U. S. C. T.
Thos. Riggs, A, 109th U. S. C. T.
F. Hunter, C, 3d U. S. C. T.
B. Harrin, C, 36th U. S. C. T.
Danl. Bledson, I, 107th U. S. C. T.
A. Duncan, E, 118th U. S. C. T.
Edwd. Boyd, A, 118th U. S. C. T.
G. W. Bailey, H, 118th U. S. C. T.

John Green, F, 115th U. S. C. T.
Thos. Morgan, I, 19th U. S. C. T.
N. Snowden, A, 38th U. S. C. T.
I. Lassing, A, 117th U. S. C. T.
Frank King, C, 38th U. S. C. T.
R. Williams, D, 36th U. S. C. T.
R. Strickfield, I, 57th U. S. C. T.
C. Reddrike, B, 38th U. S. C. T.
N. Ashbrook, A, 117th U. S. C. T.
Rich'd Asher, F, 114th U. S. C. T.
J. Thompson, D, 41st U. S. C. T.
John Dandy, A, 116th U. S. C. T.
Henry Hand, H, 19th U. S. C. T.
J. Terry, H, 114th U. S. C. T.
R. Nichols, G, 117th U. S. C. T.
D. Banket, F, 23d U. S. C. T.
Moses Possey, H, 118th U. S. C. T.
A. Ford, A, 107th U. S. C. T.
G. Maraldock, A, 6th U. S. C. T.
Wm. Roots, I, 41st U. S. C. T.
M. Plummer, B, 31st U.,S. C. T.
Jas. Wright, F, 41st U. S. C. T.
L. Carnet, F, 41st U. S. C. T.
Geo. Bell, G, 109th U. S. C. T.
Simon Askey, E, 2d U. S. C. T.
Henry Boyer, H, 5th U. S. C. T.
C. B. Taylor, I, 117th U. S. C. T.
R. Newman, D, 31st U. S. C. T.
T. Washington, E, 107th U. S. C. T.
Samuel Harris, K, 30th U. S. C. T.
John Matney, F, 7th U. S. C. T.
Joseph Aikens, G, 29th U. S. C. T.
M. Johnson, I, 23d U. S. C. T.
Thomas Roberts, U. S. C. T.
A. Dean, H, 118th U. S. C. T.
J. Berry, G, 114th U. S. C. T.
C. Hammond, F, 117th U. S. C. T.
S. Folks, H, 9th U. S. C. T.
Thomas Baisey, G, 117th U. S. C. T.
M. Taylor, C, 38th U. S. C. T.
Daniel Buchanan, D, 117th U. S. C. T.
P. Sutton, U. S. C. T.
J. Johnson, H, 29th U. S. C. T.
W. Johnson, D, 43d U. S. C. T.
Jackson Henry, E, 29th U. S. C. T.
Wm. Woosted, C, 41st U. S. C. T.
Isaac Emory, B, 114th U. S. C. T.
Samuel Price, K, 114th U. S. C. T.
B. Curby, K, 115th U. S. C. T.
Thomas Smaley, K, 31st U. S. C. T.
Philip Short, C, 7th U. S. C. T.

A. Hathaway, G, 109th U. S. C. T.
Samuel Bell, F, 117th U. S. C. T.
L. Williams, E, 117th U. S. C. T.
P. Warren, E, 23d U. S. C. T.
Noah Janes, G, 41st U. S. C. T.
James Niblet, I, 23d U. S. C. T.
Nathan Wilson, E, 4th U. S. C. T.
Daniel Banks, I, 43d U. S. C. T.
I. E. Bennett, I, 29th U. S. C. T.
N. Grider, I, 109th U. S. C. T.
Nathan Brown, I, 23d U. S. C. T.
S. Austin, E, 23d U. S. C. T.
T. Chew, G, 9th U. S. C. T.
H. Johnson, D, 7th U. S. C. T.
Wm. Elmer, E, 117th U. S. C. T.
T. Colwell, A, 8th U. S. C. T.
Wm. Stevens, I, 107th U. S. C. T.
Wm. Howerton, G, 109th U. S. C. T.
Henry Mosby, E, 127th U. S. C. T.
Geo. Collins, K, 117th U. S. C. T.
Adam Ousley, D, 109th U. S. C. T.
Harvey Jackson, G, 117th U. S. C. T.
Samuel Fry, A, 117th U. S. C. T.
Daniel Garnett, G, 118th U. S. C. T.
Sterling Couch, E, 118th U. S. C. T.
Wm. Watson, F, 127th U. S. C. T.
S. Moman, D, 107th U. S. C. T.
John Barnes, K, 109th U. S. C. T.
M. Parker, B, 127th U. S. C. T.
H. McLane, E, 118th U. S. C. T.
S. Claypoole, B, 115th U. S. C. T.
Geo. Reed, I, 29th U. S. C. T.
L. McCarey, E, 118th U. S. C. T.
Wm. Venerable, F, 109th U. S. C. T.
Jefferson Jones, D, 127th U. S. C. T.
Abram Roach, H, 118th U. S. C. T.
Thomas Sledd, K, 107th U. S. C. T.
Benjamin Turner, F, 43d U. S. C. T.
W. Vinegar, I, 115th U. S. C. T.
T. Browers, A, 41st U. S. C. T.
Thomas Jenkins, B, 41st U. S. C. T.
Wm. Benson, C, 7th U. S. C. T.
Bruce Carter, I, 107th U. S. C. T.
Sax Laws, H, 9th U. S. C. T.
Geo. Bennett, H, 117th U. S. C. T.
J. Meneker, A, 117th U. S. C. T.
Samuel Turner, U. S. C. T.
Jacob Ialus, I, 117th U. S. C. T.
C. Coffee, F, 10th U. S. C. T.
H. Shewell, K, 19th U. S. C. T.
Samuel Blaney, G, 31st U. S. C. T.

R. Harrington, I, 22d U. S. C. T.
John Nelson, C, 31st U. S. C. T.
Robert Thomas, G, 19th U. S. C. T.
James Gabriel, E, 127th U. S. C. T.
James Coggins, A, 117th U. S. C. T.
James Fuze, F, 45th U. S. C. T.
Joseph Hopkins, E, 12th U. S. C. T.
David Barker, E, 116th U. S. C. T.
Clifton Adams, F, 118th U. S. C. T.
Wm. Armstrong, I, 117th U. S. C. T.
Geo. Thomas, E, 118th U. S. C. T.
W. H. Harris, F, 45th U. S. C. T.
C. H. Thomas, D, 43d U. S. C. T.
H. Carpenter, C, 29th U. S. C. T.
I. Mitchell, U. S. C. T.
Geo. Sands, C, 29th U. S. C. T.
Samuel Grimes, B, 122d U. S. C. T.
B. Jacobs, F, 122d U. S. C. T.
Wm. Jackson, C, 29th U. S. C. T.
H. Wigglesworth, B, 45th U. S. C. T
P. Richardson, A, 115th U. S. C T.
I. Anderson, C, 22d U. S. C. T.
Samuel Baird, H, 114th U. S. C. T.
Isaac Miner, I, 117th U. S. C. T.
I. Robinson, H, 31st U. S. C. T.
Geo. Benson, C, 45th U. S. C. T.
Chas. Stovell, C, 107th U. S. C T.
D. White, F, 116th U. S. C. T
Jos. Reed, A, 29th U. S. C. T.
N. W. Bush, A, 8th U. S. C. T.
J. Booze, H, 43d J. S. C. T
Wm. Frisbie, I, 22d U. S. C. T.
Wm. Richardson, C, 22d U. S. C. T.
Henry Lewis, K, 118th U. S. C. T.
Robt. Field, B, 118th U. S. C. T.
F. Morton, E, 117th U. S. C. T.
J. Letchard, D, 118th U. S. C. T.
Everet Yates, C, 114th U. S. C. T.
R. Smith, I, 8th U. S. C. T.
Samuel Thomas, H, 109th U. S. C. T.
P. Robinson, D, 118th U. S. C. T.
Wm. Sivan, B, 38th U. S. C. T.
Wm. Dozier, B, 38th U. S. C. T.
F. Rice, D, 9th U. S. C. T.
Wm. Somerwell, K, 29th U. S. C. T.
John Average, A, 38th U. S. C. T.
G. Grosswait, A, 114th U. S. C. T.
Thomas Johnson, F, 29th U. S. C. T.
Lewis Berry, U. S. C. T.
F. Ashley, H, 118th U. S. C. T.
B. H. Miller, B, 127th U. S. C. T

L. W. Rider, I, 9th U. S. C. T.
Geo. L. Reed, C, 31st U. S. C. T.
Beverly Lee, U. S. C. T.
P. Parker, C, 117th U. S. C. T.
J. Thompson, D, 43d U. S. C. T.
Wm. Brayford, E, 41st U. S. C. T.
Saml. Bell, D, 41st U. S. C. T.
John Offort, C, 22d U. S. C. T.
Henry Daniels, C, 45th U. S. C. T.
Wm. H. Thomas, I, 43d U. S. C. T.
A. Cromwell, K, 127th U. S. C. T.
John Perry, G, 29th U. S. C. T.
G. Washington, F, 7th U. S. C. T.
R. Janes, H, 8th U. S. C. T.
R. Williams, B, 41st U. S. C. T.
P. Compton, G, 115th U. S. C. T.
M. Clellum, H, 45th U. S. C. T.
O. Washington, C, 29th U. S. C. T.
Benj. Jones, U. S. C. T.
A. Giles, I, 7th U. S. C. T.
H. Fesler, H, 109th U. S. C. T.
Saml. Mayor, U. S. C. T.
A. Witherspoon, F, 29th U. S. C. T.
I. Fazen, U. S. C. T.
L. Fox, K, 122d U. S. C. T.
H. Nelson, B, 114th U. S. C. T.
W. Sebastian, B, 116th U. S. C. T.
J. Walston, E, 36th U. S. C. T.
Friendship Matthews, E, 9th U. S. C. T.
G. Davis, I, 115th U. S. C. T.
A. Duff, C, 43d U. S. C. T.
P. Banks, C, 7th U. S. C. T.
J. Brent, A, 127th U. S. C. T.
G. Hampton, A, 115th U. S. C. T.
H. Rhudy, D, 118th U. S. C. T.
W. Hawkins, A, 41st U. S. C. T.
Robt. Lucas, E, 45th U. S. C. T.
Wm. Watkins, U. S. C. T.
Wm. Risley, D, 109th U. S. C. T.
Jas. W. Washington, B, 127th U. S. C. T.
Henry Allen, A, 115th U. S. C. T
Caleb Whitlon, F, 23d U. S. C. T.
Wm. Anes, D, 8th U. S. C. T.
P. Bell, B, 41st U. S. C. T.
Jos. Vamer, C, 29th U. S. C. T.
Peter Blanchard, U. S. C. T.
James McCombs, U. S. C. T.
John Thompson, I, 127th U. S. C. T.
Isaac Price, D, 127th U. S. C. T.
John Beard, H, 4th U. S. C. T.
Lewis Gale, G, 118th U. S. C T.

John Watson, A, 41st U. S. C. T.
S. Johnson, K, 107th U. S. C. T.
Elijah Jones, A, 109th U. S. C. T.
Jerry Evens, E, 118th U. S. C. T
I. Crosley, U. S. C. T.
S. Brown, F, 118th U. S. C. T.
O. Parker, U. S. C. T.
H. Floyd, F, 116th U. S. C. T.
David Davis, 116th Ohio, U. S. C. T.
N. McLane, H, 107th U. S. C. T.
D. Anderson, D, 107th U. S. C. T.
Chas. Coleman, E, 9th U. S. C. T.
A. Arters, H, 38th U. S. C. T.
John Spalding, D, 107th U. S. C. T.
Geo. Bromley, K, 31st U. S. C. T.
Jason Peters, H, 6th U. S. C. T.
Henry Watson, F, 5th U. S. C. T.
Jordan Hankley, H, 107th U. S. C. T.
Jesse Board, E, 107th U. S. C. T.
Lewis Delph, F, 117 U. S. C. T.
Henry Locket, G, 29th U. S. C. T.
Clifton Ellery, G, 116th U. S. C. T.
Isaac Howard, H, 41st U. S. C. T.
Wm. McIntire, G, 43d U. S. C. T.
Henderson Rock, D, 118th U. S. C. T.
John Hooper, B, 19th U. S. C. T.
N. Williams, B, 41st U. S. C. T.
James Tate, U. S. C. T.
John Wright, I, 107th U. S. C. T.
M. Chambers, I, 107th U. S. C. T.
A. Leavell, E, 116th U. S. C. T.
I. Steward, H, 117th U. S. C. T.
I. Henry, I, 127th U. S. C. T.
F. Williams, G, 109th U. S. C. T.
C. Halloway, G, 118th U. S. C. T.
G. Johnson, H, 37th U. S. C. T.
D. Johnson, H, 29th Conn. U. S. C. T.
Richard Putnam, F, 30th U. S. C. T.
Joseph Green, C, 39th U. S. C. T.
John Jordan, H, 116th U. S. C. T.
John Chew, F, 23d U. S. C. T.
Green Gross, I, 117th U. S. C. T.
Frederick Jackson, B, 29th U. S. C. T
M. Smith, G, 127th U. S. C. T.
Jack Sidner, B, 107th U. S. C. T.
George White, K, 31st U. S. C. T.
I. Curry, F, 6th U. S. C. T.
A. Young, I, 6th U. S. C. T.
E. Hughes, E, 6th U. S. C. T.
C. Woodhouse, G, 36th U. S. C. T.
Richard Varney, K, 6th U. S. C. T.

Peter Boone, U. S. C. T.
John Whiting, 6th U. S. C. T.
Joseph Banch, G, 118th U. S. C. T.
E. North, 9th U. S. C. T.
William Wilson, D, 107th U. S. C. T.
Rias Usher, B, 29th, U. S. C. T.
George Dickson, D, 36th U. S. C. T.
George Turner, G, 5th U. S. C. T.
Harrison Pedrick, G, 10th U. S. C. T.
Alex. Johns, B, 6th U. S. C. T.
Lewis Catton, H, 6th U. S. C. T.
James Banks, G, 4th U. S. C. T.
Benjamin Faulk, B, 22d U. S. C. T.
F. Smith, F, 38th U. S. C. T.
A. Jackson, G, 5th U. S. C. T.
Hen. Winslow, H, 5th U. S. C. T.
George Green, K, 22d U. S. C. T.
Silas Jones, H, 38th U. S. C. T.
Wm. Hays, C, 1st U. S. C. T.
I. Manley, D, 38th U. S. C. T.
T. Sheffield, K, 2d U. S. C. T.
J. Powell, C, 109th U. S. C. T.
James Cartler, K, 117th U. S. C. T.
Albert Boyer, C, 41st U. S. C. T.
Henry Gilbert, D, 115th U. S. C. T.
J. Woodson, B, 5th U. S. C. T.
Wm. Blair, G, 117th U. S. C. T.
H. Beverley, C, 108th U. S. C. T.
P. Brickman, D, 6th U. S. C. T.
O. Martin, C, 36th U. S. C. T.
Benjamin Sharp, G, 5th U. S. C. T.
A. Cook, H, 4th U. S. C. T.
William McEtey, F, 107th U. S. C. T.
L. McBride, H, 118th U. S. C. T.
Charles Lewis, D, 27th U. S. C. T.
Eli Proctor, H, 117th U. S. C. T.
Samuel Miles, D, 2d U. S. C. T.
J. Griffin, A, 116th U. S. C. T.
J. Cracker, K, 2d U. S. C. T.
W. H. Brown, H, 29th U. S. C. T.
R. Rendell, U. S. C. T.
A. McCann, F, 129th U. S. C. T.
William Thomas, I, 107th U. S. C. T.
W. Miller, B, 115th U. S. C. T.
L. Lockey, F, 118th U. S. C. T.
Samuel Daisey, K, 38th U. S. C. T.
James Monroe, H, 114th U. S. C. T
James McLane, E, 118th U. S. C. T
A. Cordelia, K, 27th U. S. C. T.
T. Lefever, C, 31st U. S. C. T.
Millen Stone, C, 115th U. S. C. T

Abraham Dixon, D, 30th U. S. C. T.
Charles Nealy, I, 115th U. S. C. T.
Andrew Rowen, H, 41st U. S. C. T.
G. Buchanan, 4th N. J.
C. Vernes, C, 9th N. J.
I. Munch, E, 9th N. J.
Thomas Sales, E, 9th N. J.
T. Tannings, G, 37th N. J.
I. C. Waters, 4th N. J.
E. Thomberg, H, 13th Ind.
I. Jones, A, 13th Ind.
I. Booley, B, 13th Ind.
Wm. Cable, A, 13th Ind.
I. H. Orr, I, 25th Mass.
Alexander Hayes, K, 40th Mass.
A. Bradley, H, 27th Mass.
George S. Cau, B, 40th Mass.
E. B. Hewes, A, 40th Mass.
D. R. Bruce, K, 27th Mass.
Theodore Dyse, G, 25th Mass.
A. Cook, B, 25th Mass.
Charles Horton, B, 25th Mass.
T. Magany, E, 25th Mass.
James Feeley, I, 4th Mass. Cav.
H. Davis, M, 4th Mass. Cav.
M. B. Wait, F, 25th Mass.
Lieut. C. Upton, 25th Mass
Leroy Hawes, E, 34th Mass.
Joseph Dudley, C, 34th Mass.
C. L. McIntire, 61st Mass.
D. Brew, M, 4th Mass. Cav.
John North, A, 27th Mass. Cav.
R. Wallace, G, 25th Mass. Cav.
George Baker, I, 25th Mass. Cav.
W. Townsend, F, 23d Mass. Cav.
Charles Trask, B, 24th Mass. Cav.
Silas Coles, D, 27th Mass. Cav.
T. Scoflat, 4th Mass. Cav.
G. Wayer, 4th Mass. Cav.
I. Van Martin.
I. Windson.
I. Creft.
A. Fisher.
Hen. Havvey.
Charles E. Horton.
Joseph Jones.
M. McDonnel, D, 23d Ill.
N. Smith, A, 39th Ill.
Henry Parks, D, 38th Ill.
Richard Burns, A, 23d Ill.
A. F. Moore, C, 39th Ill.

P. O. Brion, A, 23d, Ill.
John Lynch, D, 39th Ill.
W. Hodges, A, 23d Ill.
I. B. Kilburn, B, 23d Ill.
James Carr, I, 39th Ill.
A. Page, D, 39th Ill.
A. Chapman, E, 118th U. S. C. T.
E. Randell, K, 117th U. S. C. T.
C. F. Davis, F, 45th U. S. C. T.
I. Roberts, A, 118th U. S. C. T.
Jn. W. Roger, F, 19th U. S. C. T.
J. Johnson, D, 117th U. S. C. T.
J. Dillon, F, 37th U. S. C. T.
R. Reed, H, 118th U. S. C. T.
Stephen Garner, H, 43d U. S. C. T.
H. Garner, H, 31st U. S. C. T.
O. Bailey, H, 118th U. S. C. T.
W. Laskin, H, 107th U. S. C. T.
George Thomas, C, 39th U. S. C. T.
N. Anderson, D, 19th U. S. C. T.
Nox Jones, H, 118th U. S. C. T.
D. Johnson, D, 117th U. S. C. T.
William Dreads, G, 30th U. S. C. T.
Jerry Hughes, F, 117th U. S. C. T.
M. Flanigan, I, 36th U. S. C. T.
J. Nickols, K, 117th U. S. C. T.
W. Wilson, F, 29th U. S. C. T.
F. Thompson, K, 117th U. S. C. T.
I. Garrison, U. S. C. T.
John Basey, B, 118th U. S. C. T.
G. Jones, D, 118th U. S. C. T.
Wyatt Ellis, K, 118th U. S. C. T.
Areary Rogers, H, 15th U. S. C. T.
J. Hawes, F, 118th U. S. C. T.
J. Wilson, H, 117th U. S. C. T.
D. Nun, H, 117th U. S. C. T.
A. Blake, B, 7th U. S. C. T.
John Weaver, E, 8th U. S. C. T.
James Graves, K, 116th U. S. C. T.
John Crabb, K, 118th U. S. C. T.
W. Jones, F, 23d U. S. C. T.
C. McGray, C, 118th U. S. C. T.
W. Hawkins, B, 116th U. S. C. T.
M. Van Buren, G, 2d U. S. C. T.
A. Hicks, H, 23d U. S. C. T.
I. Thomas, G, 19th U. S. C. T.
Jeff. Madney, F, 107th U. S. C. T.
Edward Mitchell, C, 116th U. S. C.
C. Fraseer, C, 39th U. S. C. T.
P. Wright, D, 19th U. S. C. T.
E. Baxter, F, 39th U. S. C. T.

S. Neal, C, 27th U. S. C. T.
George Harris, C, 5th U. S. C. T.
P. Cuff, F, 127th U. S. C. T.
H. Felton, E, 37th U. S. C. T.
W. Moore, A, 1st U. S. C. T.
J. Mitchell, D, 117th U. S. C. T.
W. Reeves, K, 7th U. S. C. T.
Noah Ross, I, 29th U. S. C. T.
I. Brooklyn, D, 117th U. S. C. T.
D. Fisher, F, 107th U. S. C. T.
A. Hamlin, H, 37th U. S. C. T.
Robert Ford, D, 1st U. S. C. T.
George Taylor, K, 109th U. S. C. T.
D. Polston, K, 117th U. S. C. T.
C. Chassen, B, 36th U. S. C. T.
P. Franklin, K, 116th U. S. C. T.
W. Branch, U. S. C. T.
G. Bowey, C, 109th U. S. C. T.
W. Baynard, I, 45th U. S. C. T.
W. Scrogan, B, 116th U. S. C. T.
W. Riley, I, 107th U. S. C. T.
John Spaulding, A, 130th U. S. C. T.
Jacob Barney, B, 39th U. S. C. T.
Albert Banks, H, 41st U. S. C. T.
W. H. Raymond, I, 45th U. S. C. T.
P. Bolton, C, 1st U. S. C. T.
A. Buckett, H, 109th U. S. C. T.
Alvey Tucker, C, 127th U. S. C. T.
G. Preidea, G, 2d U. S. C. T.
R. Pitt, B, 23d U. S. C. T.
W. Stowell, K, 109th U. S. C. T.
W. Wilson, F, 39th U. S. C. T.
W. Philips, K, 2d U. S. C. T.
R. Anderson, H, 117th U. S. C. T.
John Stanley, G, 115th U. S. C. T.
W. Patten, C, 107th U. S. C. T.
W. H. Hazzard, K, 6th U. S. C. T.
W. McDowell, A, 29th U. S. C. T.
M. Johnson, G, 29th U. S. C. T.
T. Jameson, B, 23d U. S. C. T.
R. Johnson, H, 116th U. S. C. T.
N. Upclier, K, 2d U. S. C. T.
T. Johnson, K, 45th U. S. C. T.
H. Smith, K, 37th U. S. C. T.
A. Patterson, I, 109th U. S. C. T.
A. Tripp, I, 37th U. S. C. T.
George Duff, E, 41st U. S. C. T.
W. Burns, I, 127th U. S. C. T.
N. Dickson, E, 110th U. S. C. T.
A. Cann, H, 29th U. S. C. T.
H. McGee, C, 4th U. S. C. T.

W. Tucker, D, 118th U. S. C. T
A. G. Brown, C, 28th U. S. C. T
G. Valentine, H, 41st U. S. C. T.
J. Laws, K, 109th U. S. C. T.
W. Lee, K, 5th U. S. C. T.
James Bowle, D, 117th U. S. C. **T.**
J. Marshall, F, 118th U. S. C. **T.**
James Shape, B, 109th U. S. C. **T.**
H. White, H, 118th U. S. C. T.
T. Barren, G, 41st U. S. C. T.
D. Greyson, A, 45th U. S. C. T.
L. Gun, H, 107th U. S. C. T.
H. Coleman, E, 117th U. S. C. **T.**
R. Dodson, F, 23d U. S. C. T.
T. Cresler, C, 117th U. S. C. T.
S. Morman, A, 118th U. S. C. T.
John Gunner, E, 30th U. S. C. **T.**
P. Johnson, F, 29th U. S. C. T.
Ch. Turner, A, 118th U. S. C. **T.**
Hen. Clay, U. S. C. T.
Isaac Cornish, F, 30th U. S. C. **T.**
J. Vanwan, K, 107th U. S. C. T.
P. Robinson, B, 41st U. S. C. T.
Jn. Hill, B, 30th U. S. C. T.
M. Williams, A, 117th U. S. C. **T.**
J. Sivens, I, 117th U. S. C. T.
S. Bell, C, 29th U. S. C. T.
W. Cook, C, 19th U. S. C. T.
A. Hawker, F, 116th U. S. C. T.
Jn. Williams, E, 117th U. S. C. **T.**
S. Stevenson, C, 107th U. S. C. **T.**
J. Bennett, I, 118th U. S. C. T.
J. Atherson, C, 116th U. S. C. **T.**
P. Mumford, G, 19th U. S. C. T.
G. Oakey, C, 29th U. S. C. T.
J. Yelser, A, 116th U. S. C. **T.**
D. Mitchel, C, 116th U. S. C. **T.**
H. Jefferson, I, 127th U. S. C. **T.**
John Buttler, D, 39th U. S. C. **T.**
J. Harrison, E, 8th U. S. C. T.
Jeff. Craig, E, 38th U. S. C. T.
J. Moss, G, 127th U. S. C. T.
M. Mattix, I, 37th U. S. C. T.
W. Crebbs, D, 6th U. S. C. T.
J. Frances, H, 43d U. S. C. T.
E. Courser, K, 27th U. S. C. **T.**
B. Lovett, K, 6th U. S. C. T.
D. Parker, C, 117th U. S. C. **T.**
B. Henry, A, 127th U. S. C. **T.**
C. E. Turner, D, 43d U. S. C. **T.**
D. Bessy, K, 107th U. S. C. T.

J. Edwards, C, 107th U. S. C. T.
D. Tucker, K, 23d U. S. C. T.
Isaac Givens, E, 117th U. S. C. T.
S. Souper, F, 118th U. S. C. T.
J. Williams, G, 118th U. S. C. T.
P. Wicliffe, E, 118th U. S. C. T.
S. Farley, E, 28th U. S. C. T.
J. Thomas, H, 41st U. S. C. T.
R. Phillips, H, 38th U. S. C. T.
W. Taylor, C, 1st U. S. C. T.
Thomas Gough, F, 38th U. S. C. T.
T. Cammers, B, 6th U. S. C. T.
A. James, K, 22d U. S. C. T.
L. Patrick, F, 4th U. S. C. T.
M. Donald, E, —— U. S. C. T.
E. Worth, 9th U. S. C. T.
John Carr, B, 7th U. S. C. T.
James Jones, B, 107th U. S. C. T.
H. Brown, D, 5th U. S. C. T.
M. Siff, C, 107th U. S. C. T.
Peter Anty, H, 6th U. S. C. T.
N. Speen, I, 5th U. S. C. T.
A. Hall, D, 1st U. S. C. T.
John Heath, K, 2d U. S. C. T.
W. Hinton, D, 37th U. S. C. T.
John Roberts, G, 107th U. S. C. T.
S. M. Donald, A, 31st U. S. C. T.
W. Jackson, A, 4th U. S. C. T.
W. Parmer, A, 117th U. S. C. T.
B. Finman, B, 9th U. S. C. T.
A. Whatford, F, 37th U. S. C. T.
James Hall, C, 8th U. S. C. T.
W. Reymond, B, 38th U. S. C. T.
J. Burcher, B, 10th U. S. C. T.
E. North, 9th U. S. C. T.
R. Wilson, A, 22d U. S. C. T.
J. Coates, D, 4th U. S. C. T.
H. Williams, E, 10th U. S. C. T.
J. Vandergrome, D, 5th U. S. C. T.
A. Clagrate, K, 1st U. S. C. T.
Jones Edwards, B, 37th U. S. C. T.
Joseph Mead, H, 5th U. S. C. T.
G. Sterling, G, 6th U, S. C. T.
Joseph Parker, D, 2d U. S. C. T.
A. Latenhouse, U. S. C. T.
E. Morgan, E, 37th U. S. C. T.
F. Bisere, C, 38th U. S. C. T.
G. Bean, G, 1st U. S. C T.
E. Barrett, D, 118th U. S. C. T.
John Hope, I, 36th U. S. C. T.
W. Boyd, D, 30th U. S. C. T.

L. Johnson, B, 36th U. S. C. T.
Sol. Green, H, 4th U. S. C. T.
R. Jones, C, 36th U. S. C. T.
Mart. Soves, F, 5th U. S. C. T.
E. Milburn, C, 38th U. S. C. T.
George Freny, G, 22d U. S. C. T.
L. White, 6th U. S. C. T.
Conway Holt, H, 38th U. S. C. T.
J. Williamson, H, 38th U. S. C. T
M. Gough, B, 38th U. S. C. T.
Moses Brown, H, 36th U. S. C. T.
Thomas Starks, G, 5th U. S. C. T.
W. Lewis, B, 6th U. S. C. T.
G. Maxwell, H, 5th U. S. C. T.
C. Lane, H, 4th U. S. C. T.
Brack Miller, B, 122d U. S. C. T.
Daniel Tales, K, 8th U. S. C. T.
G. W. Williams, G, 43d U. S. C. T
James Walter, K, 117th U. S. C. T
John Smith, U. S. C. T.
J. Wilson, I, 3d U. S. C. T.
Nero Laven, I, 118th U. S. C. T.
T. J. Benton, E, 43d U. S. C. T.
A. Barnes, A, 109th U. S. C. T.
A. T. Myers, I, 5th U. S. C. T.
J. Stringwood, F, 4th U. S. C. T.
J. Kane, E, 4th U. S. C. T.
W. Johnson, I, 4th U. S. C. T.
J. Jackson, U. S. C. T.
W. Valentine, G, 107th U. S. C. T
Jacob Banch, G, 118th U. S. C. T.
H. Mullory, I, 5th U. S. C. T.
N. Dorsey, B, 4th U. S. C. T.
John Sanders, F, 6th U. S. C. T.
J. A. Wilson, D, 5th U. S. C. T.
Denny Goup, F, 6th U. S. C. T.
John Marshall, 6th U. S. C. T.
George Hayes, U. S. C. T.
James Wather, I, 5th U. S. C. T.
J. Shepherd, K, 1st U. S. C. T.
W. Castleman, F, 118th U. S. C. T
J. M. Coley, E, 29th U. S. C. T.
George Brown, K, 2d U. S. C. T.
N. Gilbough, D, 5th U. S. C. T.
A. Hall, D, 22d U. S. C. T.
W. Gilland, K, 27th U. S. C. T.
M. Long, G, 107th U. S. C. T.
James Gardner, G, 38th U. S. C. T.
H. Field, E, 109th U. S. C. T.
Charles Wagner, E, 107th U. S. C. T
J. Madrid, H, 38th U. S. C. T.

T. Clarkston, H, 117th U. S. C. T.
W. Johnson, I, 41st U. S. C. T.
Jesse Lee, U. S. C. T. ·
F. Dickerson, G, 107th U. S. C. T.
Jordan Burk, 4th U. S. C. T.
J. Moore, G, 30th U. S. C. T.
L. Clagghart, K, 29th U. S. C. T.
Edward Soper, G, 118th U. S. C. T.
Dorsey Taylor, A, 36th U. S. C. T.
H. Moore, F, 39th U. S. C. T.
E. Black, D, 8th U. S. C. T.
I. Bullelts, A, 29th U. S. C. T.
H. Macky, F, 29th U. S. C. T.
R Twines, G, 9th U. S. C. T.
M. Lillard, G, 117th U. S. C. T.
R. Bisley, E, 30th U. S. C. T.
Oliver Wright, A, 31st U. S. C. T.
Jerry Cecil, H, 107th U. S. C. T.
L. Board, E, 118th U. S. C. T
E. Carroll, K, 117th U. S. C. T.
F. Gay, G, 118th U. S. C. T.
A. Willetts, I, 29th U. S. C. T.
G. Mitchell, I, 39th U. S. C. T.
C. Allen, H, 107th U. S. C. T.
N. Gross, G, 9th U. S. C. T.
W. Cod, K, 23d U. S. C. T.
R. Jones, F, 37th U. S. C. T.
S. Nordike, E, 3d U. S. Art.
John Wilson, U. S. Steamer "Perry."
I. Childs, B, 8th Conn.
Daniel Sheppston, 21st Conn.
I. Cates, A, 8th Conn.
P. Dalton, E, 7th Conn.
I. Mallon, B, 7th Conn.
E. Mabb, K, 11th Conn.
Andrew Kuhn, F, 8th Conn.
Patrick Ruth, F, 1st Conn. Art.
John Brown, H, 1st Conn. Art.
F. H. Cutter, B, 11th Conn.
W. Wetherell, A, 6 Conn.
John Morse, H, 11th Conn.
Arthur Baker, F, 11th Conn.
Joshua Davis, K, 8th Conn.
E. Hanson, A, 11th Conn.
G. Brown, C, 10th Conn.
H. Dunham, G, 7th Conn.
Warren Bissell, C, 10th Conn.
Charles Howard, E, 10th Conn.
V. B. Tery, B, 6th Conn.
I. O. Brien, E, 8th Conn.
John C. Mason, F, 21st Conn.

J. Parkerson, F, 3d Conn.
H. Fitzpatrick, E, 11th Conn.
Wilson Hills, B, 21st Conn.
Wm. Brown, B, 10th Conn.
C. B. Couch, I, 7th Conn.
I. G. Littlefield, F, 11th Maine.
B. Brown, I, 9th Maine.
J. K. Green, A, 11th Maine.
G. Balcom, F, 11th Maine.
John Lombard, C, 9th Maine.
Benson Yetton, I, 9th Maine.
N. F. Sargent, C, 9th Maine.
W. Murray, G, 11th Maine.
Coba Morte, K, 11th Maine.
A. Robinson, H, 9th Maine.
H. F. Corville, K, 9th Maine.
T. Dalton, C, 11th Maine.
M. Sullivan, I, 11th Maine.
Henry Elliott, A, 9th Maine.
T. J. Robbins, I, 11th Maine.
Charles Thompson, H, 9th Maine.
J. Hamilton, F, 11th Maine.
W. Toothaker, H, 11th Maine.
G. W. Watson, G, 11th Maine.
John Murphy, D, 9th Maine.
G. H. Potter, K, 9th Maine.
W. H. Heal, H, 8th Maine.
A. Pendleton, H, 8th Maine.
M. Green, K, 9th Maine.
T. N. Ryder, C, 9th Maine.
J. Hamilton, A, 8th Maine.
Geo. Burns, K, 9th Maine.
G. Tifreld, F, 9th Maine.
I. Groves, A, 9th Maine.
W. Bean, C, 9th Maine.
G. Harmon, I, 11th Maine.
A. B. Morton, 9th Maine.
G. W. Hill, H, 9th Maine.
R. H. Bowley, H, 8th Maine.
W. H. Small, I, 9th Maine.
E. Whiting, C, 9th Maine.
H. Sprague, C, 9th Maine.
E. Austin, C, 9th Maine.
W. W. Eaton, G, 9th Maine.
W. P. Trask, G, 11th Maine.
I. Howard, G, 8th Maine.
S. Thurston, K, 11th Maine.
E. Whitney, B, 11th Maine.
Alon Prescott, H, 8th Maine.
H. H. Buise, E, 11th Maine.
Lieut. Braman, I, 11th Maine.

S. Pinckney, I, 8th Maine.
L. E. Maxwell, E, 8th Maine.
I. Tilford, K, 3d N. Y. Art.
S. Huntington, H, 142d N. Y.
A. Foster, G, 142d N. Y.
John Scott, E, 115th N. Y.
A. Guyld, B, 100th N. Y.
N. Raymond, I, 13th N. Y. Art.
Wm. Bell, M, 13th N. Y. Art.
S. Scudder, I, 20th N. Y. Cav.
Fred. Klice, 20th N. Y. Cav.
H. Myers, E, 117th N. Y.
Robt. Fortune, K, 98th N. Y.
Martin Sprague, A, 20th N. Y. Cav.
L. Crowningshield, G, 142d N. Y.
A. C. Sherman, I, 115th N. Y.
W. H. Elkins, K, 20th N. Y.
Charles Drake, K, 150th N. Y.
Patrick Degan, C, 47th N. Y.
I. Hamilton, H, 10th N. Y. A. N.
John Hurley, C, 139th N. Y.
H. Wolff, B, 1st N. Y. Eng.
I. Gunmer, B, 1st N. Y. Eng.
I. Clark, K, 3d N. Y. Art.
A. H. Simpson, C, 148th N. Y.
I. Eldridge, F, 100th N. Y.
David Roach, H, 47th N. Y.
Solomon Drake, C, 6th N. Y. Art.
T. Richards, I, 13th N. Y. Art.
S. Winters, F, 10th N. Y. Art.
Albert Senay, C. 1st N. Y. M. R.
B. F. Lossee, A, 139th N. Y.
John Walsh, G, 158th N. Y.
G. W. Bailey, A, 169th N. Y.
R. M. Ewell, M, 3d N. Y.
J. Myers, G, 100th N. Y.
Chaming Jaynes, C, 31st N. Y.
Joshua E. Bell, H, 1st N. Y. M. R.
R. H. Lymons, I, 139th N. Y.
Henry Boner, H, 13th N. Y. Art.
John Hulbert, H, 1st N. Y. M. R.
M. Bryant, 1st N. Y. Eng.
E. Wentworth, 1st N. Y. M. R.
H. H. Chamberlin, G, 148th N. Y.
Samuel Reed, 1st N. Y. M. R.
William Holland, E, 79th N. Y.
C. H. Flower, I, 89th N. Y.
Henry Odurgee, 7th N. Y. Independ't Bat.
George M. Fadder, B, 48th N. Y.
J. Smith, E, 96th N. Y.
Jacob Zeller, K, 16th N. Y. Art.

Richard Strong, G, 47th N. Y.
G. Decker, K, 16th N. Y. Art.
J. Omiston, F, 118th N. Y.
Frederick Aple, E, 118th N. Y.
J. Alfred, L, 1st N. Y. Eng.
M. Shultz, E, 158th N. Y.
G. H. Lane, L, 5th N. Y. Cav.
Sidney Norton, C, 1st N. Y. M. R.
Timothy Dillon, K, 3d N. Y. Art.
Pat. Farrell, E, 20th N. Y. Cav.
James Duyer, G, 112th N. Y.
Smith Bentley, B, 20th N. Y. Cav.
G. Auchler, A, 6th N. Y. Art.
M. Abraham, A, 16th N. Y. Art.
John P. Daniels, L, 16th N. Y. Art.
H. Starkwether, B, 20th N. Y. Cav.
John Fox, A, 158th N. Y.
J. Kegan, E, 142d N. Y.
G. Cadwell, F, 100th N. Y.
H. Laguay, H, 13th N. Y. Art.
H. Putton, F, 10th N. Y. Art.
J. Lellage, 13th N. Y. Art.
William Bishop, A, 1st N. Y. M. R.
B. L. Churchill, M, 6th N. Y. Art.
Albert Crego, M, 3d N. Y. Art.
E. Sedore, K, 16th N. Y. Art.
George M. Emmons, K, 1st N. Y. Eng
Thomas Chambers, K, 42d N. Y. Art.
E. Griffiths, G, 148th N. Y.
A. Millard, C, 142d N. Y.
H. Hoyet, G, 6th N. Y. Art.
Benjamin Potter, H, 142d N. Y.
Peter Brown, D, 89th N. Y.
G. Reynolds, I, 39th N. Y.
M. Cocherel, K, 41st N. Y.
J. Phonax, G, 6th N. Y. Art.
Isaac Maston, C, 118th N. Y.
L. Collins, A, 16th N. Y. Art.
G. F. Varlett, H, 3d N. Y. Art.
J. O. Connell, I, 13th N. Y. Art.
W. C. Cunean, D, 1st N. Y. M. R.
M. Tooney, D, 47th N. Y.
H. Rickelson, K, 118th N. Y.
H. Dutton, D, 118th N. Y.
E. Williams, B, 117th N. Y.
Alex. Shrine, H, 9th N. Y.
John Scott, E, 148th N. Y.
Lewis Brothers, B, 48th N. Y.
A. G. Vangodon, G, 98th N. Y.
Benjamin Shockton, F, 139th N. Y.
J. Van Vouno, F, 1st N. Y. Eng.

G. Swartz, E, 3d N. Y. Cav.
Eugene Sweet, K, 16th N. Y. Art.
John Kenyon, H, 8th N. Y.
George Garrow, D, 90th N. Y.
Richard Carealton, I, 139th N. Y.
O. Tripp, G, 16th N. Y. Art.
Orland Bruce, B, 16th N. Y. Art.
John Mugan, G, 117th N. Y.
C. D. Marls, D, 1st N. Y. M. R.
S. Spingteen, B, 98th N. Y.
W. Osborn, H, 89th N. Y.
J. H. Spencer, B, 98th N. Y.
George Barett, G, 118th N. Y.
George Rasbeck, B, 16th N. Y. Art.
J. Walker, I, 142d N. Y.
J. McCarty, G, 118th N. Y.
James O. Neil, C, 3d Rhode Island Art.
William H. Pierkerson, A, 53d Virginia.
J. Johnson, A, 29th Virginia.
W. Conaway, H, 9th Confederate.
W. Cawdel, H, 14th North Carolina.
Lieut. W. M. Blan, D, 1st North Carolina Cav
J. W. Horns, K, 23d, South Carolina.
W. Mason, 53d Virginia.
P. C. Johnson, C, 48th North Carolina.
J. O. Adams, G, 46th North Carolina.
Lieut. Norris, C, 5th South Carolina.
R. White, F, 3d Arkansas.
J. W. Sumkins, H, 1st Tennessee.
Eli Brewer, F, 31st North Carolina.
C. W. Ward, H, 6th South Carolina.
John Griffin, B, 44th Alabama.
G. Steadings, B, Confederate.
Lieut. P. Grizzle, C, 4th Texas.
—— Funnel, 11th South Carolina.
F. W. Baker, G, Confederate.
J. Pinsow, H, 5th Texas.
B. Harley, H, 2d South Carolina.
W. McIntyre, G, 43d U. S. C. T.
Thomas Richardson, H, 11th West Virginia.
J. Yager, H, 10th West Virginia.
P. H. Rattiff, B, 10th West Virginia.
Jeremiah Webb, G, 11th Virginia.
J. W. Rhodes, I, 10th Virginia.
Wm. Smith, E, 11th Virginia.
M. Fisher, 7th Virginia.
J. W. Deruck, 7th Virginia.
G. W. Jackson, D, 15th Virginia.
B. F. Hyman, I, 11th Virginia.
Eli Herbert, G, 12th Virginia.
W. Stoller, C, 15th Virginia.

A. J. Malsed, I. 15th Virginia.
James Keen, K, 10th Virginia.
George Drane, G, 12th Virginia.
Austin Attrey, E, 11th Virginia.
S. Henzman, C, 10th Virginia.
George Hoffman, E, 15th Virginia.
William Gilletts, A, 12th Virginia.
S. S. Scars, K, 12th Virginia.
William Frost, E, 19th Massachusetts.
Clark Gilson, D, 19th Massachusetts.
H. Fairweather, H, 19th Massachusetts.
M. H. Skinner, H, 9th Massachusetts.
John Leathers, G, 13th New Hampshire.
H. Manshey, E, 2d New Hampshire.
Pat. Cone, D, 12th New Hampshire.
Charles E. Lakeman, G, 13th New Hampshire.
H. Coburn, C, 3d New Hampshire.
H. Esty, K, 4th New Hampshire.
Charles Hall, 13th New Hampshire.
A. B. Brown, E, 10th New Hampshire.
J. Brooks, H, 3d New Hampshire.
W. Callingham, G, 7th New Hampshire.
W. Scott, A, 7th New Hampshire.
C. H. Abbott, E, 3d New Hampshire.
Charles Hill, C, 4th New Hampshire.
Leonard Wiggins, D, 3d New Hampshire.
Daniel McAllester, H, 13th New Hampshire.
Leonard Barton, E, 7th New Hampshire.
F. Fanen, D, 7th New Hampshire.
John Roach, H, 3d New Hampshire.
William Smith, K, 2d New Hampshire.
H. Limpner, B, 12th New Hampshire.
B. Hoffman, K, 4th New Hampshire.
H. D. Hall, B, 3d New Hampshire.
E. Huntoon, D, 13th New Hampshire.
Moses Ash, D, 4th New Hampshire.
J. McAlester, C, 2d New Hampshire.
Joseph Willey, I, 10th New Hampshire.
S. Rogers, A, 4th New Hampshire.
W. Pinkham, F, 10th New Hampshire.
J. E. Evers, H, 142d Ohio.
J. Johnston, D, 134th Ohio.
O. Hunter, A, 130th Ohio.
J. L. Robbins, K, 130th Ohio.
Noah Shesler, H, 132d Ohio.
J. Sheppard, F, 142d Ohio.
Frank Doty, A, 138th Ohio.
Henry Oman, B, 134th Ohio.
Philip Hunt, F, 142d Ohio.
Levi Ogden, G, 142d Ohio.
F. L. Stoockwell, D, 67th Ohio

A. J. Eldred, K, 130th Ohio.
T. Heskel, E, 148th Ohio.
John Dunham, A, 134th Ohio.
J. Colton, B, 67th Ohio.
E. Sherwood, A, 132d Ohio.
J. Neich, K, 132d Ohio.
L. Roff, C, 67th Ohio.
S. Buchanan, F, 142d Ohio.
Washington Hyatt, A, 142 Ohio.
J. L. Reames, I, 132d Ohio.
C. Hooder, K, 67th Ohio.
W. O. Griffin, I, 67th Ohio.
Hiram Root, D, 123d Ohio.
A. Winter, G, 67th Ohio.
M. R. Hitchcock, B, 116th Ohio.
A. M. Brown, G, 62d Ohio.
George Barnes, A, 67th Ohio.
P. Van Buren, C, 67th Ohio.
H. Hoffman, G, 67th Ohio.
James Bell, I, 62d Ohio.
Enas Sherwood, A, 130th Ohio.
James H. Reed, F, 142d Ohio.
G. Simms, K, 142d Ohio.
C. R. Ross, D, 130th Ohio.
James Hall, H, 148th Ohio.
C. McWilliams, I, 142d Ohio.
F. West, G, 143d Ohio.
Francis Eten, B, 67th Ohio.
J. F. Ray, B, 134th Ohio.
George Kelle, A, 132d Ohio.
Peter Miller, K, 5th Maryland.
John McPown, C, 1st Maryland.
William Smith, 1st Maryland.
M. Bourn, 1st Maryland.
John Shawgr, E, 5th Maryland.
John Hamm, H, 5th Maryland.
William Gillespie, A, 5th Maryland.
Charles Rudar, C, 5th Maryland.
John Evern, C, 5th Maryland.
T. Lane, E, 5th Maryland.
G. W. L. Stack, K, 5th Maryland.
Philip Frost, C, 5th Maryland.
G. P. Miller, H, 1st Maryland.
Joshua Turner, 5th Maryland.
T. Kelley, A, 5th Maryland.
C. O. Wilson, G, 9th Vermont.
J. Bryant, B, 9th Vermont.
William Burroughs, G, 9th Vermont.
L. Dawson, K, 9th Vermont.
William Bucks, K, 9th Vermont.
A. E. Thompson, D, 9th Vermont.

J. Blanchard, I, 9th Vermont.
Peter Ladoo, H, 9th Vermont.
John Duyer, E, 9th Vermont.
Levi Martin, B, 9th Vermont.
James Duggan, B, 9th Vermont.
A. C. Avery, H, 9th Vermont.
H. Benson, C, 9th Vermont.
A. Holman, H, 9th Vermont.
W. D. Knight, D, 9th Vermont.
S. Buzzell, E, 9th Vermont.
George Parker, G, 9th Vermont.
M. Newman, I, 9th Vermont.
S. Flanders, B, 9th Vermont.
H. W. Parkins, A, 9th Vermont.
J. P. Quackenbush, F, 9th Vermont.
G. W. H. Frost, I, 1st District of Columbia Cav.
Charles Smith, I, 1st District of Columbia Cav.
James Case, B, 1st District of Columbia Cav.
Charles Morgan, B, 11th Pennsylvania Vol.
Elisha Thorpe, C, 199th Pennsylvania Vol.
J. Lindenster, B, 5th Pennsylvania Cav.
Gideon Hass, M, 5th Pennsylvania Cav.
T. Barrington, I, 100th Pennsylvania.
E. V. Cowles, I, 199th Pennsylvania.
Sergt. Marten, D, 104th Pennsylvania.
John Fox, D, 3d Pennsylvania Art.
M. Logherman, F, 203d Pennsylvania.
William Roush, A, 206th Pennsylvania.
J. Rollison, A, 2d Pennsylvania Art.
Henry Haines, H, 50th Pennsylvania Art.
William Crawner, H, 199th Pennsylvania.
George W. Thorn, D, 199th Pennsylvania.
Robert Kinter, C, 76th Pennsylvania.
James Lynch, G, 76th Pennsylvania.
A. C. Mower, 55th Pennsylvania.
C. Mattixin, H, 199th Pennsylvania.
John Brady, I, 211th Pennsylvania.
Samuel Reed, H, 58th Pennsylvania.
J. Henry, F, 119th Pennsylvania.
J. Kirkpatrick, C, 119th Pennsylvania.
H. Sebold, A, 119th Pennsylvania.
John Holders, D, 2d Pennsylvania Art.
P. Beelman, E, 211th Pennsylvania.
C. Moise, B, 199th Pennsylvania.
H. Nicholson, E, 199th Pennsylvania.
Stephen Arnold, G, 104 Pennsylvania.
F. Button, H, 11th Pennsylvania Cav.
John White, E, 200th Pennsylvania.
George McKiffe, C, 188th Pennsylvania.
Frederick Young, A, 138th Pennsylvania.
Thomas Wilson, D, 3d Pennsylvania.

G. A. McLaugheon, A, 55th Pennsylvania.
J. W. Adams, H, 76th Pennsylvania.
Griffen Hughes, A, 3d Pennsylvania Art.
Orven Rice, C, 50th Pennsylvania.
W. P. Fouler, H, 58th Pennsylvania.
S. Scofield, K, 58th Pennsylvania.
W. Bilaston, C, 188th Pennsylvania.
G. W. Crowell, E, 206th Pennsylvania.
James Wilson, K, 58th Pennsylvania.
D. Kendrick, G, 186th Pennsylvania.
Jacob Richards, C, 188th Pennsylvania.
John Fallman, F, 199th Pennsylvania.
E. A. Cramer, A, 2d Pennsylvania.
E. Armstrong, I, 211th Pennsylvania.
J. Dafferty, K, 55th Pennsylvania.
Martin Horn, L, 2d Pennsylvania Art.
S. R. Hood, A, 211th Pennsylvania.
Wm. M. Smith, F, 106th Pennsylvania.
James A. Ageye, G, 11th Pennsylvania Cav.
W. Node, D, 2d Pennsylvania Art.
Franklin Fry, B, 200th Pennsylvania.
Samuel Welles, E, 211th Pennsylvania
M. Manderback, B, 55th Pennsylvania.
N. Fessler, E, 207th Pennsylvania.
John S. Peet, F, 97th Pennsylvania.
W. Maclem, H, 5th Pennsylvania Cav.
A. Gregory, B, 207th Pennsylvania.
M. Marcteller, E, 5th Pennsylvania.
Wm. Seyfort, E, 2d Pennsylvania Art.
Samuel Ball, E, 5th Pennsylvania Cav.
John S. Dorsham, A, 199th Pennsylvania.
Daniel Healey, L, 2d Pennsylvania Art.
E. L. Cobb, C, 203d Pennsylvania.
Wm. Henry, C, 209th Pennsylvania.
Wm. Den, I, 199th Pennsylvania.
J. D. Rollison, K, 2d Pennsylvania Art.
Joseph Ritz, I, 58th Pennsylvania.
H. Yost, G, 3d Pennsylvania.
D. Daubenspeck, K, 206th Pennsylvania.
Joseph Bitts, A, 188th Pennsylvania.
J. Bowers, F, 58th Pennsylvania.
Wm. Cook, G, 199th Pennsylvania.
Wm. Spence, E, 58th Pennsylvania.
C. McCornish, I, 206th Pennsylvania.
I. Davenport, B, 104th Pennsylvania.
I. McElwee, B, Pennsylvania Art.
L. M. Craton, I, 188th Pennsylvania.
I. L. Havens, K, 199th Pennsylvania.
I. Flemming, I, 58th Pennsylvania.
A. W. Lonnon, A, 104th Pennsylvania.
Alexander Pankers, K, 85th Pennsylvania.

James Slack, I, 11th Pennsylvania Cav.
E. Brierly, G, 3d Pennsylvania Art.
Alfred Little, K, 58th Pennsylvania.
Jos. Weaver, A, 11th Pennsylvania Cav.
Lewis Wince, K, 67th Pennsylvania.
G. W. Dutcher, B, 76th Pennsylvania.
W. Steepy, B, 85th Pennsylvania.
I. Stickle, I, 188th Pennsylvania.
Caleb Scott, I, 6th Pennsylvania.
J. Watson, D, 11th Pennsylvania Cav
I. Risinger, I, 211th Pennsylvania.
Dan Finegan, I, 55th Pennsylvania.
O. A. Bean, A, 211th Pennsylvania.
Mart. Wilson, I, 187th Pennsylvania.
W. Whitaker, F, 58th Pennsylvania.
John Ackle, H, 5th Pennsylvania Cav.
John Scotia, A, 1st Pennsylvania Art.
Wm. Hyde, G, 2d Pennsylvania Art.
G. B. Lyman, A, 211th Pennsylvania.
Joseph Conrad, H, 199th Pennsylvania.
E. Wimberger, H, 211th Pennsylvania.
John Stbern, F, 55th Pennsylvania.
James Brooks, D, 207th Pennsylvania.
Philip Kifford, F, 209th Pennsylvania.
P. M. Adder, H, 216th Pennsylvania.
G. M. Rupert, D, 211th Pennsylvania.
W. Wieland, E, 5th Pennsylvania Cav.

CITY POINT.

DEPOT FIELD HOSPITAL.

The following named are buried in the cemetery at the Depot
Field Hospital, City Point, Va.:—

J. Fields.
C. North, K, 60th Ohio.
D. Potter, F, 20th Massachusetts.
H. Vanderhird, M, 2d New York M. R.
L. Spencer, G, 9th New Hampshire.
E. C. Dyke, H, 17th Vermont.
J. Bailey, G, 179th New York
C. Bronlingan, G, 58th Massachusetts.
G. W. Jones, B, 179th New York.
C. Hager, 48th Pennsylvania.
G. Gorden, B, 37th Wisconsin.
J. Crowl, E, 109th New York.
E. Scott, H, 17th Michigan.
J. Vacht, D, 2d Pennsylvania Art.
T. Johnson, D, 109th New York.
J. Clarkson, D, 51st New York.
J. Hascall, F, 58th Massachusetts.
C. Cary, 2d Maryland.
H. Cross, C, 24th New York.
G. Averil, K, 109th New York.
W. Hill, E, 38th Wisconsin.
J. Ortell, H, 46th New York.
W. Cook, I, 37th Wisconsin.
M. Weaver, 59th New York.
S. Wilcox, I, 37th Wisconsin.
J. Wright, A, 38th Wisconsin.
J. Kramer, A, 2d Maryland.
J. Foster, K, 179th New York.
J. Cady, H, 2d Pennsylvania Art.
M. Wouldridge, K, 23d New York.
J. J. Taylor, B, 58th Massachusetts.
J. M. Cullins, F, 9th New York H. A.
J. Walker.

B. Carpenter, K, 5th Wisconsin.
Levi Pegt, I, 15th New Jersey.
J. B. Schermerhorn, A, 106th New York.
W. Wilson, E, 2d Vermont.
G. Stafford, F, 49th Pennsylvania.
H. Mitchell, 98th Pennsylvania.
J. Smith, Naval Bat.
M. Sherman, 1st Vermont H. A.
T. J. Partridge, H, 37th Massachusetts.
B. Gedrich, D, 67th Pennsylvania.
T. Messer, H, 10th Vermont.
E. Waldrum, B, 10th Vermont.
P. Boylan, G, 40th New York.
J. Fletcher, 166th New York.
A. A. Campbell, F, 1st South Carolina.
J. Osborn, F, 6th Maryland.
J. Nelovis, D, 75th Pennsylvania.
J. McGuire, G, 87th Pennsylvania.
J. Erhart, H, 119th Pennsylvania.
P. Miller, A, 9th New York Art.
C. Snyder, K, 9th New York H. A.
W. Cook, K, 2d Connecticut Art.
G. Sharps, G, 61st Pennsylvania.
George Stahl, G, 61st Pennsylvania.
George Beoins, D, 77th New York.
J. M. Meyers, F, 5th Wisconsin.
D. Sullivan, 10th New Jersey.
Charlas Riley, F, 9th New York H. A.
L. Gloughlin, 1st Maine V. V.
B. Readingler, 93d Pennsylvania.
W. Reeghard, G, 67th Pennsylvania.
J. Fitzsimmons, D, 102d Pennsylvania.
E. Martin, D, 5th Wisconsin.
Wm. Oliver, D, 5th Vermont.
J. Gavron, H, 93d Pennsylvania.
1st Lieut. F. B. Hunter, 1st Maine.
1st Lieut. H. Saulbrig, I, 98th Pennsylvania
J. Beirce, B, 98th Pennsylvania.
H. Eppauline, D, 1st New York Eng.
C. Benson.
F. Wambyer, F, 41st New York.
N. Rugg, I, 3d Vermont.
A. Rhodes.
N. Cray, I, 122d Ohio.
C. Miller.
C. A. Barpee, K, 5th Wisconsin.
A. Bailey, A, 1st Michigan S. S.
A. M. Rese, A, 1st Maine S. S.
A. Keller.
John Noyes.
C. Carr, 60th New York.

P. J. Linger, K, 7th New York.
H. Surtyam, I, 58th Pennsylvania.
W. Simpson, A, 153d New York.
J. Northway, E, 43d Michigan.
Charles Tuttle, F, 2d Connecticut H. A.
C. P. Hartman, C, 49th Pennsylvania.
G. W. Smith, F, 77th New York.
J. Glace, H, 102d Pennsylvania.
D. Harding, H, 67th Pennsylvania.
A. W. Aldrich, B, 4th Vermont.
1st Lieut. Restolick, F, 122d Ohio.
Lieut. A. F. Perrine, C, 62d New York.
W. J. David, H, 102d Pennsylvania.
J. Dutton, F, 11th Vermont.
J. P. Morse, F, 4th New Jersey Art.
F. Brackett, H, 37th Massachusetts.
W. Milford, L, 11th Pennsylvania Art.
C. Wagner, H, 93d Pennsylvania.
R. Simmers, F, 93d Pennsylvania.
T. McNamara, I, 7th Maine.
J. Malone, G, 3d N. Y.
L. Rupell, D, 1st Vermont.
John Caul, F, 122d Ohio.
J. Yokem, F, 1st Delaware.
P. Phiney, B, 11th Vermont.
David H. Mead, E, 122d N. Y.
Wm. Sly, H, 4th Vermont.
A. L. Sparrow, F, 110th Ohio.
W. Meyers, F, 15th N. Y.
G. C. Hovey, M, 11th Vermont.
J. H. Pritchard, D, 2d Connecticut H. A.
J. M. Carr, B, 1st Vermont.
Amos Ives, L, 2d Connecticut.
S. M. Stodart, E, 9th N. Y. Art.
Wm. Messer, K, 98th Pennsylvania.
H. W. Smith, B, 4th Vermont Art.
E. Ward, H, 11th Vermont.
D. Rinehart, H, 82d Pennsylvania.
Richard Webb, C, 1st Delaware.
W. Stillwell, A, 14th N. Y.
H. Goodyear, A, 6th Vermont.
W. Walston, B, 4th Vermont.
John Cook, A, 1st N. Y. Art.
C. Gurnsey, B, 2d Connecticut H. A.
H. Knoble, K, 2d Wisconsin.
A. Craigne, H, 10th Vermont.
F. Condon, F, 110th Pennsylvania.
J. Dernuth, D, 2d Connecticut.
H. Peas, H, 2d Connecticut.
Wm. Lane, F, 6th Vermont.
John Loth, A, 6th N. Y.

F. Howard, A, 1st Vermont H. A.
M. Lee, C, 1st Maine.
W. W. Conklin, E, 15th N. Y.
C. McCorson, H, 1st Ohio.
H. Harding, C, 139th Pennsylvania.
F. Boxburg, A, 32d N. Y.
G. Wright, H, 9th N. Y.
C. Johnson, G, 49th Pennsylvania
J. Miller, A, 62d N. Y.
N. Lockwood, H, 1st Ohio Art.
J. Miller, C, 97th Pennsylvania.
F. Laird, B, 9th N. Y.
Joel Kenedy, H, 2d Connecticut.
L. R. Wood, D, 10th U. S. Infantry.
G. R. Fivetack, H, 149th Pennsylvania.
J. Elderkin, C, 21st Pennsylvania Cav.
A. L. Pyle, B, 187th Pennsylvania.
J. Simmonds, A, 7th Wisconsin.
G. S. Bailey, D, 16th Michigan.
Levi Klingensmith, I, 11th Pennsylvania
C. F. Churchill, I, 6th New Hampshire H. A.
H. Thompson, K, 6th New Hampshire H. A.
P. J. Miller, I, 11th Pennsylvania.
A. Myers, C, 14th U. S. Infantry.
Sergt. E. J. Messick, B, 3d Delaware.
N. M. Reede, H, 83d Pennsylvania.
J. Mann, A, 187th Pennsylvania.
H. Barr, B, 15th N. Y. H. Art.
E. Stewart, C, 157th Pennsylvania.
John Fultz, H, 149th Pennsylvania.
J. Williams, F, 15th N. Y. H. Art.
L. Hassiage, I, 15th N. Y. H. Art.
J. Thompson, C, 6th N. Y. H. Art.
J. Foster, C, 15th N. Y. H. Art.
W. Pergh, A, 88th Pennsylvania.
A. Cobb, E, 16th Maine.
L. D. Crouch, H, 150th Pennsylvania.
Francis West, K, 39th Massachusetts.
J. Livingston, L, 16th Michigan.
G. W. Stevens, B, 94th N. Y.
N. Hockman, I, 19th Indiana.
J. Shaw, G, 190th Pennsylvania.
A. Mowry, C, 11th Pennsylvania.
G. C. Arnold, 7th Co., N. Y. S. S.
B. F. Wells, K, 187th Pennsylvania.
H. Alwines, 4th U. S. Infantry.
J. Ritter, B, 21st Pennsylvania Cav.
W. F. Hallus, I, 21st Pennsylvania.
W. Shaffer, H, 83d Pennsylvania.
Thomas Pugh, M, 21st Pennsylvania Cav.
G. M. Shaffer, D, 11th Pennsylvania.

Wm. Chillingworth, H, 4th Delaware.
Sergt. James Kearns, G, 94th N. Y.
D. E. Eldrid, B, 11th Pennsylvania.
D. Armstrong, F, 143d Pennsylvania.
A. Glasen, K, N. Y. H. Art.
John A. Smith, D, 38th Pennsylvania.
W. Baker, C, 21st Pennsylvania Cav.
Ross McKenney, B, 21st Pennsylvania Cav.
Q. M. Sergt. C. E. Fay, 17th U. S.
J. McMullen, K, Pennsylvania R.
J. Gorden, H, 2d Pennsylvania R.
W. Miller, H, 7th Wisconsin.
J. McSam, E, 40th New Jersey.
F. B. Ayers, B, 10th New York.
W. Gray, E, 2d Rhode Island,
A. Goodwin, D, 87th Pennsylvania.
H. Thompson, E, 1st Michigan Cav.
C. K. Lewis, G, 121st N. Y.
E. Morely, A, 37th Massachusetts.
P. Wayman, B, 91st N. Y.
J. Treville, D, Hampton Legion.
J. A. Robertson, I, 5th N. C.
E. Deway, H, 1st Rhode Island Art.
F. Sullivan, G, 2d Rhode Island.
H. Snodgrass, A, 4th Virginia Bat.
H. M. Lisley, I, 1st Maine.
W. M. Gawyer, B, 5th Vermont.
G. Sheldon, B, 93d Pennsylvania.
Lieut. C. H. Meyon, A, 5th Wisconsin.
B. Ostrander, H, 91st N. Y.
J. Bender, G, 67th N. Y.
A. Pelton, K, 37th Massachusetts.
T. M. Meyers, C, Naval Bat.
George Barry, D, 19th Virginia.
George Merson, C, 121st N. Y.
E. Willsie, C, 91st N. Y.
Thomas Dorsey, G, 1st Maryland.
Wm. Cars, K, 91st N. Y.
Thomas Smith, F, 146th N. Y.
Frederick Miller, A, 91st N. Y.
Robert Closes, E, 16th Michigan.
H. Beech, I, 146th N. Y.
Joseph Thomas, H, 189th Pennsylvania.
A. G. Wagner, C, 5th N. Y.
Sergt. S. F. Trahern, D, 3d Delaware.
Amos Smith, A, 7th Maryland.
Frederick Pryor, F, 3d Delaware.
Tobias Michael, K, 198th Pennsylvania.
Chap. E. P. Crosby, 185th N. Y.
Henry Sims, I, 210th Pennsylvania.
F. Ensilis, L, 15th N. Y. H. A.

John H. Hyler, I, 20th Maine.
Anson Verill, D, 20th Maine.
L. Schaap, A, 4th Maryland.
Wm. Brown, B, 5th N. Y.
Emil Kraft, E, 15th N. Y. H. A.
J. A. Murphy, C, 9th N. Y.
E. F. Johnson, G, 185th N. Y.
Enoch Lee, E, 146th N. Y.
Wm. Baxter, H, 1st Maryland.
Samuel Hagadern, H, 91st N. Y.
J. Bowers, 7th Maryland.
N. Stanton.
Frederick Nutt, 104th Pennsylvania.
W. Dewitt.
F. Buggs, A, 97th N. Y.
N. Allen, K, 142d Pennsylvania.
W. Brown, G, 38th Wisconsin.
S. Emphy.
G. Thompson, 27th N. Y. Bat.
J. Thomas, H, 8th Michigan.
J. Groan, I, 51st N. Y.
Theodore Prosser, K, 27th Michigan.
E. P. Pierce, B, 6th N. H. Bat.
Sergt. J. M. Mercer, M, 13th Ohio Cav.
Job Bavser, C. 205th Pennsylvania.
J. Froggett, C, 186th N. Y.
M. McClintic, M, 14th N. Y. H. A.
G. Knightlinge, F, 8th Michigan.
James Fritz, A, 209th Pennsylvania.
M. S. Morgan, K, 8th Michigan.
Thomas Commons, D. 2d Pennsylvania Bat.
Peter Folay, A, 14th N. Y. H. A.
Sergt. C. Gastim, D, 37th Wisconsin.
Sergt. D. Waltz, D, 37th Wisconsin.
F. Scott, G, 158th N. Y.
G. Brooks.
S. Hoys, D, 59th Massachusetts.
J. Babb, C, 13th Ohio.
W. Kinney, K, 51st Pennsylvania.
J. Wade, G, 50th Pennsylvania.
W. Snyder, K, 14th N. Y.
A. Mason, B, 60th Ohio.
W. Barnes, B, 37th Wisconsin.
L. Kilbun, G, 6th New Hampshire.
C. Shelley, K, 60th Ohio.
I. M. Davis, H, 31st Maine.
E. Baldwin, A, 60th Ohio.
W. Prithen, G, 38th Wisconsin.
H. Otterson, C, 186th N. Y.
John Knoid, A, 79th N. Y.
Sergt. C. P. Brown, I, 37th Wisconsin.

C. Sherry, 57th N. Y.
R. H. Baldwin, 4th N. Y. Art.
S. Ackerman, 69th N. Y.
J. Blair, 14th Connecticut.
E. Fritch, 88th N. Y.
G. Thompson, 61st N. Y.
J. Mitchell, 105th Pennsylvania.
S. Eckstein, 8th New Jersey.
J. Kuhn, 8th New Jersey.
G. W. Smith, 28th Massachusetts.
T. A. Glading, 7th N. Y. H. A.
J. H. Horssley, 7th N. Y. H. A.
P. Meyers, 52d N. Y.
J. Gannagle, 40th N. Y.
C. O. Goodrich, H, 12th Virginia.
L. M. Coffine, 1st Maine Art.
P. Schmiltz, 7th New Jersey.
O. D. Watson, 5th New Hampshire.
E. Cushman, 4th N. Y. Art.
J. Bunting, 91st Pennsylvania.
G. Welch, 5th New Hampshire.
A. Ford, 8th New Jersey.
F. Martin, 11th New Jersey.
T. Donley, 20th Massachusetts.
G. Hyde, 120th N. Y.
Lewis Hunt, 19th Maine.
Hiram Moore, 52d N. Y.
James Cromwell, 53d Pennsylvania.
E. Turgan, 7th N. Y. Art.
S. Dearwood, 1st Minnesota.
G. Dolt, 124th N. Y.
T. Sellers, 69th N. Y.
G. Merritt, 7th New Jersey.
Michael Welch.
N. S. Frail, C, 1st Massachusetts.
John Bray, 73d N. Y.
Frederick Shann, 61st N. Y.
M. J. Jenkins, D, 61st N. Y.
John Lynch, F, 7th N. Y.
J. Pease, H, 81st Pennsylvania.
Charles Conlard, K, 20th Maine.
Charles Siebert.
Wm. H. Ellison, 33d Pennsylvania.
J. A. Simmons, A, 120th N. Y.
M. A. Hyde, A, 111th N. Y.
James Carney, A, 77th N. Y.
P. Eagan, 2d U. S. Infantry.
Wm. F. De Morest, D, 2d N. Y.
P. Florence, 1st Connecticut Art.
James Lucas, B, 52d Pennsylvania.
G. Michelfelder, E, 7th N. Y. Art.

Arthur Bacon, 28th U. S. C. T.
Charles Goldsboro, I, 28th U. S. C. T.
Joseph Isaacold, Government employee.
Robin Cox, G, 10th U. S. C. T.
Eleven Bailey, K, 30th U. S. C. T.
Henry Williams, G, 28th U. S. C. T.
Lafayette Williams, H, 28th U. S. C. T.
G. H. Robinson.
Isaac Moden, 28th U. S. C. T.
Nelson Roberts, 10th U. S. C. T.
Joseph Heck, B, 10th U. S. C. T.
Edward Paderger, E, 115th U. S. C. T.
Thomas Snowder (colored citizen.)
Henry Currey, C, 28th U. S. C. T.
Andrew Fichett, C, 10th U. S. C. T.
David James, K, 28th U. S. C. T.
George W. Follbuer, D, 28th U. S. C. T.
Richard Bell, K, 28th U. S. C. T.
George H. Hall, C, 28th U. S. C. T.
Wm. Jeffrey, C, 28th U. S. C. T.
Wm. Murry, 28th U. S. C. T.
Joseph Turner, B, 28th U. S. C. T.
J. Hersh, K, 4th U. S. Infantry.
Wm. Smith, 1st Engineers.
E. Stevenson, E, 4th U. S. Infantry.
J. Monroe, H, 106th N. Y.
E. Joslyn.
S. L. Wardard, 16th Michigan.
N. Porter, M, 8th N. Y.
J. Kauffman, A, 61st Pennsylvania.
George C. Booze, C, 119th Pennsylvania.
W. H. Hawkins.
Sergt. G. Phipps, K, 65th N. Y.
J. P. Willett, I, 8th Michigan.
H. Mentor, H, 1st Connecticut Cav.
G. McCown, C, 107th N. Y.
C. Huff, A, 16th Maine.
W. H. Vannest, G, 107th Pennsylvania.
J. Bowls, E, 6th Wisconsin.
C. Hulshiser, E, 198th Pennsylvania.
C. L. Harvey, H, 1st N. Y. Art.
George Wyman, D, 18th New Hampshire.
H. Cash, D, 189th N. Y.
J. Lindler, L, 15th N. Y. H. A.
K. Craimer, I, 198th Pennsylvania.
Charles Oberly, B, 185th N. Y.
Ira Dupont, D, 32d Massachusetts.
Edward McLueer, H, 1st N. Y. Art.
G. W. Frost, I, 16th Maine.
Henry Slade, K, 15th N. Y.
A. W. Gould, A, 188th N. Y.

Joshua Bryant, E, 155th Pennsylvania.
Elias Tubbs, J, 43d Pennsylvania.
W. Clanden, B, 155th Pennsylvania.
Amos Lamb, D, 189th N. Y.
E. McCaffery, Bat. I, —— Rhode Island.
Sergt. Frank Duroll, A, 16th Michigan.
David Speels, B, 83d Pennsylvania.
Sergt. C. Schlieff, F, 15th N. Y. H. A.
Frishin Chrysler, 91st N. Y.
C. Deity, L, 15th N. Y. A.
G. Tackeling, A, 155th N. Y.
Edward Ford, G, 4th Delaware.
E. Nashot, B, 83d Pennsylvania.
Lewis Carl, F, 20th Maine.
Sergt. T. O. Conor, G, 11th U. S.
John Wise, A, 185th N. Y.
A. T. Hartwell, I, 1st Michigan.
J. Brazee, K, 20th N. Y.
Adam Noise, G, 107th Pennsylvania.
Wm. Hurst, B, 1st N. Y. Art.
J. Lacher, I, 115th N. Y.
J. Collins, C, 4th Maryland.
J. Bussker, F, 104th N. Y.
M. Fitzpatrick, G, 5th N. Y.
James Hutchins, E, 91st Pennsylvania.
J. Dick, A, 187th N. Y.
W. C. Hunter, 190th Pennsylvania.
J. Seinden, F, 1st Maryland.
Isaac Seaman, E, 1st Michigan.
J. Druig, B, 104th N. Y.
S. Green, D, 15th N. Y. H. A.
O. French, D, 20th Maine.
A. C. Gold, L, 155th Pennsylvania.
J. Kending, H, 198th Pennsylvania.
J. D. Fisher, H, 83d Pennsylvania.
Dan Stockley, 118th Pennsylvania.
C. H. Bancroft, B, 16th Michigan.
G. E. Wines, H, 56th Pennsylvania.
Sergt. J. Bradley, C, 16th Michigan.
T. P. Powel, B, 124th N. Y.
J. Font, B, 1st N. Y.
J. A. Burch, A, 94th N. Y.
L. Jestive, F, 56th North Carolina.
J. McKinney, B, 49th North Carolina.
J. Harlow, K, 56th Pennsylvania.
Corp. C. Whiteheart, C, 56th North Carolina.
Richard Simmons, K, 104th N. Y.
E. L. Studt, N, 198th Pennsylvania.
Sergt. J. Ackland, G, 3d U. S. Infantry.
O. Simpson, F, 121st Pennsylvania.
Capt. John Lamney, D, 6th Wisconsin.

Robert Hamilton, B, 200th Pennsylvania.
W. Cunnines, H, 187th N. Y.
W. P. Durtin, C, 83d Pennsylvania.
E. Haight, G, 189th N. Y.
S. Crocker, F, 210th Pennsylvania.
T. Hollinger, G, 3d Delaware.
Sergt. L. Brown, I, 1st Maryland.
A. Carrell, D, 189th Pennsylvania.
D. A. Strong, K, 21st N. Y.
F. Killink, F, —— New Hampshire.
C. H. Granger, H, 20th Maine.
J. Eyer (or Ezer,) D, 210th Pennsylvania.
A. Wood, B, 24th N. Y. Cav.
Charles Reiman, M, 15th N. Y. H. A.
J. Dippy, M, 15th N. Y. H. A.
M. J. Powers, D, 6th Wisconsin.
Wm. Moore, B, 104th N. Y.
A. Heckathorn, F, 121st Pennsylvania.
J. Mitterman, A, 16th Michigan.
H. Loveall, E, 3d N. Y. Art.
Robert Mickey, C, 11th Pennsylvania,
J. L. Pessley, F, 20th Pennsylvania.
W. Brown, A, 16th Maine.
J. Davidson, M, 198th Pennsylvania.
J. Leroy, F, 94th N. Y.
J. Berghans,
Samuel Colwell, I, 11th Pennsylvania,
C. M. Main, D, 118th N. Y.
D. C. Hollenbach, E, 118th N. Y.
J. Leonard,
G. W. Nathans, H, 8th Maryland,
Daniel Bruce, C, 119th N. Y.
J. Lamance, A, 32d Massachusetts.
J. Smith, A, 11th Pennsylvania.
James McCarthy, A, 5th N. Y.
Ira Audley, Dixon's Light Art.
E. Howland, I, 16th Maine.
G. H. Reynolds, A, 20th Maine.
O. Lawrence, F, 140th N. Y.
A. Swasey, A, 107th Pennsylvania.
S. Fogg, C, 20th Maine.
F. Fisher, H, 6th Wisconsin.
Daniel Canfield, C, 118th N. Y.
S. Church, A, 189th N. Y.
F. Crane, C, 16th Maine.
C. Later, G, 198th Pennsylvania.
W. McSherler, A, 83d Pennsylvania.
J. Shoemaker,
J. Williams, A, 83d Pennsylvania.
J. Saa Stone, A, 45th Pennsylvania.
C. D. Slatterly, —— 14th Massachusetts

O. Vera, D, 1st N. Y. Art.
J. E. Stoufer, F, 11th Pennsylvania.
A. Alonzo, —— 32d Massachusetts.
E. Lamb.
William Hettinger, F, 190th Pennsylvania.
D. Van Steinburg, M, 15th N. Y. H. A.
D. Burkhart, F, 115th Pennsylvania.
J. Eicheneour, F, 21st Pennsylvania Cav.
W. Smith, A, 97th N. Y.
J. L. Chapman, H, 118th N. Y.
T. C. Major, A, 198th Pennsylvania.
A. L. James, H, 185th N. Y.
H. Wheaton, H, 189th N. Y.
F. Phippen, H, 185th N. Y.
O. McDonald, G, 56th Pennsylvania.
J. Doyle, B, 4th U. S. Art.
D. B. Stout, B, 1st Pennsylvania Art.
J. Haft, G, 1st Michigan.
N. Guyyer, —— 90th Pennsylvania.
R. Coleman, E, 83d Pennsylvania.
M. Scoff, K, 21st South Carolina.
James E. Paine, D, 44th N. Y.
C. W. Lessley, K, 25th South Carolina.
Corpl. C. K. Shumway, A, 187th Pennsylvania,
C. A. Sayle, —— 1st Rhode Island.
C. Corney, —— 21st South Carolina.
John Swift, A, 146th N. Y.
L. Reicor, —— 10th U. S. Band.
S. S. Tryon, G, 95th N. Y.
E. Orr, —— 9th N. Y. Art.
Comby, A, 8th Maryland.
M. S. Buckingham, B, 1st N. Y. Art.
H. Shultz, G, 8th Maryland.
M. Parker, 1st Confederate Bat.
J. E. Joiner, G. 41st Virginia.
J. Ravelle, C, 95th N. Y.
Wm. Cross, K, 41st Virginia.
P. Mitchell, A, 17th U. S. Infantry.
Sergt. C. M. Atkinson, E, 7th S. C. Bat.
E. McCannon, E, 76th N. Y.
J. Brissent, B, 11th U. S. Infantry.
E. Bentimg, F, 15th N. Y. H. A.
J. T. Martin, —— 4th Miss.
J. Jones, G, S. C.
Chas. Jenkins, Bat. A, —— Wisconsin Art.
J. H. Ray, —— 23d Georgia.
T. Comlow, K. 51st N. C.
Corp. A. Voyeritz, I, 14th U. S.
A. Perry, H. 15th N. Y. H. A.
H. Mower, —— 1st N. Y. Bat.
S. Sheffield, B, 4th Delaware.

S. S. Seiger, B, 90th Pennsylvania.
G. E. Aspforth, B. 146th N. Y.
F. Knight, K, 187th Pennsylvania.
W. H. Estus, H, 143d Pennsylvania.
G. D. Gardner, G, 37th Massachusetts.
W. Schmidt, D, 15th N. Y. H. A.
G. Thiebold, G, 15th N. Y. H. A.
P. Purval, C, 83d Pennsylvania.
P. Rupert, E, 1st N. Y. Light Art.
Wm. Wallace, K, 187th Pennsylvania
J. M. Bankhard, C, 7th Maryland.
L. Darling, Bat. B. 4th U. S.
D. Canford, G, 15th N. Y. H. A.
G. Mayle D, 15th N. Y. H. A.
A. C. Eldridge, D, 50th N. Y. Engineers.
F. A. Nanday, F, 50th N. Y. Engineers.
M. Lananley, B, 94th N. Y.
G. Smith, B, 94th N. Y.
E. Murphy, C, 27th N. Y. Bat.
W. Snyder, A, 50th Pennsylvania.
L. Weaver, F, 2d N. Y. Rifles.
J. Morse, L, 14th N. Y. Art.
R. Pattet, B, 2d N. Y. M. R.
C. C. Carpenter, D, 24th N. Y. Cav.
W. Brinit, A, 38th Wisconsin.
R. Young, H, 109th N. Y.
F. Lueny, F, 48th Pennsylvania.
H. Shepperd, F, 44th N. Y.
E. Bradley, E, 187th Pennsylvania.
E. J. Vincent, C. 21st Pa. Cav.
P. Wolf, H, 88th Pennsylvania.
S. Raymond, E, 1st New Hampshire Cav.
A. Mooller, D, 157th Pennsylvania.
J. Good, K, 90th Pennsylvania.
J. Bradley, H, 12th U. S.
W. W. Fox, H, 6th N. Y. H. A.
A. Woolheater, K, 157th Pennsylvania.
W. C. Johnson, B, 187th Pennsylvania.
P. Burnett, F, 3d Delaware.
Joseph Carson, F, 7th Wisconsin.
H. Smidt, A, 88th Pennsylvania.
H. S. Windle, E, 150th Pennsylvania.
Del. Cathen, A, 187th Pennsylvania.
J. Kensey, C, 157th Pennsylvania.
H. Barnes, C, 187th Pennsylvania.
Daniel Yoder, K, 187th Pennsylvania.
Robert Conners, H, 21st Pa. Dis. Cav
Jacob Straser, K, 15th N. Y. H. A.
P. O. Miller, 88th Pennsylvania.
Wm. Hartung, B, 15th N. Y. H. A.
Chas. Smith, F, 187th Pennsylvania.

Michael Casey, G, 97th N. Y.
Alexander Carson, D, 155th Pennsylvania.
Frank Martin, H, 12th U. S.
P. Gilbert, D, 87th Pennsylvania.
G. U. Shlaffer, L, 21st Pennsylvania Cav.
Sam. Carey, 16th Michigan S. S.
G. Erginger, C, 97th N. Y.
J. Adams, C.
G. Horn, A, 15th N. Y. H. A.
Wm. W. Bangs, F, 12th Massachusetts.
H. Hinds, M, 21st Pennsylvania Cav.
Andrew Sharp, D, 11th Pennsylvania.
G. A. Tinker, B, 11th U. S.
Thos. Erskin, C, 15th Maine.
Stn. Urshler, G, 83d Pennsylvania.
Chas. Crise, H, 91st Pennsylvania.
I. N. Nash, B, 7th Indiana.
F. F. Lawner, G, 83d Pennsylvania.
Asbury Bates, A, 6th Wisconsin.
A. Nichols, 6th N. Y. H. A.
E. Parsner, 1st N. Y. Art.
Wm. Horner, H, 155th N. Y.
Xor. Duchtler, B, 15th N. Y. H. A.
A. Allbright, 1st Pennsylvania Rifles.
W. J. Morris, H, 155th Pennsylvania.
Chas. Kelsey, F, 146th N. Y.
S. H. Wright.
M. C. Baker, 21st Pennsylvania Cav.
J. T. Freeman, H, 62d Pennsylvania.
A. Sinniman, L, 15th N. Y. H. A.
W. C. B. Steeles, M, 15th N. Y. H. A.
Clark Davis, B, 24th Michigan.
Wm. Brown, H, 95th N. Y.
Sergt. G. A. Jacobs, I, 83d Pennsylvania.
Wesley Fyer, D, 107th Pennsylvania.
M. D. McOmick, E, 4th Delaware.
Henry Reich, I, 107th Pennsylvania.
Wm. Hedrick, F, P. L. Maryland.
L. Laird, F, 147th N. Y.
Sergt. L. Bropby, E, 91st Pennsylvania Rifles.
Dav. Habald, G, 97th N. Y.
Dav. Burgess, F, 6th N. Y. H. A.
Saml. Spencer, E, 12th Massachusetts.
A. Erline, G, 2d Pennsylvania Reserves.
Abr. Eschelman, C, Bucktail R.
John Rusk, D, 91st Pennsylvania.
Jos. Palmerston, E, 76th N. Y.
Jacob Johnston, E, 12th U. S. I.
Saml. O. Burger, B, 187th Pennsylvania.
Jas. S. Thompson, H, 91st Pennsylvania.
D. F. Chapel, L, 1st N. Y. Art.

J. Barkholder, 21st Pennsylvania Cav.
Alex. Sopher, A, 6th N. Y. H. A.
Lieut. Philips, Adjt., 7th Wisconsin.
Horace Kirk, G, 6th N. Y. H. A.
Lewis Wenkle, D, 15th N. Y. H. A.
Ed. Nephry, K, 83d Pennsylvania.
Henry Plrugh, C, 155th Pennsylvania.
Lewis Spoteathe, B, 187th Pennsylvania.
Chas. Blazor, L, 6th N. Y. H. A.
E. Smith, 12th Massachusetts.
Dan. L. Repler, K, 5th Pennsylvania Reserves.
Pat. Dance, B, 11th Pennsylvania Res.
G. W. McClarry, G, 4th Delaware.
Pat. Coyle.
Henderson Stevens, C, 19th U. S. C. T.
Ed. Gozney, A, 30th U. S. C. T.
H. Wells, 23d U. S. C. T.
John Garett, 23d U. S. C. T.
Geo. Washington, C, 29th U. S. C. T.
O. Farthing, G, 27th U. S. C. T.
G. Mattleber, B, 43d U. S. C. T.
Lewis Enes, B, 30th U. S. C. T.
Corp. Geo. Williams, A, 29th U. S. C. T.
S. Mercer, (teamster.)
Thos. Brooks, E, 23d U. S. C. T.
Moses Porter, H, 29th U. S. C. T.
Jas. J. Ant, F, 29th U. S. C. T.
Wm. Campbell.
Frank Engler.
Sergt. D. Brown, 27th U. S. C. T.
Jas. Netts.
S. Boon, C, 28th U. S. C. T.
J. O. Cox, K, 4th U. S. C. T.
John Price, A, 23d U. S. C. T.
A. White, H, 28th U. S. C. T., (Reserves.)
John Johnson, D, 29th U. S. C. T.
Jas. Wing, B, 10th U. S. C. T.
John E. Capern, A, 10th U. S. C. T.
Jas. Ferrill, E, 29th U. S. C. T.
Wm. Hyatt, A, 30th U. S. C. T.
Radon Cofeer, A, 37th U. S. C. T.
Thos. W. Bond, H, 4th U. S. C. T.
John Holland, I, 30th U. S. C. T.
John Connard, C, 27th U. S. C. T.
Jos. Evans, B, 28th U. S. C. T.
Andrew Evans, B, 28th U. S. C. T.
Nat. Henson, F, 39th U. S. C. T.
Levi Stewart, C, 19th U. S. C. T.
S. Williams, I, 39th U. S. C. T.
Isaac Hughes, C, 39th U. S. C. T.
W. Russell, A, 23d U. S. C. T.

H. Henmon, H, 19th U. S. C. T.
Julius Freman, B, 31st U. S. C. T.
Wm. Dawsey, G, 9th U. S. C. T.
Wm. H. Clay, H, 30th U. S. C. T.
L. Johnson, (servant.)
J. T. Harmon, A, 43d U. S. C. T.
N. Walker, C, 4th U. S. C. T.
S. Sharp, C, 4th U. S. C. T.
N. A. Nailom, 4th U. S. C. T.
F. Forseman, K, 30th U. S. C. T.
G. Green, G, 43d U. S. C. T.
Wm. Pipkins, D, 23d U. S. C. T.
Wm. Hires, G, 14th U. S. C. T.
Jas. Catch, C, 43d U. S. C. T.
Jas. Stark, (servant.)
Philip McKissick, F, 43d U. S. C. T.
S. Chambers, G, 19th U. S. C. T.
E. Henson, A, 19th U. S. C. T.
F. Jones.
L. Tann, (servant,) B, 28th U. S. C. T.
O. Manck, E, 23d U. S. C. T.
Wm. Better, A, 23d U. S. C. T.
H. Hannan, 69th N. Y.
S. Arnold, 99th Pennsylvania.
J. Meyer, 30th N. Y.
C. Rullman, 64th N. Y.
R. McClosky, —— 23d Massachusetts.
J. Feltman, —— 84th Pennsylvania.
J. Springslomyer, —— 184th Pennsylvania.
D. Dany, —— 19th Maine.
J. Waterhouse, —— 53d Pennsylvania.
W. Pearson, —— 114th Pennsylvania.
J. Boyson, —— 5th New Hampshire.
J. Coney, —— 5th Michigan.
L. Putnam, E, 37th Wisconsin.
W. Galiger, K, 57th Massachusetts.
W. Bush, C, 2d N. Y.
H. Tillman, F, 14 N. Y. H. A
L. S. Gardner, D, 109th N. Y.
J. K. Rowe, C, 100th Pennsylvania.
E. Gunnier, C, 2d Pennsylvania Art.
H. M. Brown, K, 32d Maine.
G. Smith, D, 2d Michigan.
J. Smith, H, 35th Massachusetts.
G. Prafest, —— 2d Pennsylvania Art.
F. Grant, I, 32d Maine.
J. Weston, —— Wisconsin.
A. D. Dennis, A, 14th N. Y.
A. Dennison, L, 24th N. Y. Cav.
E. W. Belcher, H, 27th Michigan.
W. H. Hamilton, I, 109th N. Y.

C. Hamilton, K, 14th N. Y. H. A.
L. Bennett, K, 32d Maine.
G. Meyer, B, 2nd Pennsylvania Art.
J. G. Yackwell, G, 39th Pennsylvania.
G. Norton, G, 24th N. Y. Cav.
G. R. Williams, E, 14th N. Y. H. A.
D. Buchanan, D, 2 Pennsylvania Art.
B. White, —— 11th Massachusetts Bat.
S. S. Tucker, H, 17th Vermont,
J. Warner, C, 13th Ohio.
C. D. French, I, 59th Massachusetts.
M. Dudley, G, 9th New Hampshire.
A. Epp, B, 27th Michigan.
W. M. Barnes, C, 1st Michigan.
J. Dehorne, G, 9th New Hampshire.
F. K. Jacobs, G, 100th Pennsylvania.
S. D. Philips, C, 109th N. Y.
W. Clift, G, 2d N. Y.
J. Bruer, F, 27th Michigan.
R. Harris, H, 2d N. Y. M. R.
C. Pocket, G, 57th Massachusetts.
C. Mitchel, K, 100th Pennsylvania
E. W. Eldridge, K, 32d Maine.
D. Lenry, —— 45th Pennsylvania.
R. Jimerson, —— 14th N. Y. Art.
G. P. Cole, A, 14th N. Y. H. A.
J. T. Decker, G, 2d N. Y. M. R.
F. F. Craighead, M, 100th Pennsylvania.
G. Matt, F, 57th Massachusetts.
C. Heburn, G, 13th Ohio.
A. Tutler, A, 2nd N. Y. M. R.
C. Whitecar, B, 22d Maine.
G. Y. Shepherd, G, 15th N. Y.
J. Smith, B, 19th New Hampshire.
A. Ireland, I, 50th Pennsylvania,
L. Kinney, E, 27th Michigan.
J. Dunham, E, 31st Maine,
J. H. Gray, M, 14th N. Y. H. A.
T. Graves, I, 27th Michigan.
G. D. Conden, I, 60th Ohio.
C. W. Sprecker, C, 179th N. Y.
D. Arnold, D, Dunell Bat.
R. Smith, I, 2d Maryland.
D. Morton, B, 2d Pennsylvania M. R.
Laroy M. Palmer, G, 31st Maine.
W. Hitner, 5th Excelsior.
W. Potter, 2d Pennsylvania Art.
E. Edinger, 2d Michigan.
C. Grobis, 2d N. Y.
A. Town, 32d Maine.
J. Houghtling, B, 24th N. Y. Cav.

D. Wheeler.
J. S. Fisher, B, 2d N. Y. M. R.
S. W. Coock, 57th Massachusetts.
E. A. Adams, 59th Massachusetts.
W. H. Allen, B, 2d Michigan.
B. O. Wold, 29th Pennsylvania.
D. Flynn, 155th Pennsylvania.
G. Morehouse, 1st Michigan.
J. Hurd, 51st Pennsylvania.
H. Wilday, 61st N. Y.
A. Aldrich, G, 58th Massachusetts.
J. Aurell, 14th N. Y. H. A.
A. Shiffer, 2d Michigan.
J. Davis, 31st Maine.
T. Corier, 11th New Hampshire.
L. Burgess, 86th N. Y.
S. Hemphill, 2d Pennsylvania Art.
D. Houser, B, 48th Pennsylvania.
S. Dunham, F, 20th Michigan.
I. Brownsangh, 105th Pennsylvania.
E. A. Kelly, 1st U. S. S. S.
L. Ingalsbe, 1st U. S. S. S.
L. J. Russel, 4th Ohio.
J. H. Geriosh, 1st Maine.
A. Inglo, 184th Pennsylvania.
Sergt. J. Connor, Bat. I, 5th U. S. Art.
W. Riley, 61st N. Y.
M. Clemihern, 6th South Carolina.
D. O. Conor, 7th N. Y. Art.
N. M. Shaw, 1st District of Columbia Cav,
G. Lee, 1st Maine Art.
J. Coch, 4th N. Y.
C. Ecker, 69th Pennsylvania.
G. S. Merchant, 125th N. Y.
W. Sullivan, 69th Pennsylvania.
S. Emerson, 2d U. S. S. S.
W. L. Wallace, 1st Maine Art.
E. J. Wright, 5th Michigan.
F. Greneger, 73d N. Y.
J. Kent, 39th N. Y.
J. Beebe, 6th N. Y.
C. Eckley, 110th Pennsylvania.
R. J. Stewart, 183d Pennsylvania.
J. Lynch, 183d Pennsylvania.
J. M. Herington, 7th W. Va.
J. Gardner, 15th South Carolina.
A. Agan, 81st Pennsylvania.
J. Sammer, 8th Ohio.
P. Strickland, 7th North Carolina.
A. Compton, 184th Pennsylvania
W. C. Peer, 125th N. Y.

Reuben Hutchison, H, 140th Pennsylvania.
M. H. Dean, 2d N. Y. Art.
J. C. Dungan, 37th North Carolina.
J. McGinnis, 61st' N. Y.
J. L. McGlannel, 4th N. Y. Art.
E. B. Pearson, 4th N. Y. Art.
Sergt. P. Kall, 39th N. Y.
S. R. T., on left arm.
G. W. Grant, 1st Massachusetts Art.
G. W. Lake, E, 26th Michigan.
L. Brandt, 7th N. Y.
P. Donovan, 2d N. Y. Art.
Lieut. E. Greenfield, 1st Pennsylvania Rifles.
P. Blackall, 7th N. Y. Art.
Corp. E. Jones, 16th Mass.
D. Noland, 170th N. Y.
A. Swede, 6th New Hampshire.
L. Bragg, 1st Maine Art.
J. Wagner, 7th N. Y. Art.
J. Hefner, 53d Pennsylvania.
Wm. Henry, 53d Pennsylvania.
L. D. Perkins, 1st Maine Art.
Wm. Upwright, 36th Wisconsin.
L. A. Sturtervean, 1st Maine Art.
F. C. Balby, 7th N. Y. Art.
Mich'l McGratn, 170th N. Y.
Geo. Ruttle, 7th Ohio.
Geo. B. White, 179th N. Y.
J. R. Orne, 1st Maine Art.
Jas. Reed, 105th Pennsylvania.
H. A. Aiken, 1st Massachusetts.
Geo. Ceahon, 8th N. Y. Art.
Maj. Wm. A. Kirk, 57th N. Y.
D. J. Morehouse, 8th N. Y. Art.
M. Field, 111th N. Y.
E. Tolby, 1st Maine Art.
H. Reed, 1st Maine Art.
F. Burness, 88th N. Y.
C. Smith, 126th N. Y.
G. W. Burk, 1st Maine Art.
W. Blystone, 63d Pennsylvania.
J. S. Wallace, 2d N. Y. Art.
P. Derhan, 39th N. Y.
Sergt. A. Sprowl, 1st Maine Art.
H. Erwin, 20th Indiana.
E. Justice, 110th Pennsylvania.
Corp. P. Welch, 72d N. Y.
A. Sheppard, 1st Massachusetts.
L. Blanchard, 8th N. Y. Art.
W. S. Brown, 4th N. Y. Art.
G. H. Earlel 36th Wisconsin.

L. Lord, 1st Maine Art.
G. M. Mites, 106th Pennsylvania.
A. Sandass, 1st Maine.
S. Hufman, 7th N. Y. Art.
H. L. Brown, 1st Massachusetts Art.
F. Hathway, 2d N. Y. Art.
F. A. Dearburn, 1st Maine Art.
M. Barnes, 184th Pennsylvania.
D. Richardson, 17th Maine.
C. A. Voorhees, 2d N. Y. Art.
H. C. Croker, 111th N. Y.
H. McCaffaity, 115th Pennsylvania.
P. Matree, 8th N. Y. Art.
M. Gunner, 57th N. Y.
J. Marshel, 1st Maine.
T. Tiff, 2d N. Y. Art.
G. Lamer, 8th N. Y. Art.
O. Churches, 2d N. Y. Art.
E. Rowllins, 7th N. Y. Art.
J. Finley, 170th N. Y.
A. Harrington, 8th N. Y.
W. Sopher. 11th Massachusetts.
I. Brown, 17th Maine.
T. Keecher, 170th N. Y.
A. Thomas, 4th N. Y. Art.
W. W Johnson, 1st Maine Art.
W. L. Coston, 53d Pennsylvania.
J. Davis, 36th Wisconsin.
W. Collins, 2d N. Y. Art.
J. W. Heseldon, 5th New Hampshire.
W. Dewyen, 63d N. Y.
N. Long, 184th Pennsylvania.
J. Lee, 36th Wisconsin.
J. Silverman, 88th N. Y.
J. H. Winons, 11th New Jersey.
C. Rowley, 26th Michigan.
S. Maynard, 28th Massachusetts.
J. Vanderpool, 57th Pennsylvania.
J. M. Decker, 53d Pennsylvania.
J. Cortis, 1st Maine Art.
G. Rikard, 52d N. Y.
F. Hall, 63d N. Y.
J. Sheable, 73d N. Y.
Lieut, P. Cronin, H, 155th N. Y.
J. O. Brien, 8th New Jersey.
J. Brannen, 40th N. Y.
N. J. Kein.
G. Young, 61st N. Y.
J. Ryans, 73d N. Y.
M. Machentrutz, 5th Michigan.
L. Howard, 10th N. Y.

W. Backett, 5th New Jersey.
J. Barry, 28th Massachusetts.
M. McAuliffe, 4th N..Y. Art.
F. Faulkner, K, 10th N. Y.
M. Flamburg, 52d N. Y.
J. Allen, 116th Pennsylvania.
J. C. Phillips, 86th N. Y.
W. Hill, 2d N. Y. Art..
S. Sanders, 52d N. Y.
F. Smith, 1st Maine Art,
G. Felmly, 7th New Jersey.
J. M. Shove, 141st Pennsylvania.
W. H. Shove, 1st Maine Art.
J. Tidmarsh, Bat. A, 1st New Hampshire
J. Albus, 7th Virginia.
N. Hignet, 1st Delaware.
W. Finnegan, 17th Massachusetts.
A. Lonefield, 8th N. Y. Art
W. A. Austin, 2d N. Y. Art,
E. Newbert, 164th N. Y.
E. Green, 8th N. Y.
A. D. Hall, 1st Maine Art.
J. H. Brown, 3d Vermont Bat.
W. A. Hood.
D. McMann, 19th Maine.
D. Brown, 120th N. Y.
P. Jones, 5th U. S. Bat.
J. Lawless, 2d N. Y. Art.
J. Foley, 40th N. Y.
E. Lillienstein, 64th N. Y.
I. Adams, 1st Maine Art.
I. C. Fulton, 4th N. Y. Art.
T. Mitchel, 1st Delaware.
J. Logan, 110th Pennsylvania.
G. Corbin, 8th N. Y.
H. Sharo, 8th N. Y. Art,
H. Mertrin, 42d N. Y.
A. Hapel, 46th Virginia.
C. A. Chandler, 19th Maine.
E. Wentworth, 8th N. Y. Art,
G. Heastley, 53d Pennsylvania.
J. Miles, 184th Pennsylvania.
C. Chace, 32d Maine.
G. W. Tuestay, 1st Maine Art.
V. Messer, 2d N. Y. Art.
G. Hays, 4th Connecticut.
W. W. Osburn, 57th N. Y.
G. Rose, 8th N. Y.
J. Trees, 116th Pennsylvania,
G. T. Osburn, 1st Maine Art.
Lieut. R. Glass, 8th N. Y. Art.

J. Henry, 8th N. Y. Art.
A. Keny, 152d N. Y.
T. W. Morison, 2d N. Y. Art.
J. H. Jamison, 57th Pennsylvania.
Corp. E. Lyman, 1st U. S. S. S.
A. Miller, 1st Maine Art.
W. Prescott, 105th Pennsylvania.
J. J. Jackson, 1st Maine Art.
P. Brenner, 1st Maine Art.
J. Mushlee, 7th New Jersey.
G. Persales, 152d N. Y.
T. Savage, 1st Maine Art.
C. Winters, 20th Indiana.
L. Maguire, 20th Massachusetts.
G. Frothingham, 1st Massachusetts **Art.**
J. E. Ritchie, 1st Maine Art.
R. S. Donahue, 2d N. Y. Art.
E. D. Bree, 99th Pennsylvania.
G. Vungan, 111th N. Y.
M. Remine, 155th N. Y.
J. F. Haynes, 1st Maine Art.
A. J. Cole, 1st Maine Art.
W. McGlaughlin, 1st Massachusetts **Art,**
P. P. Black, 37th Massachusetts.
H. H. Harpster, 184th Pennsylvania.
F. Desmona, 5th Michigan,
E. Jennison, 1st Maine Art.
W. P. Hamilton, 64th N. Y.
G. Stewart, 8th N. Y. Art.
F. A. Leech, 1st Maine Art.
H. Brownan, 20th Massachusetts.
A. H. Concher, 184th Pennsylvania.
J. Hynn, 5th N. Y. Art.
H. Cesar, 7th N. Y. Art.
T. O. Brien, 69th N. Y.
S. H. Crocker, 152d N. Y.
Chas. Tompkins, 57th Pennsylvania.
H. C. Crocker, 4th N. Y. Art.
J. Vasnier, 57th N. Y.
Wm. Dugeon, 69th Pennsylvania.
P. Murphy, 19th Massachusetts.
R. H. Walker, 57th Pennsylvania.

CITY POINT LIST.

John Crowley, E, 189th N. Y.
Wallace Corham, B, 118th N. Y.
—— Shider.
Wm. B. Conaver, G, 2d Pa. Art.
Daniel Perkins, F, 8th Maine.
James Rutley, C, 142d N. Y.
Clinton Stratton, I, 118th N. Y.
Albert Atwood, K, 4th N. H.
James Dalley, E, 169th N. Y.
John C. E. Benudetz.
J. D. Otis, D, 10th N. Y. Art.
Edward Carroll, H, 10th N. Y. Art.
Nelson Clennents, H 169th N. Y.
D. C. Clark, K, 188th Pennsylvania.
Lewis Hiny, J, 96th N. Y.
M. Kelly, I, 188th Pennsylvania.
J. H. Cole, I, 115th N. Y.
Louis Byron, B, 169th N. Y.
Geo. Asobson, H, 22d Conn. C. T.
Samuel Peabody, F, 9th Maine.
Henry F. Williams, D, 1st Conn. Art.
Jesse Harvey, G, 76th Pennsylvania.
Geo. W. Ryeson, F, 9th Maine.
Geo. Jenkins, F, 25th Mass.
J. Lamklerer, D, 5th U. S. C. T.
James Thomas, E, 22d U. S. C. T.
Daniel Jackson, K, —— U. S. C. T
Cyrus Westcott, F, 118th N. Y.
Samuel Hair, I, 98th N. Y.
Aaron Wade, 10th N. Y.
Daniel Goward.
Elias B. Smith, I, 10th N. Y. Art.
Patrick Farrell, G, 25th Mass.
Wm. M. Pinkham, D, 8th Maine.
Henry Crane, 16th U. S. C. T.
James Winchester, G, 4th U. S.
Chas. Shushell, H, 98th N. Y.
Geo. Sprouts, F, 188th Pennsylvania.

Corp. David Webber, G, 12th N. Y.
Moses Cummings, D, 98th N. Y.
John H. Bird, H, 3d N. Y. Art.
J. H. Robinson, C, —— N. J.
Samuel Rogers, F, 38th U. S.
Davy Wilson, 4th U. S. C. T.
Wm. Harris, A, 10th N. Y.
John Tart, B, 118th N. Y.
Henry Neigonfind, F, 19th Wis.
John Dougherty, E, 8th Conn.
Henry N, Loomis, H, 21st Conn.
Henry D. Armalar, D, 27th Mass.
Chas. Hendig, C, 37th U. S.
Jacob Winfield F, ——
Wm. Jones, H, 22d U. S. C. T.
Thos. Malcom, E, 21st Mass.
S. W. Abbott, G, 23d Mass.
Wm. D. Little, drummer, 12th N. H.
O. Foster, E, 58th Pennsylvania.
Geo. Lutton, K, 112th N. Y.
J. Wilson, G, 4th U. S. C. T.
C. B. King, B, 58th Pennsylvania.
R. Whitehall, K, 22d U. S. C. T.
P. Bush, K, 22d U. S. C. T.
Chas. Golding, 6th U. S. C. T.
S. Stewart, G, 4th U· S. C. T.
—— Taylor D, 22d U. S. C. T.
P. F. Fox, C, 10th N. H.
Lewis Osborne, G, 139th N. Y.
David Breah, K, 118th N. Y.
Geo. Hanno, C, 9th N. J.
Geo. W. Smith, F, 89th N. Y.
Daniel Jeffers, B, 8th Conn.
Elbridge A. Mirim, "?" E, 23d Mass.
Frank Petollo, E, 4th Mass. Cav.
Geo. Handslan, H, 139th Pennsylvania.
Jas. A. Grover, I, 81st N. Y.
Samuel Street, A, 19th ——
Jacob Shoff, C, 188th Pennsylvania.
Wm. Roberts, A, 22d U. S. C. T.
Wm. E. Glover, 115th or 25th N. Y.
Ferdinand Shilling, D, 9th N. J.
Thos. Patten, B, 188th Pennsylvania.
Wm. Reihsnider, B, 55th Pennsylvania.
Geo. Denton, G, 22d U. S. C. T.
John Ross, I, 22d U. S. C. T.
W. H. Atwood, K, 96th N. Y.
Jas. Hagon, G, 76th Pennsylvania.
Wm. Debout, C, 142d Ohio.
J. B. Stoplin, B, 10th N. Y.
W. G. Butler, G, 19th Wis.

Jas. Myers, K, 29th Conn.
Geo. W. Smith, C, 29th Conn.
John Kedont, A, 7th U. S. C. T.
Harison Mines, 22d U. S. C. T.
Murray Higgins, 7th U. S. C. T.
Chas. Fields, C, 5th U. S. C. T.
Corp. L. Beal, D, 9th Mass.
Henry Barker, H, 4th U. S. C. T.
Abram Sulud or Sneud, D, 22d U. S. C. T.
Chas Sportes, A, ——
Samuel L. Sherman, B, 21st Mass.
Wm. Hutchinson, B, 9th Maine.
Thos. Fremble, K, 96th N. Y.
G. S. Siebrecht, A, 2d Pa. H. A.
Lawrence Shields, B, 76th Pennsylvania.
Edward Delmore, D, 6th U. S. C. T.
Fred Humphrey, K, 1st U. S. C. Cav.
S. C. Harding, H, 10th N. Y.
Geo. Rickett, E, 10th N. Y.
L. Bundy, D, 1st N, Y. M. R.
Freeman Bain, G, 142d N. Y.
E. W. Zaner, B, 55th Ponnsylvania.
Nathan H. Pierson, H, 81st N. Y.
Henry Beder, K, 76th Pennsylvania.
W. H. Silvers, A, 9th N. J.
Smith L. Peacock, K, 112th N. Y.
J. D. Fretby, H, 76th Pennsylvania.
Sergt. J. W. Carson, D, 2d N. Y.
S. G. Smith, E, 148th N. Y.
Levi C. Eames, D, 25th Mass.
Albert Heimstead, E, 3d N. Y, Art.
Thos. J. Armstrong, H, 16th N. Y. H. A.
Edmond Lyon, F, 11th Conn.
John I. Messer, E, 10th N. H.

CITY POINT. CAVALRY CORPS CEMETERY.

Names of persons buried in Cavalry Corps Cemetery at City Point, Va.

A. Y. Graham, M, 17th Pa. Cav.
Thos. Foley, B, 6th Ohio Cav.
J. D. Foders, A, 18th Pa. Cav.
D. Stevenson, C, 1st N. H. Cav.
C. P. Howard, E, 10th N. Y. Cav.
J. Ballinger, C, 13th S. C. Infantry.
B. Quigley, A, 1st Mass. Cav.
J. W. Milton, A, 11th Pa. Cav.
M. Telyea, D, 10th N. Y. Cav.
C. O. Thompson, D, 6th Ohio Cav.
Lieut. W. H. Bradman, M, 1st Maine Cav.
H. S. Janvrin, I, 1st Mass. Cav.
D. McCarty, K, 1st N. J. Cav.
J. H. Miller, B, 11th Pa. Cav.
W. Hubbard, K, 1st N. J. Cav.
H. Haight, B, 8th Pa. Cav.
J. Conaman, M, 2d Pa. Cav.
J. Jacobs, C, 20th S. C. Infantry.
W. S. Farris, F, 1st Maine Cav.
Geo. Gould, D, 16th Pa. Cav.
W. Sourwine, E, 10th N. Y. Cav.
S. R. Booland, L, 16th Pa. Cav.
Richard Ansel, B, 5th U. S. Cav.
John Metcalf, F, 5th U. S. Cav.
R. Clements, L, 24th N. Y. Cav.
F. Kramer, C, 3d U. S. Cav.
J. H. Ferguson, C, 4th S. C. Cav.
D. R. Elsington, E, 1st N. C. Infantry.
Jas. Craft, D, 12th S. C. Infantry.
J. Stone, E, 1st S, C, Infantry.
Wm. Onweller, B, 6th Mich. Cav.
A. Tuick, A, 16th Pa. Cav.
H. S. Sams, F, 1st N. J. Cav.
J. W. White, L, 2d U. S. Cav.
M. Sargent, I, 1st Vt. Cav.
G. Taylor, I, 1st Mass. Cav.
W. Kern, M, 1st N. J. Cav.
Jas. Long, C, 5th Mich. Cav.

J. McCallister, B, 1st Maine Cav.
G. M. Harris, M, 1st N, H. Cav.
E. D. Kendig, E, 21st Pa. Cav.
H. Groff, G, 21st Pa. Cav.
G. C. Besse, K, 1st Maine Cav.
G. Philipson, G, 1st N. J. Cav.
J. Ratwell, E, 16th Pa. Cav.
J. Brownsaugh.
W. D. Taylor, C, 4th Pa. Cav.
C. S. King, L, 4th Pa. Cav.
W. H. Bollinger, I, 21st Pa. Cav.
Wm. Collins, K, 1st Mass. Cav.
J. DeWolffe, K, 1st Conn. Cav.
J. Thomas, M, 6th Ohio Cav.
L. Green, M, 6th Mich. Cav.
Henry A. Reed, E, 7th Mich. Cav.
J. Bunting, I, 4th Mass. Cav.
B. F. Critenden, M, 10th N. Y. Cav.
S. L. Shater, I. 8th N. Y. Cav.
J. Glancy, I, 2d Pa. Cav.
F. G. Armstrong, G, 6th Mich. Cav.
M. Kiger, E, 1st N. J. Cav.
H. Sommermuir, I, 15th N. Y. Cav.
E. O. Rice, B, 10th N. Y. Cav.
L. J. Peck, C, 6th Mich. Cav.
E. F. Sisco, I, 4th Pa. Cav.
F. A. G. Hall, C, 1st R. I. Cav.
Wm. Brame,—1st Pa. Cav.
S. J. Jenkins, B, 2d Pa. Cav.
G. Hart, A, 1st Conn. Cav.
J. Coup, K, 1st Pa. Cav.
J. T. Cook, K, 2d N. Y. Cav.
G. Campbell, E, 6th Ohio Cav.
T. D. Hance, K, 3d N. Y. Cav.
J. Auger, (Citizen.)
J. Seebach, B, 13th Pa. Cav.
S. McNaspy, D, 13th Pa. Cav.
D. M. Tibbets, D, 1st D. C. Cav.
A. L. West, C, 1st N. J. Cav.
M. T. Naugle, F, 5th Pa. Cav.
J. E. Rood, A, 1st N. Y. Dragoon.
David Way, K, 6th Mich. Cav.
M. D. Bossard, L, 2d Pa. Cav.
T. Tulley, A, 11th Pa. Cav.
C. H. Robinson, F, 1st D. C. Cav.
J. Smith, I, 4th Pa. Cav.
H. H. Ware, E, 2d Pa. Cav.
I. B. Conant, C, 1st Maine Cav.
Lieut. E. Greenfield,—1st Pa Rifles.
Maj. G. M. Crawford.
P. Kremer, L, 16th Pa. Cav.

F. Brice, K, 16th Pa. Cav.
W. O. Haruret, G, 1st Va. Infantry.
P. S. Sides, K, 35th N. C. Infantry.
E. Comstock, E, 1st U. S. Cav.
Lieut. O. S. Mathews, A, 11th Pa. Cav.
A Nicholy, A, 21st Pa. Cav.
D. Myers, A, 21st Pa. Cav.
J. Donlon, A, 2d N. Y. Cav.
T. Grucyr, E, 10th N. Y. Cav.
P. Quin,—10th N. Y. Cav.
Benj, Denson, G, 1st Del. Cav.
T. Welsh, F, 2d Pa. Cav.
F. LaDuke, I, 24th N. Y. Cav.
C. O. Reed, B, 4th Pa. Cav.
Augustus Dearbeau, D, 24th N. Y. Cav.
C. E. Dearborn, K, 1st Maine Cav.
P. Downs, F, 10th N. Y. Cav.
J. Bevins, M, 21st Pa. Cav.
J. Cochran, E, 2d Va. Cav.
W. Ward, M, 21st Pa. Cav.
Lieut. J. A. Welton, K, 4th Pa. Cav.
J. Madill, L, 2nd N. Y. M. R.
B. Bumcrantz, M, 10th N. Y. Cav
J. Duncan, H, 4th Pa. Cav.
W. Wilson, B, 8th Pa. Cav,
C. Millinger, A, 2d Ohio Cav.
B. Munson, B, 13th Ohio Cav.
G. Berwick, B, 8th Pa. Cav.
J. Pike, L, 4th Pa. Cav,
A. S. Nichols,
Thos. O. Brien, A, 1st N. J. Cav.
Henry Bartsuff, M, 16th Pa. Cav.
J. B. Fox, G, 4th Pa. Cav.
J. R. Getschell, D, 1st D. C. Cav.
G. Tracy, 2d U. S. Battery.
S. Parker, E, 2d Pa. Cav.
E. S. Girt, E, 4th Pa. Cav.
W. Cocks,—6th Ohio, Cav.
J. Shan, G, 21st Pa. Cav.
L. H. McQuistion, C, 4th Pa. Cav.
J. Zimmerman, A, 13th Pa. Cav.
A. Gloze, A, 13th Pa. Cav.
L. Emmons, C, 6th Ohio Cav.
B. Warren, E, 1st Maine Cav.
G. Stevenson, K, 8th Pa. Cav.
J. H. Rhodes, A, 16th Pa. Cav.
W. C. Reedy, B, 14th Pa. Cav.
J. Hill, H, 16th Pa. Cav.
R. C. Lewis, D, 1st Pa. Cav.
J. Stearns, C, 8th N. Y. Cav.
S. W. Lane. L. 10th N. Y. Cav.

W. W. Pope, K, 4th Pa. Cav.
W. Leach, K, 10th N. Y. Cav.
J. A. Little, C, 28th N. C. Infantry
C. Climan, B, 1st N. J. Cav.
P. Decker, K, 1st N. J. Cav.
C. Carny, K, 6th Ohio Cav.
P. H. McArdle, H, 4th Pa. Cav.
R. Brady, I, 2d Pa. Cav.
J. Dunninge, F, 6th Ohio Cav.
L. Randall, A,—N. Y. M. R.
H. Harlan, K, 4th Pa. Cav.
Sergt. W. F. Lent, E, 1st Pa. Cav.
J. B. Johnson, I, 1st Maine Cav.
C. P. Hubbard, E, 1st Maine Cav.
F. Brown, D, 1st Mass. Cav.
R. Kendrick, K, 1st Maine Cav.
W. M. Platt, C, 5th S. C.
P. Seigel, H, 2d Pa. Cav.
G. W. Reed, 1st S. C. Rifles.
J. F. Cook, 15th N. Y.
D. McCarty, K. 5th U. S. Cav.
G. W. Stallman, A, 4th Pa. Cav.

CITY POINT. ON LINE OF R. R.

The tollowing named are buried at City Point, Va.—along the line of the Rail road between the "Point," and the defenses.

C. P. Beekman, D, 189th N. Y.
L. Berbere.
S. H. Linpuk.
Benj. Dingee, C, 20th N. Y.
I. Leve, I, 8th U. S. C. T.
Wm. Purnell, K. 10th U. S. C. T.
Thos. Jackson,—28th U. S. C. T.
Francis Hartman.
Pleasant Crooke, (Citizen.)
Ferdinand Reul, I. 47th Pennsylvania.
Thos. Chester, (Colored man.)
H. Murphy, H, 57th N. Y.
Edward Barnes.
John Gilroy.
Hubert Laettchel.
J. W. Jones, F, 15th N. Y. Eng.
Demsey Sumner, (Colored Teamster.)
John Knowles, C, 20th Maine.
Lewis Cappell, F, 7th New Hampshire.
Thos. Nuby, North Carolina.
John Welsh, G, 8th Maryland,
Geo. W. Leop, 65th New York,
Chas. Burns, Confederate Navy.
Lieut. Alexander, D, 211th Pennsylvania.
W. R. Hawkins, 1st Div. 9th A. C.
Fred. Meure,—13th Pennsylvania.
Henry Contras, E, 10th U. S. C. T.
Sergt. Cornelius Fagan, H, 209th Pennsylvania.
Wm. Ruse, (Colored man.)
L. W. Shattuck, B, 11th Vermont.
I. More, G, 109th U. S. C. T.
Mosier Mascar.
David Cochre.
James Anderson.
Albert Fry, 9th N. Y. Cav.
Geo. Hubbard, F, 23th U. S. C. T.
Eli S. Gillett,—186th N. Y.
Lieut. G. O. French, 1st Vermont Art.

7

Andrus Weaver, H, 54th Pennsylvania.
John Mead, F, 82d N. Y.
Alex. Davis, E, 10th U. S. C. T.
Joseph Keeler, F, 10th U. S. C. T.
Winslow Bryant, A 1st Maine S. S.
Chas. F. Green.
DeWitt C. Pelton, Corp. 2d N. Y. M. R.
Martin Soble, K, 1st Maryland.
Wm. Carney, E, 10th U. S. C. T.
John Steinbach, (Citizen.)
Wm. H. Fardell,—7th N. Y.
James Clayton, (Colored man.)
Geo. Taylor, (Colored man.)
Wm. C. Baber,—56th North Carolina.
E. J. Effreds,—1st Maine H. A.
Sergt. E. Curtis.
W. Austin,—N. Y. Engineers.
J. W. Collins, A, 155th N. Y.
Hiram Archer, G, 41st New Jersey.
Albert Henry,—U. S. C. T.
Condy Montgomery, H, 122d U. S. C. T
Wm. Klander, B, 15th N. Y. Eng.
Isaac Edmond.
John Leippe.
John J. Stein, B, 15th N. Y. Eng.
Chas. Shepard, (supposed deserter.)
John F. Miller, (unassigned.)
Wm. Heise, (unassigned.)
Chas. Zeek, G, 68th Pennsylvania.
Daniel Sickler, B, 20th N. Y.
Andrew Sweeney, F, 20th N. Y.
Joseph Smith, I, 10th U. S.
Oliver Thomas, 2d New Hampshire.
Edwin Coonts, H, 15th Virginia.
James H. Wade, (citizen.)
Wm. Willis, 8th N. Y.
George L. Setch, I, 11th Pa. Cav
James Mummert, (unassigned.)
Thos. Floyd, H, 10th U. S. C. T.
Race Rosby, 1st U. S. C. T.
Art. Bakeman, 185th N. Y.
H. G. Myers, D, 107th Pennsylvania
Solomon Carley, 4th N. Y. H. A.
John Williams, G, 8th U. S. H. A.
S. Beal, (unassigned.)
Chas. Stevens, 8th U. S. C. Art.
Henry Lee, (Colored man.)
Monzo Slayter, C, 188th N. Y.
Jos. Van Weet, D, 20th N. Y. S. M.
Isaac Tremper, I, 20th N. Y. S. M.
Mark Deans, D, 3d Pennsylvania Cav.

Sylvester Linn, A, 3d Pennsylvania Cav
Jos. B. Trym, C, 61st Massachusetts.
W. B. Southwick, F, 21st N. Y. Cav.
Ebia Shackles, C, 5th Massachusetts Cav.
J. C. Skinner, L, 22d N. Y. Cav.
P. Hunter, (colored laborer.)
Augustus Groser, C, 2d N. Y.
A. Dawson, F, 6th U. S. C. T.
J. P. Hill, F, 6th Michigan.
James Dorce, 6th U. S. C. T.
George G. Elliott, E,——
James Gray, E, 4th U. S. C. T.
James Green.
Sam Grant, A, 14th N. Y. H. A.
Thos. Price, 22d U. S. C. T.
Chas. D. Cadwell, C, 16th Massachusetts.
Henry H. Widfodt, A, 13th N. Y. Art.
Augustus Graset, 26th N. Y.
P. McConskin, E, 170th N. Y.
Chas. E. Duff, F, 1st U. S. C. T.
A. E. Blanchard, E, 1st D. C. Cav.
C. B. Davenport, M, 3d N. Y. Cav.
D. Goodwin, A, 8th Maine.
Edward Delensy, I, 118th N. Y.
John Weeks, B, 1st Minn.
Jos. Pien, D, 19th Wis.
David Smith, II, 5th U. S. C. T
Abram Mason, H, 118th N. Y.
John Smith, A, 139th N. Y.
Jas. Dorlander, D, 76th P. V.
Geo. Derchner, H, 97th P. V.
Robt. McClintock, E, 6th U. S. C. T.
Corp. Geo. Garvine, D, 37th N. J.
Jas. Roach, K, 16th N. Y. H. A.
Sergt. Saml. H. Brink, G, 39th Ill.
Wm. Williams, E, 13th Ind.
Archibald Collins, I, 115th N. Y.
Ruel W. Rowe, G, 9th Maine.
Reuben Small, A, 11th Maine.
John Redmond, A, 16th N. Y. Art
Patrick Logan, G, 16th N. Y. Art.
Jas. Mulholand, K, 16th N. Y. Art
Jas. Perkins, F, 7th N. H.
Nehemiah Peulis, —— 5th N. J. B
Geo. L. McCorison, —— 1st D. Cav.
Geo. Brown, —— 9th U. S. C. T.
John Hamilton, —— 5th N. J B
Erza Ayers, —— 1st U. S. Art
Edward Harris, G, 8th U. S. C. T.
S. R. Godfren, A, 76 P. V.
Hosey Robinson, F, 37th N. J.
Thos. Lyick, F, 16th N. Y.
John Phaler, F, 169th N. Y.

Wm. Wilson, D, 8th U. S. C. T.
A. Richardson, E, 22d U. S. C. T.
Geo. S. Porter, D, 29th Conn.
Jas. Lang, Colored.
Gilbert Voorheeves, A, 16th N. Y.
Chas. Shaffer, —— 95th P. V.
Wm. Cosgrove, C, 3d N. H.
Chas. H. Evans, K, 29th Conn.
Geo. Benson, B, 7th N. H.
Cyrus G. Hardy, G, 17th Maine.
Jeremiah McGuire, G, 17th Maine.

On the banks of the Appomattox, a little below **Broadway Land-ing.**

Jas. McCormick, K, 1st Conn. Art.
Jas. Smith, E, 1st Conn. Art.
Wm. Rolleston, I, 1st Conn. Art.
John Homer, G, 1st Conn. Art.
Jacob Torfe, C, 1st Conn. Art.
Richard B. Tucker, I, 1st Conn. **Art.**
Michael Houk, G, 1st Conn. Art.
Chas. Pollard, G, 1st Conn. Art.
Jas. McCarty, M, 1st Conn. Art.
Wm. Althoff, B, 1st Conn. Art.
Ransom N. Reynolds, K, 1st Conn. **Art.**
Richard S. Baxter, I, 1st Conn. Art.
Truman Foote, L, 1st Conn. Art
Jas. Kelley, I, 1st Conn. Art.
Frank Smith. K, 1st Conn. Art.
Edwin A. Johnson, A, 1st Conn. **Art.**
Henry W. Cady, C, 1st Conn. Art.
John F. Bailey, D, 1st Conn. Art.
Augstus Talmage, E, 1st Conn. Art.
Byron Tucker, B, 1st Conn. Art.
Frank Allenback, E, 1st Conn. Art.
Sidney Townsend, D, 1st Conn. Art.
Julian Griffin, A, 1st Conn. Art.
Geo. Chapman, A, 1st Conn. Art.
Edwin B. Chipman, D, 1st Conn. **Art.**
Nathan T. Lyon, I, 1st Conn. Art.
John Lambrecht, F, 1st Conn. Art.
Jos. Fitzsimmons, I, 1st Conn. Art.
Herman Foote, L, 1st Conn. Art.
Wm. H. Quindar, I, 1st Conn. Art.
John W. Caton, C, 1st Conn. Art.
Levi Simes, I, 1st Conn. Art.
Cornelius Malloy, E, 1st Conn. Art.
Francis Davison, G, 1st Conn. Art.
Samuel R. Rose, F, 1st Conn. Art.
Horace R. Hedloy, I, 1st Conn. Art.
Preston Griswald, I, 1st Conn. Art.
Jas. H. Huntly, I, 1st Conn. Art.
Owen W. Millingan, E, 3d Pa. Art.

THE RUFFIN PLANTATION.

Graves found on the Ruffin Plantation, one mile north of Meade Station, and east of the Rail-Road.

John Sheridan, B, 4th N. Y. Art.
R. Hane, F, 155th N. Y.
W. Nash, E, 8th N. Y.
Fred. Pennel, I, 19th Maine.
Robt. Medowes, E, 170th N. Y.
I. Allen, D, 155th N. Y.
Sergt. T. Wilson, A, 155th N. Y.
Corp. E. Jones, A, 170th N. Y.
Sergt. Geo. Chambers, C, 72d Pennsylvania.
A. Burns, I, 164th N. Y. Art.
Corp. P. Musgrave, I, 1st Mass. Art.
Corp. I. Murphy, C, 155th N. Y.
Sergt I. Welch, E, 170th N. Y.
Ruben Carlon, E, 19th Maine.
John Wiley, A, 155th N. Y.
John Matthews, E, 170th N. Y.
Harvey Dunham, L, 8th N. Y. Art.
Geo. Johnes, G, 8th N. Y. Art.
John Bailey, F, 108th N. Y.
Asa Smith, H, 4th N. Y. Art.
Isaac Peck, A, 8th N. Y. Art.
Edward Lyke, H, 4th N. Y. Art.
Corp. W. Kelley, A, 15th Mass.
John Aker, B, 4th N. Y. Art.
Adolph Wolfran, B, 20th Mass.
Darvan Cole, C, 36th Wisconsin.
Sergt. S. Edwards, E, 8th Ohio.
James Steward, D, 155th N. Y.
Elias Condo, F, 184th Pennsylvania.
Joseph Liberty, E, 1st Mass.
H. Allen, K, 8th N. Y. Art.
Wm. Duffey, D, 155th N. Y.
Sergt. C. Williams, H, 69th Pennsylvania.
Thos. Atkins, E, 155th N. Y.
H. McFarlan, D. 69th N. Y.
Corp. I. Staysa, B, 184th Pennsylvania.
Pat. Sheridan, A, 69th N. Y.
Corp. R. McClore, C, 164th N. Y.
Lein O'Connell, K, 155th N. Y.

Lieut. Samuel Gilbreth, 1st Co., S. S. 20th Mass.
Lieut. Elias F, Gallaway, K, 36th Wis.
Wm. Bentley, F, 4th N. Y. Art.
Patrick McKeen, H, 170th N. Y.
Corp. Ern. Myers, D, 7th Virginia.
Mat. Bittles, K, 36th Wisconsin.
John Vanoute, F, 4th N. Y.

Enclosed ground near 2d Division Hospital, 9 A. C., at Meade
Station.

Seth Knowles, A, 2d Michigan.
Wm. Mahar, K, 1st Conn. Art.
I. Long, C, 50th Pennsylvania.
I. Alwine, E, 50th Pennsylvania.
Thos. B. Western, D, 2d Michigan.
Wm. Cartwright, F, 2d Michigan.
Jeremiah Everhart, 19th N. Y. Bat.
Francis Hazel, Bat. G, 1st N. Y. Art.
Lieut. M. V. Stanton, 126th N. Y.
Wm. H. Baird, 126th N. Y.
Corp. Albert Green, D, 125th N. Y.
B. Finnegan, F, 125th N. Y.
C. Walters, K, 28th Mass.
A. Custard, D, 145th Pennsylvania.
G. Bowen, H, 7th N. Y.
I. McMillan, H, 5th N. Y.
I. Cusick, 28th Massachusetts.
Gillingham, D, 2d Delaware.
L. Ducat, F, 63d N. Y.
I. Coffin, H, 111th N. Y.
D. Lapham.
Sergt. W. Woods, G, 5th New Hampshire.
Corp. Chas. Eaton, H, 5th New Hampshire.
A. McCarthy, G, 111th N. Y.
I. Metcalf, 11th N. Y., Bat. I.
G. Williams, 7th N. Y. Art.
H. C. Adams, K, 21st Michigan.
R. B. Nephem, D, 53d Pennsylvania.
Lieut. S. Peters, G, 81st Pennsylvania.
F. Wadleigh, K, 5th New Hampshire.
I. Shults, H, 116th Pennsylvania.
R. Entwistle, D, 2d N. Y. Art.
F. Carey, F, 7th N. Y. Art.
R. Dever, B, 52d N. Y.
I. F. Baring, H, 148th Pennsylvania.
I. Huttenhoun, E, 140th Pennsylvania.
Wm. Smith, E, 53d Pennsylvania.
Sergt. Ebenezer Barrett, G, 4th N. Y. Art.
Robt. McCaully, G, 28th Mass.
Joseph Dubois, G, 39th N. Y.
Wm. Lane, D, 69th N. Y.

Emilels, A, 61st N. Y.
Ernest Hoofman, C, 57th N. Y.
M. Churdel, C, 64th N. Y.
Vergneray, B, 7th N. Y. Art.
Chas. Jones, H, 4th N. Y. Art.
Melchar Garting, E, 66th N. Y.
John Casey, Bat. K, 4th N. Y. Art.
Arthur Donelly, B, 170th N. Y.
John McManus, A, 10th N. Y.
John Waltz, I, 8th N. Y. Art.
John S. Wilson, H, 19th Maine.
I. W. Swift, A, 20th Mass.
Patrick Curtin, E, 152d N. Y.

Cemetery 3d Division, 9th A. C. Hospital, Meade Station.

Chas. W. Partlen, K, 1st Conn. Art.
Wm. Kaske, K, 1st Conn. Art.
Patrick Duff, K, 1st Conn. Art.
Enoch Sykes, F, 209th Pennsylvania.
Amandes Moyer, H, 209th Pennsylvania.
Wm. P. H. Clark, H, 209th Pennsylvania
Wm. Stonebraker, C, 209th Pennsylvania.
Jacob Hummer, B, 209th Pennsylvania.
Sergt. C. E. Hemphill, F, 211th Pennsylvania.
Thos. H. Kitchen, C, 211th Pennsylvania.
Orin E. Campbell, A, 207th Pennsylvania.
John Stryker, I, 207th Pennsylvania.
John Stedman, C, 207th Pennsylvania.
Wm. H. Stull, I, 207th Pennsylvania.
J. I. Young, A, 207th Pennsylvania.
Mikel Juggel, I, 207th Pennsylvania.
Jas. P. Stevenson, D, 211th Pennsylvania.
Henry M. Dowell, C, 211th Pennsylvania.
Wm. Nulf, C, 211th Pennsylvania.
Geo. T. Rarick, F, 205th Pennsylvania.
Jas. B. Logue, F, 211th Pennsylvania.
Sergt. Harvey D. Hickey, C, 211th Pennsylvania.
Joseph Casmer, K, 205th Pennsylvania.
Sergt. Jas. W. Barich, K, 205th Pennsylvania.
Westmarland, D, ——
Simon P. Foot, K, 208th Pennsylvania.
Geo. Harning, E, 207th Pennsylvania.
John Shupe, K, 211th Pennsylvania.
Jabez N. Swift, A, 186th N. Y.
John Myers, D, 205th Pennsylvania.
Solomon Leahman, E, 207th Pennsylvania.
Wm. Decker, E, 207th Pennsylvania.
Frank L. Fisk, H, 186th N. Y.
Jas. Francis, B, 186th N. Y.
P. W. Cady, G, 207th Pennsylvania.
Wm. Bell, F, 205th Pennsylvania.
Sergt. Wm. Troxel, F, 205th Pennsylvania.

John Hite, I, 205th Pennsylvania.
Henry Y. Miller, B, 208th Pennsylvania.
Saml. Laughbaugh, E, 209th Pennsylvania
John Wallace, E, 200th Pennsylvania.
W. G. Barton, F, 200th Pennsylvania.
Eli Duer, A, 114th Pennsylvania.
Jas. Decker, I, 211th Pennsylvania.
Almon Crittenden, B, 186th N. Y.
A. P. Bancraft, D, 207th Pennsylvania.
Bartell Hammond, D, 207th Pennsylvania.
Lieut. Cane, 207th Pennsylvania.
Geo. L. Putman.
Joseph Elden, D, 209th Pennsylvania.
L. F. Brown, G, 211th Pennsylvania.
T. Morris, 207th Pennsylvania.
Lieut. Sharks, 106th.

2d Division Ground, adjoining 3d Div., 9th A. C., Meade Station.

C. L. Haskell, B, 26th Mass.
Chas. B. Lebold, F, 45th Pennsylvania.
Chas. Hozon, 179th N. Y.
Henry Works, E, 31st Maine.
R. King, H, 48th Pennsylvania.
Wm. Donnelly, H, 48th Pennsylvania.
Jas. Evans, I, 179th N. Y.
Geo. T. Pomeroy, 186th N. Y.
Corp. Bery A. Stanchfield, K, 31st Maine
H. A. Webster, Bat. C, 1st N. Y. A.
Norman A. Pease, K, 186th N. Y.
Crutipher Fry.
Geo. C. Deane, E, 186th N. Y.
Chas. B. Lincoln, E, 31st Maine.
I. E. Kitton, I, 31st Maine.
I. P. Blanchard, G, 207th Pennsylvania.
Wm. W. Taylor, I, 211th Pennsylvania.
Sergt. Eugene Reid, A, 207th Pennsylvania.
Lewis Snook, F, 205th Pennsylvania.
John Hunter, E, 31st Michigan.
Jos. Reifer, K, ———
Sergt. Johnson, C, 186th N. Y.
Philip Riner, F, 45th Pennsylvania.
Jefferson Harland, D, 186th N. Y.
John W. Dustine, 211th Pennsylvania.
Peter Osborn, K, 208th Pennsylvania.
Jacob Richwen, I, 45th Pennsylvania.
Dustin Lamb, K, 186th N. Y.
Frederick Stanley, D, 186th N. Y.
Thos. Martin, G, 56th Mass.
Samuel Smith, K, 186th N. Y.
Wm. H. Tibbetts, L, 31st Maine.
Chas. R. Cook, K, 179th N. Y.

Victor Emanuel, A, 6th N. H.
Sergt. John G. Brown, D, 6th N. H.
Ashael Tobias, C, 179th N. Y.
Henry L. Nutter, L, 31st Maine.
Stephen B. Capron, G, 17th Vermont.
Jas. Norton, D, 6th N. H.
Henry Hanson, G, 179th N. Y.
Corp. Wm. Myer, M, 31st Maine.
Oscar Dunham, I, 186th N. Y.
Elisha A. Brown, B, 186th N. Y.
Geo. Miller, G. 11th N. H.
John Carley, F, 179th N. Y.
Thos. Doway, C, 56th Mass.
John H. McMannis, C, 179th N. Y.
Capt. W. F. Williams, I, 2d N. Y. M. R.
John Hancock, E, 179th N. Y.
Edwin H. Fowler, A, 179th N. Y.
John Savley, H, 2d N. Y. M. R.
D. L. Longhouse, M,—N. Y. M. R.
John Brow, C, 179th N. Y.
Thos. Ghe, B, 2d Maryland.
Sergt. I. S. Watson, D, 2d Maryland.
Corp. John Thomas, D, 2d Maryland.
Wm. Dohart, C, 179th N. Y.
A. Russ, A, 31st Maine.
Wm. Daker, F, 11th N. H.
John Darha, C, 9th N. H.
Aaron Tracy, K, 31st Maine.
Geo. Benton, G,—N. Y. M. R.
John Manning, K,—N. Y. M. R.
G. W. Eldred, F, 17th Vermont.
T. L. Thomas, E, 179th N. Y.
T. A. Barker, C,—N. Y. M. R.
John C. Luff, K, 32d Maine.
A. C. Gill, H, 32d Maine.
Jas. O. Clemont, D, 6th N. H.
C. S. Hubbard, K, 32d Maine.
Calvis S. Perkins, 32d Maine.
Lieut. I. L. Atwood, E, 2d N. Y. M. R.
Marons B. Smith, F, 17th Vermont.
Chas. Archer, G, 17th Vermont.
A. D. Banker, D, 31st Maine.
C. B. Frost, G, 32d Maine.
Robt. M. Sellen, E, 2d N. Y. M. R.
Henry Carman, H, 2d N. H.
Sergt. E. S. Parsons, D, 9th N. H.
L. S. Sherwood, 19th N. Y. Bat.
H. N. Chafman, A, 9th N. H.
Alva Allen, —— 6th N. H.
Thos. Johnson, A, 9th N. H.
Omri K. Eastman, B, 11th N. H.

Ezra Cozzen, H, 32d Maine.
E. J. Sewell, A. 31st Maine.
Franklin Eggart, L,—N. Y. M. R.
H. A. Nelson, F, 11th N. H.
Thos. McGuire, H, 2d Md.
E. D. Foster, E, 11th Maine.
Larhett Wescott, H, 17th Vermont.
Isaac Raymond, C, 31st Maine.
I. M. Mansfield, K, 6th N. H.
Michael Gillan, F, 32d Maine.
Henry C. Clark, F, 31st Maine.
W. P. Wallace, K, 2d Pennsylvania V. R.
I. B. Johnson, M, 2d N. Y. M. R
Daniel Prescott, G, 31st Maine.
T. C. Tupper, E, 31st Maine.
John F. Bliss, F, 17th Vermont.
R. S. Muddy, F, 2d N. Y. M. R.
Albion O. Page.
S. A. Grommett, E, 31st Maine.
Wm. F. Bean, L, 31st Maine.
Corp. Oscar P. Fisk, D, 179th N. Y.
Wm. C. Braden, F, 32d Maine.
I. W. Brown, F, 32d Maine.
Wm. Woodrough, F, 56th Mass.
Henry L. Thomas, A, 186th N. Y.
Sergt. Parris Carnhe, F, 2d N. Y. M. R.
Fred. Tiflil, L, 2d N. Y. M. R.
E. Erion, I, 2d N. Y. M. R.
W. H. Foster, H, 2d N. Y. M. R.
Peter Clark, H, 2d N. Y. M. R.
Wm. Lindsly, I, 2d N. Y. M. R.
Samuel I. Knox, D, 2d N. Y. M. R.
Egbert W. Robbins, B, 2d N. Y. M. R.
Wm. Rogers, H, 31st Maine.
F. F. Cole, A, 31st Maine.
A. Hutchinson, C, 11th N. H.
W. Follansbe, C, 11th N. H.
Joseph Pero, F, 11th N. H.
G. C. Swift, G, 11th N. H.
Hiram Passage, C, 2d N. Y. M. R.
Perry G. Williams, L, 2d N. Y. M. R.
Daniel Morrison, G, 11th N. H.
F. C. Newman, G, 2d N. Y. M. R.
H. S. Applin, E, 6th N. H.
John H. King, I, 2nd Md.
Sergt. Elzah S. Rawson, G, 6th N. H.
Peter Hellishhar, K, 6th N. H.
R. E. Dwinnell, C, 17th Vermont.
Lieut. H. C. Gage, G, 31st Maine.
Geo. Weeks, I, 2d N. Y. A.
Henry L. Clarke, E, 2d N. Y. A.

Corp. Jas M. Blake, A, 6th N. H.
Jos. Shaffee, K, 6th N. H.
Jos. Gray, K, 11th N. H.
Marshall Mercey, H, 17th Vermont.
Sergt. Chas. B. Copp. F, 31st Maine.
F. Rafferty, A, 31st Maine.
Patrick Dreaish, G, 35th Mass.
John Widgell, C, 48th Pennsylvania.
John Kilroy, I, 7th R. I.
Wm. H. Johnson, G, 7th R. I.
A. Chapman. K, 36th Mass.
Simon Devlin, F, 48th Pennsylvania
Wm. Simpson, G, 48th Pennsylvania.
Jesse D. Gleason, F, 36th Mass.
Wesley Packard, B, 36th Mass.
Wm. Pye, E, 45th Pennsylvania.
Thos. Oakes, A, 36th Mass.
Hugh Conevay, D, 45th Pennsylvania.
Wellington Wilson, D, 45th Pennsylvania.
Nathan Rich, K, 48th Pennsylvania.
G. W. Morey, H, 48th Pennsylvania.
Isaac Lewis, F, 48th Pennsylvania.
John Macdonald, C, 35th Mass.
E. H. Dillingham, D, 58th Mass.
Wm. Folley, D, 51st N. Y.
Michael Devine, D, 51st N. Y.
Newton Wellman, E, 21st Mass.
Ira Pierce, M, 24th N. Y. Cav.
I. Baker, —— 24th N. Y. Cav.
Sergt. D. G. Howe, G, 24th N. Y. Cav.
Capt. Chas. Goss, —— 21st Mass.
C. F. Piggery, 5th N. J. Bat.
Wm. C. Ray, A, 21st Mass.
L. F. Alexander, F, 21st Mass.
Sergt. C. P. Myrick, B, 4th R. I.
Jerry Harrigan, K, 36th Mass.
I. K. Belts, I, 48th Pennsylvania.
Geo. Neidell, A, 8th Ohio.
A. Calagher, H, 48th Pennsylvania.
Henry Russell, D, 36th Mass.
Geo. Osgood, A, 48th Pennsylvania.
John Henry, E, 4th R. I.
S. Satvenson, I, 97th Pennsylvania.
John McKuhn, C, 51st N. Y.
Phileam Stolte, G, 45th Pennsylvania.
Timothy Barry, H, 51st N. Y.
L. Beablehimer, E, 48th Pennsylvania.
Geo. Martin, C, 4th R. I.
I. F. Hauber, G, 45th Pennsylvania.
S. Branstetter, E, 45th Pennsylvania.
Daniel O. Knap, H, 51st N. Y.

Reuben Bailey, F, 45th Pennsylvania.
Sergt. James Farley, C, 4th R. I.
John Major, E, 48th Pennsylvania.
Thos. M. Dermoth, F, 58th Mass.
Seward Houghton, I, 51st N. Y.
John Homar, B, 48th Pennsylvania.
Schnarel, F, 39th N. J.
Edward Aspinal, H, 45th Pennsylvania.
Geo. E. Holliday, G, 39th N. J.
John Doty, G, 39th N. J.
Sergt. E. T. Brown, C, 21st Mass.
Chas. Giarraro, K, 35th Mass.
E. S. Ward, H, 36th Mass.
R. A. Whitman, D, 7th R. I.
Corp. Geo. Shoop, 27th N. Y. Bat.
Edwin Bronson, B, 51st N. Y.
Chas. W. Gilman, C, 35th Mass.
Nicholas Delaney, K, 48th Pennsylvania.
Henry Tholheim, H, 48th Pennsylvania.
Henry Sankoff, E, 35th Mass.
Geo. Heiss, A, 45th Pennsylvania.
Adolph Leissener, C, 35th Mass.
Wm. Livingston, C, 48th Pennsylvania.
John Kelly, K, 82d Pennsylvania.
Corp. Joseph Chase, A, 31st Mass.
Sergt. John Nunumaker, D. W. Va. Cav.
Byron Taylor, F, 51st N. Y.
C. Shultz, E, 35th Mass.
Betram Badenshartz, B, 39th N. J.

1st Division Cemetery, 9th A. C., near Meade Station.

Robt. Guthrie, A, 27th Mich.
E. H. Rood, D, 27th Mich.
Chas. W. Skank, E, 27th Mich.
A. Arrent.
I. Cartrig, A, 109th N. Y.
Geo. Galligher, G, 27th Mich.
Burrett Hummison, D, 109th N. Y.
M. E. Wildey, D, 109th N. Y.
David Leonhart.
H. H. Peck.
N. Cummings, A, 38th Wis.
E. Banderson, A, 37th Wis.
Corp. Geo. Gamble, C, 27th Mich.
Austin Panstle, A, 27th Mich.
Sanford Davis, G, 109th N. Y.
Sergt. Alex. H. Atherton, K, 109 N. Y.
Corp. Wm. H. Newton, C, 109th N. Y.
John F. Ackerman, B, 51st N. Y.
Geo. B. Carnes, G, 8th Mich.
John Perry, A, 109th N. Y.

Robt R. Felton, I, 51st Pennsylvania.
Wm. Chase, B, 8th Mich.
O. F. W. Eckerman, I, 8th Mich.
Chas. Wilson, G, 8th Mich.
John Ronan, D, 51st Pennsylvania.
F. W. Evans, —— 109th N. Y.
A. Youno, B, 57th Wis.
H. S. Bosart, —— 109th N. Y.
John Greenhouse, —— 37th Wis.
Wm. Gibson, K, 27th Mich.
Moses Boyer, E, 37th Wis.
Jas. Markle, C, 109th N. Y.
D. Huver.
Richardson.
F. H. Racey, C, 37th Wis.
C. O. Dana, A, 38th Wis.
B. W. Licester, A, 37th Wis.
Henry H. Howe.
E. Leon D. Green, —— 27th Mich.
Robt. Hicks. C, 38th Wis.
Henry Gauer, F, 38th Wis.
Stephen Ware, G, 8th Mich.
John Dergnett, B, 27th Mich.
Barber McCall, D, 8th Mich.
Thos. Smith, E, 27th Mich.
Sergt. Mippies Peaches, F, 38th Wis.
O. Sa—si—ka, E, 38th Wis.
Stephen Schott, F, 38th Wis.
T. Foster, K, 51st Pennsylvania.
Wm. DeBell, A, 109th N. Y.
Christian Sheets, G, 51st Pennsylvania.
Alfred Meckleg, —— 51st Pennsylvania.
Corp. Geo. M. Aurand, E, 50th Pennsylvania.
C. D. Miller, —— 27th Mich.
Corp. Jos. Kenned, E, 51st Wis.
E. L. Bullard, B, 109th N. Y.
P. Scoott, H, 27th Mich.
Thos. McDaniels, A, 109th N. Y.
Wm. Young, G, 51st Pennsylvania.
Harlon Haines, G, 27th Mich.
E. R. Wirth, F, 51st Pennsylvania.
Samuel Gillespie, F, 51st Pennsylvania.
Sergt. F. T. Bentley, —— 8th Mich.
M. Whitt, K, 37th Wis.
K. D. Fruitman, —— 37th Wis.
Chas. Weaver, E, 109th N. Y.
J. E. Cole, F, 27th Mich.
Jeremiah Troy, G, 51st Pennsylvania.
S. I. Gibson, —— 51st Pennsylvania.
Corp. Wm. Kooker, G, 51st Pennsylvania.
Sergt. Thos. Pierce, K, 51st Pennsylvania.

B. McHarry. G, 51st Pennsylvania.
S. Pearson, E, 109th ——
S. Baker, —— 109th N. Y.
S. Williams, K, 109th N. Y.
M. Mulfar.
R. W. Scott, A, 37th Wis.
A. H. Smith, D, 27th Mich.
Willer Springstead, C, 109th N. Y.
Conrad Schafer, A, 38th Wisconsin.
Jas. Brown, H, 109th N. Y.
Geo. Sloan, C, 27th Michigan.
A. M. Young, E, 109th N. Y.
Geo. B. Shumway, D, 37th Wisconsin.
Ever A. Hittstead, I, 38th Wisconsin.
Michael Setzer, I, 38th Wisconsin.
Wm. Dunn, G, 38th Wisconsin.
Geo. Newcomb, E, 38th Wisconsin.
John Raines, D, 38th Wisconsin.
Sergt. C. H. Churchill, I, 38th Wisconsin.
Francis Nichols, G, 27th Michigan.
Joel Wood, G, 109th N. Y.
John McFall, C, 51st Pennsylvania.
S. J. Himtoon, D, 27th Michigan.
A. Page, G, 37th Wisconsin.
N. Dock, I, 27th Michigan.
Oscar Gould, C, 8th Michigan.
Chas. Bakeman, D, 79th N. Y.
Geo. Narberger, D, 79th N. Y.
Louis Kemp, D, 79th N. Y.
Jas. A. Florance, A, 79th N. Y.
Alex. Miller, A, 79th N. Y.
Wellington Kendrickson, G, 17th Mich.
Adam Beard, C, 27th Michigan.
Corp. W. H. Bruce, G, 1st Rifles.
C. L. Gould, H, 37th Wisconsin.
—— Whitney, A, 37th Wisconsin.
Fred Rohle, H, 37th Wisconsin.
I. W. Wilcox, K, 50th Pennsylvania.
Frank Artush, F, 38th Wisconsin.
Thos. James, F, 38th Wisconsin.
Wm. Drayer, E, 50th R. P. V. V.
A. Bellanger —— Wisconsin
—— Sterns, C, 38th Wisconsin.
John B. Clago, C, 38th Wisconsin.
C. H. Gray, 1st Conn Art.
Corp. Henry Dane, K, 37th Wisconsin.
Wm. S. Perriga, G, 38th Wisconsin.
Corp. Wm. E. Hussey, G, 37th Wisconsin.
John Kennedy, H, 8th Michigan.
Reuben Chambers, C, 27th Michigan.
Wm. H. Dunton, I, 60th Ohio.

Patrick Haley, K, 60th Ohio.
Robt. Moore, D, 60th Ohio.
I. McElvey, A, 60th Ohio.
S. L. Runyon, F, 60th Ohio.
Wm. Louis, 10th Co., O. V. S. S. Art. 60th Ohio.
Jesse E. Berry, L, 60th Ohio.
Jasper Fultz, A, 60th Ohio.
Sergt. Austin Hudson, F, 60th Ohio.
Corp. Jos. Mayhue, C, 60th Ohio.
Willard Hugh Fawkes, C, 60th Ohio.
Nelson Stevens, E, 60th Ohio.
Sergt. R. W. Hull, B, 60th Ohio.
Sergt. Major, Giles N. Cowles, 60th Ohio.
Fred. Kohler, F, 50th R. P. V. V.
Wm. Biery, I, 50th R. P. V. V.
John T. Mays, E, 50th R. P. V. V.
John Strohn, H, 50th R. P. V. V.
Jacob Getler, C, 50th R. P. V. V.
Jos. Walmer, E, 50th R. P. V. V.
Chas. Beach, A, 50th R. P. V. V.
Peter Fox, A, 50th R. P. V. V.
A. Burns, E, 50th R. P. V. V.
Levi Lews, E, 50th R. P. V. V.
I. Tobias, E, 50th R. P. V. V.
J. W. Wilcox, K, 50th R. P. V. V.
Hiram Miller, F, 50th R. P. V. V
A. A. Gretton, K, 50th R. P. V. V.
Wm. Struler, F, 50th R. P. V. V.
Fred Koothe, F, 50th R. P. V. V.
C. Burket, C, 50th R. P. V. V.
Wm. Wagner, C, 50th R. P. V. V.
Capt. Henry A. Lantz, E, 50th R. P. V. V.
Jas. Hodges, G, 2d Mich.
Robt. Ford, H, 2d Mich.
Asa Terleson, E, 2d Mich.
Theodore Dand, H, 2d Mich.
I. E. Simmons, B, 2d Mich.
Alfred Rowe, G, 2d Mich.
R. Gardner, I, 2d Mich.
John Newel, I, 2d Mich.
W. F. Hawley, C, 2d Mich.
—— Klinheen, K, 46th N. Y.
Jacob Schirmer, G, 46th N. Y.
Ph. Hermann, C, 46th N. Y.
—— Krieg, A, 46th N. Y.
Wm. Yokers, H, 46th N. Y.
Geo. Wieland, H, 46th N. Y.
Rudolph Belge, I, 46th N. Y.
Anton Straka, K, 46th N. Y.
John A. Peard, C, 60th Ohio
L. Killer, —— 2d Mich.

—— Clemmins, 50th Pennsylvania.
Corp. Wallace Litcher, Independent **S. S.**
Wm. Boyer, H, 60th Ohio.
O. Whole, —— 46th N. Y.
Sergt. Jacob Repel, K, 46th N. Y.
Jos. S. Wilson, C, 60th Ohio.
John Fritz, C, 50th Pennsylvania.
—— Lofflin, —— 46th N. Y.
—— Muller, —— 46th N. Y.
—— Banker V. Steingingle, B, 46th **N. Y.**
Sergt. Adam Murray, A, 46th N. Y.
Sergt. Otto Schenck, —— 46th N. Y.
Sergt. John A. Tighe, K, 29th Mass.
Corp. Jas. Nicholas, A, 46th N. Y.
Sammay Maddis.
J. D. Schonmaker, —— 60th Ohio.
J. C. Cooper, E, 14th N. Y. A.
Sergt. A. Beach, G, 14th N. Y. A.
W. Young, M, 14th N. Y. A.
Ames Cromer, B, 14th N. Y. A.
E. Raynor, B, 14th N. Y. A.
D. E. Bell, L, 14th N. Y. A.
A. C. Rowne, L, 14th N. Y. A.
G. Pethord, A, 14th N. Y. A.
H. W. Thompson, A, 14th N. Y. **A.**
C. H. Turner, L, 14th N. Y. A.
John Brook, D, 14th N Y. A.
F. Hudson, M, 14th N. Y. A.
Henry Benton, M, 14th N. Y. A.
—— Jones, M, 14th N. Y. A.
E. Adams, E, 14th N. Y. A.
H. Carey, K, 14th N. Y. A.
Jas. Armstrong, B, 14th N, Y. A.
I. Pierce, K, 14th N. Y. A.
Corp. Albert H. Hall, K, 14th N. Y. **A.**
Levi Closs, K, 14th N. Y. A.
M. McTaggart, K, 14th N. Y. A.
W. S. Allen, K, 14th N. Y. A.
M. Lawrence, K, 14th N. Y. A.
Corp. S. O. Potter, K, 14th N. Y. A.
W. Ormsbey, M, 14th N. Y. A.
Sergt. I. D. Seaman, M, 14th N. Y. A.
Sergt. James Clark, K, 14th N. Y. A.
Wm. McCauley, M, 14th N. Y. A.
—— Hughes, M, 14th N. Y. A.
J. Robinson, K, 14th N. Y. A.
G. Smither, A, 14th N. Y. A.
Lorenzo Streeter. L. 14th N. Y. A.
I. Arrance, F, 14th N. Y. A.
Sergt. C. E. Dority, K, 14th N. Y. A.
Stephen A. Woods, D, 14th N Y. A.

G. A. Cowan, H, 14th N. Y. A.
I. Schlosser.
A. Barber, B, 14th N. Y. A.
M. McMann, E, 14th N. Y. A.
Patrick Mulligan, M, 14th N. Y. A.
Jas. Colins, B, 14th N. Y. A.
John Hinds, M, 14th N. Y. A.
Wm. Joslin, M, 14th N. Y. A.
John G. Swarz, A, 14th N. Y. A.
Peter Hart, K, 14th N. Y. A.
Jos. Barker, A, 14th N. Y. A.
Corp. Martin Briggs, K, 14th N. Y. A.
A. Mason, A, 14th N. Y. A.
Edwin D. Clark, I, 14th N. Y. A.
Sergt. Jacob Rhedan, C, 14th N. Y. A.
Martin Day, C, 3d Maryland.
Alexander Barber.
John McPhetridge, L, 14th N. Y. A.
Michael King, —— 19th N. Y. Bat.
H. W. Maril, —— 7th Maine Bat.
John Barver, —— 34th N. Y. Bat.
Martin Wilson, —— 14th N. Y. A.
Jesse Zimmerman, —— 14th N. Y. A.
Thos. C. Philpit, E, 14th N. Y. A.
Lyonau W. Ellinwood, I, 14th N. Y. A.
I. Respick, C, 3d Maryland.
H. D. Lutman, B, 3d Maryland.
T. Blair, B, 3d Maryland.
John McAvoy, B, 3d Maryland.
Ernico Cremonin, B, 59th Mass.
H. F. Chapman, B, 59th Mass.
Sergt. John A. Tiche, K, 29th Mass.
I. Scandlon, E, 59th Mass.
Martin Minton, B, 29th Mass.
Corp. Richard Gurney, H, 29th Mass.
Sergt. S. N. Grosvenor, C, 29th Mass.
Sergt. Wm. F. Willis, H, 29th Mass.
Jas. C. Powers, —— 59th Mass.
John C. Stewart, B, 29th Mass.
Jacob Wagner, E, 29th Mass.
Fred. Pottit, C, 100th Pennsylvania.
E. Heasy, B, 100th Pennsylvania.
Wm. Gray, A, 100th Pennsylvania.
Samuel F. Wilson, F, 100th Pennsylvania.
John Sharks, H, 100th Pennsylvania.
Geo. Martin, I, 59th Mass.
L. W. Rawson, K, 57th Mass.
D. Flynn, A, 57th Mass.
Sergt. I. J. Coaley, A, 57th Mass.
H. Streeter, H, 57th Mass.
S. A. Byam, K, 57th Mass.
Sergt. Chas. Dearing, E, 3d Maryland.
8

J. G. Brady, G, 3d Maryland.
Corp. E. D. Richards, C, 59th Mass.
Ambrose Upton, D, 59th Mass.
P. Lucas, H, 59th Mass.
Lyrons Barker, —— 100th Pennsylvania.
M. O. Doyle, H, 59th Mass.
I. H. Rogers, H, 59th Mass.
Mtn. Dumpey, E, 59th Mass.
Thos. Kelty, K, 100th Pennsylvania.
Capt. W. C. Oliver, B, 100th Pennsylvania.
Sergt. Saml. L. Moore, C, 100th Pennsylvania.
Philip Anthony, F, 100th Pennsylvania.
Wm. S. Simcox, —— 100th Pennsylvania.
J. Forney, F, 100th Pennsylvania.
Harvey A. Squers, G, 100th Pennsylvania.
John Brentliff, G, 100th Pennsylvania.
Wm. Rinkler, E, 29th Mass.
Chas. Richards, M, 100th Pennsylvania.
Herbert D. Beckwith, F, 57th Mass.
Sergt. C. F. Harlow, C, 29th Mass.
Sergt. Orrin D. Holmes, E, 29th Mass.
Edwin Cudworth, E, 57th Mass.
Fard. W. Park, F, 57th Mass.
Corp. Fred. H. Cheyney, C, 57th Mass.
Jas. Leisless, G, 57th Mass.
Chas. B. Grases, —— 57th Mass.
Uriah Hecter, —— 100th Pennsylvania.
David Gerica, B, 100th Pennsylvania.
David Smith, G, 100th Pennsylvania.
Corp. Dotleff Haase, 3d N. J. Bat.
Thos. Isaacs, H, 29th Mass.
Geo. E. Snow, G, 29th Mass.
Marity Renter, E, 29th Mass.
John Mars, A, 100th Pennsylvania.
John Lonnry, A, 100th Pennsylvania.
John S. Atherton, M, 100th Pennsylvania.
John O. Tanfield, ⎫
Miron Wescott, ⎪
Geo. Wags, ⎬ On one board.
Royal C. Griffis, ⎭
C. W. Wise, A, 2d Pennsylvania Art.
Geo, Metz.
Jas Reed.
—— Potsgrove, I, 2d Pennsylvania Art.
—— Webster, —— 18th N. H.
Henry Roberson.

Enclosed on Prince George Road, half a mile east of Meade Station.

Thos. Martin, I, 155th Pennsylvania.

Chas. Thomas, A, 91st Pennsylvania.
Henry Keen, D, 91st Pennsylvania.
Wm. Pierson, F, 21st Pennsylvania Cav.
T. R. Poyles, D, 187th Pennsylvania.
Geo. Weiser, H, 155th Pennsylvania.
Corp. Andrew Brown, C, 91st Pennsylvania
Jas. Hood, H, 91st Pennsylvania.
A. H. Harrison, A, 21st Pennsylvania.
Oakley Amerman, K, 187th Pennsylvania.
A. P. Enstreet, I, 146th N. Y.
Saml. Sorbear, B, 187th Pennsylvania.
Henry Fish, —— 2d N. Y. A.
Saml. J. Harris, F, 187th Pennsylvania.
Sergt. G. Bentley, D. 22d Mass.
David McAllister, E, 187th Pennsylvania.
Wm. G. Bingamin, G, 21st Pennsylvania Cav
Wm. McKee, B, 91st Pennsylvania.
Wm. D. Miller, B, 91st Pennsylvania.
Wm. F. Cain, F, 83d Pennsylvania.
Albert Ides, A, 187th Pennsylvania.
L. R. Sherwood, O, 83d Pennsylvania.
Jas. Holler, E, 21st Pennsylvania Cav.
Jos. H. Bricket, E, 91st Pennsylvania.
Martin Walls, A, 16th Michigan.
Wm. Minick, H, 21st Pennsylvania Cav.
Jos. Guinin, H, 150th Pennsylvania.
Chas. Jones, G, 187th Pennsylvania.
Wm. Hodgson, A, 83d Pennsylvania.
M. Gronter, H, 16th Michigan.
Seth English, —— 4th Michigan.
Geo. Wonderley, E, 187th Pennsylvania.
Nat. Hays, —— 22d Massachusetts.
John Keys, H, 91st Pennsylvania.
David Ripley, —— 142d Pennsylvania.
Jos. Bellis, A, 143d Pennsylvania.
Jas. L. Pell, A, 21st Pennsylvania Cav.
Neal Gurrens, E, 150th Pennsylvania.
David McAllister, E, 187th Pennsylvania.
Perry Philips, C, 155th Pennsylvania.
A. I. Martin, L, 21st Pennsylvania Cav.
Peter W. Weaver, L, 16th Michigan.
I. A. Hallinger, A, 21st Pennsylvania Cav.
Thos. R. Boyle, D, 187th Pennsylvania.
Henry V. Brooks, E, 143d Pennsylvania.
M. H. Scanlan. C, 16th Michigan.
Sergt. F. B. Welch, D, 83d Pennsylvania.
Linsley.
Sergt. J. E. George.
Danl. Flemming.
Corpl. G. E. Evers, G, 59th Massachusetts.
Solomon Derr, —— 2d Pennsylvania Art.

Graves found in lower end of garden at the house of Peter Burchard on Prince George Road.

- T. Moarhad, —— I, 148th Pennsylvania.
- H. G. Hogi.
- S. Dun, H, 4th N. Y.
- A. Hamlen, H, 26th N. H.
- Jacob Dierce, B, 7th N. Y. Art.
- P. Fitzpatrick, G, 81st Pennsylvania.
- E. Davis, A, 125th N. Y.
- L. Rooney, F, 63d N. Y.
- P. Fitzsimons, C, 4th N. Y. Art.
- H. I. Ginkin, B, 5th N. Y.
- T. Huck, E, 61st N. Y.
- R. Bunn, C, 6th N. Y.
- E. Ewirett, D, 61st N. Y.
- C. Clark, F, 64th N. Y.
- Wm. Rockwell, B, 64th N. Y.

Graves to the left of Prince George Road, nearly opposite the enclosed ground, on the hillside towards road.

- Chas. Curns, H, 7th Maryland.
- J. C. Caldwell, Bat. C, Massachusetts Art.
- J. Fitzgerald, —— 11th U. S.
- Louis Lanser, G, 8th Maryland.
- Sergt. Wm. N. Lent, A, 6th N. Y. Art
- Patrick Cartland, F, 12th U. S.
- G. A. Maine, E, 7th Maryland.
- Albert Ankerson, G, 11th U. S.
- Ira A. Simons, F, 146th N. Y.
- Corp. John Britt, F, 5th N. Y.
- G. D. Bailey, K, 4th U. S.
- John Holland, F, 1st Maryland.
- Oliver P. Stewart, A, 10th U. S.
- Louis Lashine, Bat. D, 1st N. Y.
- H. Blake, I, 15th N. Y. Art.
- G. Jaring, K, 146th N. Y.
- Capt. Franz. Sleckner, I, 15th N. Y. A.
- Chas. Hegeman, K, 6th N. Y.
- Corp. Patrick Edwards, 15th N. Y., I, Bat.
- Abial Green, M, 6th N. Y. Art.
- Sergt. Leonard Cronk, I, 6th N. Y. Art.
- Wm. Bloom, —— 4th Maryland.
- C. T. Heintze, L, 15th N. Y. Art.
- Corp. W. E. Devins, M, 15th N. Y. Art.
- C. Price, G, 15th N. Y. Art.
- Jas. McDonald, 10th U. S.
- Jos. W. Warrenco, —— Cav.
- Chas. Preman, Bat., H, 1st N. Y. Art.
- Jas. Christian, C, 6th N. Y.
- Geo. Max, K, 1st Maryland.

Jas. S. Lipe, —— 10th U. S.
Jas. Dalton, D, 146th N. Y.
Simon Galey, G, 7th Md.
John Williams, D, 146th N. Y.
Andrew Rosenstron, — 140th N. Y
Thos. Lee, — 4th Maryland.
Chas. Myers, — 10th U. S

FAIR GROUNDS HOSPITAL, PETERSBURG, VA.

J. T. Matton, —— 2d N. Y. Cav.
N. P. Bristol, H, 1st Michigan.
Sergt. J. T. Lockington, H, 97th N. Y.
Albert Wright, I, 48th Pennsylvania.
Geo. Curtis, A, 20th Maine.
G. T. Adams, G, 210th Pennsylvania.
J. Benning, A, 15th N. Y. H. A.
W. Heath, K, 2d Michigan.
Wm. Valentine, C, 5th N. Y.
J. Brown, D, 1st Connecticut H. A.
A. Calhoun, C, 211th Pennsylvania.
Jas. Barnes, A, 146th N. Y.
Chas. Logan, F, 14th U. S.
T. S. Laird, F, 16th Pennsylvania.
H. Moore, D, 29th U. S. C. T.
J. W. Jones, I, 127th Pennsylvania C. T.
J. Wright, K, 1st U. S. C. T.
Thos. White, H, 127th U. S. C. T.
A. Parey, A, 2d U. S. C. T.
J. Eignor, H, 120th N. Y.
Sergt. E. G. Lemons, E, 16th Pennsylvania Cav.
W. I. Graylee, A, 109th U. S. C. T.
E. Mayes, H, 104th Pennsylvania.
R. Sheppard, E, 8th U. S. C. T.
W. H. Miller, D, 45th U. C. S. T.
Daniel Thomas.
C. H. Clarke, Lakeville Massachusetts.
John Holmes, C, 127th Pa. C. T.
O. Fitchett, B, 7th U. S. C. T.
L. Reasure, K, 29th U. S. C. T.
A. H. Giles, F, 6th N. Y. Art.
H. LaGrange, E, 6th N. Y. H. A.
D. Lawson, G, 38th New Jersey.
E. Wentworth, F, 1st Maine Cav.
W. Jones, C, 11th U. S. C. T.
J. Stevens, E, 2d Pennsylvania.
Steph. J. Loftcet, M, 10th N. Y.
R. Weaver, H, 23d U. S. C. T.
J. Robinson, I, 18th N. Y.
T. Biard, H, 109th U. S. C. T.
D. Gehr, G, 17th Pennsylvania Cav.

T. H. Poke, —— 9th U. S. C. T.
Geo. Clayton, C, 26th U. S. C. T.
W. T. Reynolds, A, 4th Delaware.
Corp. Christopher Thomas, B, 2d Pennsylvania Art.
M. Bonnister, H, 155th Pennsylvania.
Sergt. I. Statca, B, 41st U. S. C. T.
A. Wright, F, 31st U. S. C. T.

Graves found in Fort "Hell."

Wm. Nellis, F, 121st Pennsylvania.
L. W. Baatman, A, 187th Pennsylvania.
Wm. H. Johnson, G, 187th Pennsylvania.
J. M. Putney, D, 39th N. Y.
Lieut. Emit Sick, F, 7th N. Y.
Peter Powel, I, 12th New Jersey.
John Mahony, A, 73d New York.
Lewis Johnson, H, 11th Massachusetts.
Jas. W. Lunt, G, 1st Maine Art.
A. R. Bixby, F, 2d U. S. S. S.

East of Fort "Hell."

L. Hemmenger, A, 149th Pennsylvania.
L. S. Jordon, B, 143d Pennsylvania.
S. I. Dodson, F, 149th Pennsylvania.
John Woodruff, F, 143d Pennsylvania.
Levi Malloy, E, 40th Pennsylvania.
A. E. Hutchings, E, 19th Maine.
Geo. G. King, C, 124th N. Y.
J. Nelson, G, 19th Maine.

Between Fort "Hell," and Fort Davis.

—— Benson, G, 19th Maine.
John Kelly, K, 170th N. Y.

North side of Fort Davis.

John Burke, —— 20th Massachusetts.
Sergt Jas. Burke, K, 20th Massachusetts.
Thos. Blaig, E, 105th Pennsylvania.
John Barlelman, F, 39th New Jersey.
Jas. Idel.
John Ischi, F, 39th New Jersey.
Jas. Idol, B, 205th Pennsylvania.

Near Orchard east of Fort Davis.

Sergt. Michael Brady, G, 104th N. Y.
Sergt. Henry Brunyan, D, 104th N. Y.
Robt. Cowles, L, 21st Pennsylvania Cav.
Jas. Crosbie, D, 52d N. Y.

Near the Avery House.

John Fuchs, H, 6th Wisconsin.
Sergt. J. Fox, B, Purnell Legion, Md.
John Thorp, D, 5th U. S. Art.

Near Point of Woods, North of Avery House.

> Jas. Stewart, F, U. S. C. T.
> Corp. Geo. W. McKeen, D, 24th Massachusetts.
> Geo. Gamball, I, 24th Massachusetts.
> Corp. Horace Enox, B, 4th Ohio.
> Lewis Hemitaran, F, 63d U. S. C. T.
> Geo. Jackson, K, 30th U. S. C. T.
> 'Corp. Thos. D. Tainter, A, 11th Maine.
> Asa. A. Arthurs, I, 11th Maine.
> Sergt. A. F. Bassett, D, 11th Maine.

Bet. Avery House and Norfolk R. R. near Bridge.

> John Plunket, —— 157th Pennsylvania.

Near Point of Woods S. W. Avery House.

> I. O. Conrad, A, 107th Pennsylvania.
> John Beaumont, A, 88th Pennsylvania.
> Milton C. Goheen, C, 62d Pennsylvania.

Half mile N. W. Avery House.

> Edw. Harris, —— 11th Massachusetts Bat.
> Geo. M. Grath.

Half mile North Avery House.

> C. R. Dutton, —— 26th Michigan.
> Benj. Clark and 3 others in one Grave, 111th N. Y.
> I. S. McConnel, Bat. D, —— Pennsylvania.
> John Bruce, D, 88th N. Y.
> W. A. Stone, C, 88th N. Y.
> Lieut. T. C. Sharp, C, 2d Pennsylvania Art.

Half mile East Avery House near the grove.

> Peter Brennan, D, 40th N. Y.
> Edwd. Kupferschun, D, 5th New Jersey.
> Earl Hulbert, F, 5th Michigan.
> Jas. Murray, F, 86th N. Y.
> Reuben Boyd, C, 40th N. Y.
> Lines D. Richards, K, 57th Pennsylvania.
> Sergt. Geo. H. Coffin, D, 2d U. S. S. S.
> Pat'k Hughes, D, 6th New Jersey.
> Peter Conlon, G, 11th New Jersey.
> Jas. Mulligan, K, 11th New Jersey.
> Jas. Ryerson, D, 124th N. Y.
> Thos. Odonell, C, 52d N. Y.
> Geo. Cockran, E, 99th Pennsylvania.
> Michael Keller, A, 8th New Jersey.
> Isaac Horr, B, 105th Pennsylvania.
> Jas. H. Hall, E, 17th Maine.
> Wm. Grinder, L, 99th Pennsylvania.
> Lewis Shores, I, 120th N. Y.
> John Barnes, K, 120th N. Y.
> Geo. Wagner, A, 4th N. Y. H. A.
> M. V. Campbell, B, 124th N. Y.

Grant B. Benjamin, G, 124th N. Y.
Jas. Furman, E, 120th N. Y.
Chester Judson, H, 124th N. Y.
Simon P. Post, K, 124th N. Y.
John R. Doxie, I, 73d N. Y.
Henry George, B, 40th N. Y.
Thos Corby, —— 43d N. Y.
John Leo, B, 11th New Jersey.
John W. Trout, F, 11th New Jersey.
A. F. Büchard, K, 141st Pennsylvania.
Lemuel Hall, F, 40th N. Y.
Nicholas Sherry, —— 10th N. Y.
Danl. E. Kirk, F, 40th N. Y.
Sergt. Peter Petffor, I, 5th Michigan.
Corp. David A. Chase, L, 1st Maine H. A.
Thos. Woodman, K, 1st Maine H. A.
Hugh Shantro, I, 4th N. Y. Art.
Jas. Jevine, F, 120th N. Y.
D. Borrus, F, 4th N. Y. Art.
Dubois Beacraft, G, 40th N. Y.
Thornton E. Pearcy, G, 1st Maine Art.
John Marsh, D, 63d Pennsylvania.
Robt. Parrent, G, 11th N. Y.
Jas. Miller, B, 105th Pennsylvania.
Wm. A. Miller, I, 105th Pennsylvania.

In cornfield near *"Burnside's Mine."*

Thos. Malony, K, 45th Pennsylvania.
Sergt. I. O. Hunt, H, 35th Massachusetts.
Lieut. Saml. Berry, G, 35th Massachusetts.
Solomon Richardson, F, 35th Massachusetts.
Jacob C. Bugh, K, 67th Ohio.
H. Thornton, K, 67th Ohio.
Capt. John Cartright, —— 27th U. S. C. T.

Yard 50 Rods S. W. Pitkin's Station, near R. R.

Saml. Wood, I, 40th Massachusetts.
T. I. Sullivan, E, 40th Massachusetts.
W. H. Kelley, D, 87th Pennsylvania.
Geo. Bogart, F, 16th N. Y. H. A.
Henry Henkelgury, B, —— N. Y. Eng.
Edwd. Sandford, C, 8th Maine.
Wm. I. Thomas, A, 8th Pennsylvania.
John Kestry, F, 2d Pennsylvania H. A.
R. A. Ketcham, H, 10th N. Y. Art.
I. P. Donham, F, 81st N. Y.
Henry McGee, L, 2d Pennsylvania H. A.
Corp. Thos. Cosrello, D, 8th Connecticut.
Alonzo E. Harrington, I, 114th N. Y.
Luke Bowker, F, 2d New Hampshire.
Levi Barrows, F, 2d New Hampshire.

I. C. Hadsell, II, 2d Pennsylvania Art.
John Cochrane, R, 55th Pennsylvania.
I. B. Laaman, II, 5th Maryland.
Wm. A. Lewis, A, 8th Maine.
John Allen, B, 142d N. Y.
I. B. Little, G, 188th Pennsylvania.
H. F. Foster, H, 89th N. Y.
H. Wolffer, L, 4th U. S. Art.
1. Robinson, B, 2d Pennsylvania Art.
I. A. Stines, C, 126th Pennsylvania.
W. B. Kemp, B, 26th Virginia.
E. Stevens, B, 25th Massachusetts.
G. W. Mitchell, E, 8th Connecticut.
D. Hannah, M, 102d Pennsylvania.
I. Houston, D, 5th Vermont.
I. McDonnell, K, 11th Connecticut.
G. A. Feagles, I, 148th N. Y.
Sergt. A. Ballard, D, 102d Pennsylvania.
Napoleon Beck, E, 90th N. Y.
Jos. Marquis, —— 13th Indiana.
Corp. S. Carr, E, 169th N. Y.
I. Lynch, A, 4th New Hampshire.
Ben. Judd, M, 10th N. Y. H. A.
S. T. Elliott, C, 13th New Hampshire.
G. H. Hutchins, D, 2d Connecticut.
Jas. Leddis, E, 118th N. Y.
Johann Nuller, I, 117th N. Y.
Jas. Conahy, D, 142d N. Y.
L. D. Inell, C, 10th New Hampshire.
Robt. Bonner, D, 2d Pennsylvania Art.
D. Kelley, F, 12th New Hampshire.
Moses Edmunds, H, 4th New Hampshire.
Sergt. E. B. Ferris, I, 118th N. Y.
I. Conaly, A, 142d N. Y.
C. Addams, B, 188th Pennsylvania.
E. C. Schaffer, D, 76th Pennsylvania.
I. Waltons, D, 97th Pennsylvania.
H. Donahue, F, 55th Pennsylvania.
M. Rogan, F, 97th Pennsylvania.
Henry Potts, B, 8th Maine.
Wm. Sargent, B, 8th Maine.
N. Derwin, C, 97th Pennsylvania.
C. Berger, H, 2d Pennsylvania.
Hartley Roe, F, 2d Pennsylvania.
I. Strunk, A, 12th New Hampshire.
Robt. Henry, D, 112th N. Y.
W. A. McKinney, D, 92d N. Y.
D. Goodwin, K, 4th New Hampshire.
J. Buckley, G, 118th N. Y.
D. Greely, H, 102d Pennsylvania.
B. Wise, D, 93d Pennsylvania.

E. McElheny, I, 93d Pennsylvania.
Ulric Beck, B, 2d Pennsylvania H. A.
Ben. Decker, C, 148th N. Y.
A. Green, F, 2d Pennsylvania H. A.
Capt. I. M. McIntosh, E, 142d N. Y.
H. Ford, I, 76th Pennsylvania.
I. H. Lamb, B, 13th Indiana.
M. Hocum, B, 96th N. Y.
I. Scully, — 9th New Jersey.
E. Y. Porter, D, 4th New Hampshire
Corp. I. Sullivan, G, 139th N. Y.
Antiune Felio, K, 118th N. Y.
M. Stephen, B, 1st N. Y. Eng.
B. F. Robins, B, 10th New Hampshire.
Henry Smith, H, 8th Connecticut.
Caleb Kulefish, A, 9th New Jersey.
David Metcalf, G, 76th Pennsylvania.
Sergt. Jas. E. Barker, D, 3d N. Y.
John Hoghan, A, 115th N. Y.
Lewis Linburgher, H, 23d U. S. C. T.
Jerome Etheridge, L, 10th N. Y.
Geo. T. Teft, K, 117th N. Y.
Daniel McKiel, A, 40th Massachusetts.
Thos. I. Putnam, B, 9th New Jersey.
R. B. Leffingwell, G, 169th N. Y.
Albert Nesberg, H, 48th N. Y.
Jos. R. Emmett, K, 4th New Hampshire.
Silas T. Tiffany, F, 112th N. Y.
Henry Addiss, E, 48th N. Y.
Jos. McDade, G, 4th New Hampshire.
Jos. Morris, H, 11th Connecticut.
Geo. Wilding, I, 4th New Hampshire.
John A. Crossley, F, 2d Pennsylvania.
Robt. M— W———, F, 97th Pennsylvania.
Corp. — P. W———
Sergt. I. M. L———, — 13th Indiana.
Corp. Jas. Gallagher, F, 47th N. Y.

Near Friend House.

Henry C. Blake, C, 139th N. Y.
Wm. I. Lynch, B, 63d N. Y.
Hesleton Huntress, A, 10th New Hampshire.
Jas. Cramley, B, 62d N. Y.
T. H. Gotham, G, 10th N. Y.
Corp. Jas. Johnston, B, 62d N. Y.

South of Friend House; near the Run.

Albert W. Jones, I, 89th N. Y.
Sergt. I. H. Peassall, G, 89th N. Y.
Chas. Bell, E, 89th N. Y.
Alex. Dunlap, ———
Wm. Shatock, I, 23d Massachusetts.

B. Katterman, B, 55th Pennsylvania.
Fred Shandeum, ———
Alfred Jackson, D, 4th New Hampshire.
I. W. Martin, K, 4th New Hampshire.
H. C. Lund, B, 4th New Hampshire.
Samuel A. Fitch, K, 89th N. Y.

Hill Side; few rods South of Fort Friend.
Michael Huzzy, D, 11th Connecticut.

Between Fort "Hell" and Fort Rice, east of Breast Works.
John Ralmstine, I, 184th Pennsylvania.
Corp I. A. Darnel, C, 20th Indiana.
Jacob James, H, 20th Indiana.
F. M. Waggoner, B, 20th Indiana.
Michael Heafey, B, 20th Indiana.
Z. Craiger, E, 20th Indiana.
Sergt. Robt. Deyo, B, 20th Indiana.
I. D. Stininger, I, 184th Pennsylvania.
A. Bush, G, 40th N. Y.
John Dunlan, I, 73d N. Y.
Frederick Cook, G, 17th Maine
C. L. Miller, I, 17th Maine.
Capt. A. C. Gammon, F, 17th Maine.

At Fort Rice.
Lewis Poolex, K, 146th ———
Fred. Miller, D, 10th N. Y.
E. Boothe, C, ——— Cav.

Back of Fort Rice.
C. North, D, 7th N. Y. H. A.
Jas. M. Tyler, H, 19th Maine.
G. S. Cobb, I, 19th Maine.
Mark Ryder, H, 73d N. Y.
I. Stork, F, ——— U. S. Infantry.
Sergt. Theo. Barraclough, F, 6th N. Y.
Samuel Bell, C, 6th N. Y. H. A.
Jas. Stevens, I, 10th Massachusetts.
Lyman R. Blood, F, 20th Massachusetts.
Adam Heidy, B, 4th Maryland.
Sergt. G. T. Shipley, E, 4th Maryland.
T. T. Daggett, F, 20th Maine.
H. E. Dunbar, G, 20th Maine.
I. T. Myres, D, 11th U. S. Infantry.
Hurburt Stone, ——— 11th U. S. Infantry.
Renauld A———.

Under a tree S. W. of Meade Station.
Jos. Givisiez, ——— 27th N. Y. Bat.

Near strip of Woods opposite Meade Station.
Sergt. Geo. W. Russell, K, 5th New Hampshire.
Henry Bullard, K, 5th New Hampshire.
Aug. Studtman, C, 9th New Jersey.

Lieut. Louis Wolf, B, 52d N. Y.
Hiram H. Barnes, F, 118th N. Y.
Sanford Botham, G, 7th New Hampshire.
Peter Rudwick, L, 19th Maine.

Yard between Meade Station and " *Strip of Woods*."
Benj. Croff, —— 2d Pa. Art.
—— Broughman, —— 2d Pa. Art.
Norman Green, F, 2d Pa. Art.
Sergt. Jos. F Passmore, F, 2d Pa. Art.

East side of Ravine between Meade Station and " *Strip of Woods*."
A. Kiein, C, 5th New Hampshire.

Half mile S. E. of Meade Station.
Leander Myers, K, 148th Pennsylvania.

Back of Meade Station, *West.*
Corp. M. A. Rankin, G, 6th Pennsylvania.
Lieut. Jas. Shuter, C, 40th N. Y.
A. I. Locke, F, ——
Geo. F. ——

Back of 9th A. C. Head Quarters, *in Woods.*
Walter Walling, A, 36th Wisconsin.
Mathias R. Morgan, B, 184th Pennsylvania.
Jason Cook, G, 8th N. Y. H. A.

Near Fort Macgilvery.
Irving P. McCaubey, —— 96th N. Y.
E. Weed, A, 87th N. Y.
Chas. A. McFarland, B, 25th Massachusetts.
Patrick Smith, A, 2d New Hampshire.
Wm. Lennen, E, 188th Pennsylvania.
Jas. Godsey, I, 188th Pennsylvania.
R. Green, H, — Conn. V.
Chas. E. Jones, K, 117th N. Y.
Jas. Lovell, A, 117th N. Y.

On City Point Wagon Road, back of the Defences, near the *Creek.*
Geo. A. Lee, G, 188th Pennsylvania.
Geo. H. Myers, C, 95th Pennsylvania.
Corp. Chas. Nevins C, 95th Pennsylvania.
O. P. Corson, B, 188th Pennsylvania.
Edward Ripley, B, 10th N. Y. Art.
Thos. Johnson, I, 2d Pa. Art.
Wm. Peck, H, 61st N. Y.
Adelbert Rich, I, 81st N. Y.
Jas. M. Flood, B, 10th New Hampshire.
Geo. Dull, D, 2d Pa. Art.
Geo. Rohr, E, 2d Pa. Art.
Michael Haish, C, 2d Pa. Art.
Sergt. S. H. Glass, A, 122d N. Y.
John Pinter, —— 5th U. S. C. T.

Between Picket Lines front of Fort Steaaman.
I. C. Gray.

Back of Fort Steadman.

Albert Richmond, F, 117th N. Y.
Jason Harget, I, 117th N. Y.
Daniel Ulster, A, 13th Indiana.
Jos. R. Smith, B, 8th U. S. C. T.
Calvin —nass, ——
H. F. Robison, E, 10th N. Y. Art.
F. A. Ahein, —— 10th N. Y. Art.
John F. Lamb, —— 9th Maine.
I. H. B., I, 9th.——
Fred. Rachner, B, 117th N. Y.
John H. Buster, I, 9th Maine.
Sergt. C. H. Burgess, G, 9th Maine.
C. S. Cloud, D, 97th ——
Tho. Campbell, C, 3d N. Y.
I. Krisel, I, 97th Pennsylvania.
Geo. T. Morrill, B, 23d Massachusetts
V. Yarnal, A, 97th Pennsylvania.
John Guest, G, —— Pennsylvania.
Jas. R. Saville, I, 23d Massachusetts.
Jos. Weatha —, —— 142d N. Y.
Geo. Watson, B, 142d N. Y.
Hiram Hyde, A, 142d N. Y.
Rich'd Muller, K, 40th N. Y.
Wm. G. Seymour, B, 8th N. Y.

Back of Fort Steadman.

Jacob Kramer, D, 40th N. Y.
I. C. Holbrook, F, 17th Maine.
John Stacy, I, 164th N. Y.
Fred'k Helberg, K, 155th N. Y.

East of Fort Steadman.

Thos. Williams, B, 5th New Jersey.
Wm. B. Howe, C, 115th N Y.
Alfred C. Snyder, I, 115th N. Y.
H. E. Fulkerson, A, 76th Pennsylvania.
Miles G. Kinsel, F, 76th Pennsylvania.
Jos. D. Hagerty, F, 76th Pennsylvania.
Corp. John Flessining, H, 11th New Jersey
Corp. Chas. P. Smith, D, 9th New Jersey.
Sergt. E. B. Smith, C, 9th New Jersey.
L. Midget, F, 36th U. S. C. T.
Corp. F. V. Dougherty, A, 6th New Jersey.
I. O. Spencer, K, 7th New Jersey.
Edwd. Crozby, E, 7th New Jersey.
Thos. Wallraven, E, 7th New Jersey.
Henry A. Ryther, C, 27th Massachusetts.

South of Fort Steadman.

    Geo. Snathel, D, 6th Connecticut.
    Andrew J. Neff, E, 6th Connecticut.
    Geo. W. Russel, —— 5th New Jersey
    Henry Bonland, —— 5th New Jersey.

Near Meade Station.

    J. T. Johnson.
    Wm. Johnson, —— 23d U. S. C. T.
    T. H. Fryer, A, 53d Pennsylvania.

South of Fort Haskel.

    Hugh Hays, I, 14th N. Y. H. A.
    Tac. Aeberle, C, 7th N. Y.
    Otto Behm, B, 7th N. Y.
    Corp. Terchmann, F, 7th N. Y.

At Fort Steadman.

    L. Burgmire, G, 55th Pennsylvania.
    John Williams, B, 4th New Hampshire.
    B. F. Gliddin, E, 9th Maine.
    Corp. H. Chambers, H, 169th N. Y.
    J. Ende, ——, N. Y.
    Corp. P. McConkey, F, 169th N. Y.
    M. Marvin, H, 169th N. Y.
    Nat. Martin, F, 169th N. Y.
    A. Graham, G, 169th N. Y.
    Clement Carr, E, 169th N. Y.
    O. Fish, H, 4th New Hampshire.
    C. McKenney, E, 9th Maine.
    O. T. Patterson, E, 9th Maine.
    L. M. Work, B, 9th Maine.
    T. B. Crowell, D, 9th Maine.
    A. F. Saunders, D, 9th Maine.
    J. W. Philbrick, E, 9th Maine.
    D. Russell, D, 9th Maine.
    Winthrop L. Presby, D, 4th New Hampshire.
    D. F. Perkins, B, 4th New Hampshire.
    D. T. Caulfield, B, 169th N. Y.
    A. M. Abbott, E, 9th Maine.
    J. McKanna, D, 51st Pennsylvania.
    John W. Barker, K, 4th New Hampshire.
    Wm. B. Ealf, I, 8th Michigan.
    J. P. Joslin, E, 36th Wisconsin.
    Frederic D. Port, C, 7th Michigan.
    E. Boothe, C, Purnell Cav.
    Fred. Mulless, D, 10th U. S. Inf'y.
    Lewis Pool, K, 146th —
    S. W. Van Driver, K, 4th Delaware.
    F. C. Gray, F, 18th Maine.

Yard near Parke's Station.

Wm. H. Young, D, 198th Pennsylvania
T. Y. Pollard, B, 189th N. Y.
John Quigley, A, 189th N. Y.
Wm. C. Fuller, A, 185th N. Y.
D. Vanbuskirk, N, 198th Pennsylvania.
Moses Luther, I, 188th N. Y.
A. M. Gibney, I, 188th N. Y.
I. D. Akres, A, 189th N. Y.
John S. Cott, —— 21st Pennsylvania Cav.
Chas. E. Adams, F, 20th Maine.
S. McMinen, K, 189th N. Y.
Joel Bryant, E, 188th N. Y.
D. V. Hall, E, 189th N. Y.
John Lewis, C, 188th N. Y.
H. Hibbard, D, 189th N. Y.
S. Vandike, B, 188th N. Y.
Wm. Smith, D, 188th N. Y.
P. Eveland, H, 189th N. Y.
Lewis Harder, L, 198th Pennsylvania.

Half mile West of Parke's Station.

Ezra T. Warner, E, 40th New Jersey.
Wm. J. Reynolds, C, 15th New Jersey.
Sylvester Smith, E, 4th New Jersey.
David D. Russell, H, 10th New Jersey.
Alfred Tompkins, C, 1st New Jersey,
Manuel Silver, E, 10th New Jersey.
John O. Neal, I, 40th New Jersey.
Corp. E. D. Vallette, D, 2d Rhode Island.
Wm. Haverill, H, 37th Massachusetts.
Sergt. John T. Rimpell, B, —— Maryland Cav.
Thos. W. Twyford, D, 109th Pennsylvania.
Corp. B. Higdon, G, 7th Indiana.
Geo. Rosison, D, ——
John Johnston, C, 97th N. Y.
Joshua T. Copper.
John Waitknight, F, 118th Pennsylvania.
John Stenner, A, *Purnell Legion.*
I. T. Davis, D, 4th Rhode Island.
Sylvester Prout, G, 2d Connecticut.
David Cramner, I, 2d Connecticut.
P. Heggekjar, I, 5th Wisconsin.
Michael Apal, K, 5th Wisconsin.
John Southmayde, E, 5th Wisconsin.
Milton S. Frazier, C, 82d Pennsylvania.
Near by:—Capt. J. B. Doughty, A, 5th Wis.

Near House at Parke's Station.

Wm. Bowman, H, 24th U. S. C. T.
Philip Sembly, E, 23d U. S. C. T.

Henry Crosson, C, 28th U. S. C. T.
Abraham Kalloway, E, 28th U. S. C. T.
Thomas Scott, F, 39th U. S. C. T.
Geo. Tibos, A, 23d U. S. C. T.
Andrew Morgan, G, 19th U. S. C. T
John Hatchel, C, 28th U. S. C. T.

North-west of Parke's Station, near Works.
Adolph Cafuld, —— U. S. C. T.

Large yard west of Parke's Station.
Hiram Horton, F, 140th N. Y.
Wm. C. White, E, 210th Pennsylvania.
Hen. Erwen, C, 210th Pennsylvania.
Wm. Paynter, A, 157th Pennsylvania.
James Cambell, I, 4th Delaware.
Archibald Woodruff, M, 15th N. Y. Art.
L. W. Hurlburd, I, 140th N. Y.
Ferdinand Yeager, K, 1st Md.
John E. Ward, B, 4th Delaware.
Levi T. Moon, E, 44th Wis.
Wm. Chiseltine, C, 1st Md.
John Befurt, B, 157th Pennsylvania.
Emmanuel Boon, B, 210th Pennsylvania.
Warren Bradford, A, 190th Pennsylvania.
Francis Galloway, D, 1st Mass. Cav.
Charles McKinstry, F, 210th Pennsylvania
Thomas Davis, C, 3d Delaware.
John Richie, A, 3d Delaware.
Wm. H. Palemtory, G, 4th Delaware.
Nathan Tobs, —— 210th Pennsylvania.
Robt Ackley, G, 210th Pennsylvania.
T. Allen, K, 198th Pennsylvania.
G. H. Sampler, 188th N. Y.
S. McIntire, A, 185th N. Y.
Sergt. Fitz Simmons, K, 91st Pennsylvania
I. Matteson, F, 185th N. Y.
Corp. M. I. Moss, H, 189th N. Y.

Near the House of Mr. Kane.
Lieut. W. S. Collins, E, 1st Maine Cav.
Wm. H. Ellis, E, 14th Conn.
H. Murphy, ——
Capt. Wm. C. Wallace, C. S. A.
Max Limbach, K, 1st Maryland.
Fred Smith, (colored.)

Near Warren Station, on Weldon R. R.
Henry Toomy, D, 187th Pennsylvania.
O. F. Bowers, E, 21st Pa. Cav.
Jos. A. Johnston, I, 6th Wisconsin.
Corp. John B. Shillinly, B, 187th Pennsylvania
M. McNamara, 3d Mass. Bat.

9

A. Wood, Batt'y, L, 1st N. Y. **Art.**
Alonzo Ketchum, ——
Wm. Senn, I, 15th N. Y.
Weldon R. R near — House.
Milton Noggle, G, 21st Pa. Cav
O. F. Bowers, E, 21st Pa. Cav.
Near Patrick Station to the South East.
Geo. Wilson, B, 64th N. Y.
Geo. Kebboe, D, 52d N. Y.
John Pratt, B, 5th New Hampshire.
John Redmond, I, 7th N. Y. H. A.
Chris. Madden, A, 63d N. Y.
Seaman Nic, F, —— N. Y. H. A.
Lawrence E. Babcock, C, 125th N. Y.
Perry Forrest, E, 64th N. Y.
Max Leemgruber, H, 7th N. Y.
David Sloan, C, 61st N. Y,
Chas. Tonsay, D, 11th N. Y.
John McCoy, K, 69th N. Y.
Allen Runnington, I, 5th New Hampshire.
J. A. Logue, B, 53d Pennsylvania.
A. Mesick, E, 111th N. Y.
Geo. White, C, 28th Massachusetts.
Andrew Dowen, C, 28th Massachusetts.
Owen Brennan, A, 28th Massachusetts.
S. L. Putney, H, 69th N. Y.
Jesse Hopkins, G, 61st N. Y.
Wm. Huffman.
W. A. How, D, 183d Pennsylvania.
Henry Burgess, G, 52d N. Y.
W. Slattery, H, 2d N. Y.
John Howard, A, 111th N. Y.
Hugene Straham, D, 64th N. Y.
W. I. Parson, B, 148th Pennsylvania.
Albert Linton, B, 81st Pennsylvania.
James Kern, G, 111th N. Y.
John White, G, 5th N. Y.
Orland Golder, H, 111th N. Y.
Chas. Bott, H, 61st N. Y.
H. Grotten, —— 28th Massachusetts.
M. Hofferand, H, 64th N. Y.
A. O. Carter, A, 179th N. Y.
Geo. Webster, B, 44th N. Y.
Freman Elwell, I, 20th Maine.
Mos. Burkheal, D, 16th Michigan.
Chas. Colflesh, G, 118th Pennsylvania.
Sergt. Sam. Johnson, I, 16th Michigan.
John White, L, 16th Michigan.
Mitchel Laplant, L, 16th Michigan.
Sergt. John Roublemar, A, 16th Michigan.

J. Johnson, —— 37th North Carolina.
Sergt. Jacob Dexheimer, E, 69th N. Y.
Sergt. John Miller, B, 69th N. Y.
Chas. Frainer, F, 69th N. Y.
F. Smallon, K, 69th N. Y.
Corp. Wm. Leabey, K, 69th N. Y.
Jas. Signal, E, 69th N. Y.
Geo. Stackpole, H, 69th N. Y.
Jos. Collins, H, 69th N. Y.
Corp. John Murphy, B, 28th Massachusetts.
John Lee, H, 69th N. Y.
John Anderson, I, 145th Pennsylvania.
H. Cromfar, D, 148th Pennsylvania.
Henry Lawrence, A, 2d N. Y. A.
John Winter, A, 64th N. Y.
H. Philips K, 8th N. Y. A.
H. Niles, I, 8th N. Y. A.
W. P. Griggs, I, 121st N. Y.
John Thornton, B, 8th N. Y. A.
E. Townsend, A, 3d Pa. Cav.
J. S. Moore, D, 19th Maine.
A. Charles, A, 19th Maine.
S. A. Bingham, K, 148th Pennsylvania.
Renaldo I. Walker, F, 12th New Jersey.
Gabl. Day, E, 155th Pennsylvania.
Peter Winters, L, 8th N. Y. A.
John Smith, H, 1st Delaware.
Lt. Col. F. I. Spantler, —— 4th Ohio.
Corp. A. Baker, F, 12th New Jersey.
Wm. H. Stockton, E, 12th New Jersey.
Rich. Birch, C, 10th N. Y.
Lieut. H. G. Maclavish, A. A. A. G. 2d B. 2d D. 2d A. C
Moses Granley, A, 69th Pennnsylvania.
Geo Poole, L, 8th N. Y. A.
J. D. Dugeon, D, 10th N. Y.
John Smith, E, 69th N. Y.
Chas. H. Thomas, B, 23d U. S. C. T.
Louis Harris, H, —— U. S. C. T.
Preston Cook, H, 28th U. S. C. T.
Wm. Brown, I, 23d U. S. C. T.
Jas. H. Buck, G, 4th N. Y. A.
Sergt. Chas. D. Harper, A, 40th N. Y.
F. H. Freadmore, F, 120th N. Y.
Michael Mahar, I, 120th N. Y.
Frederick Bunte, D, 120th N. Y.
Sergt. Sam. Syme, I, 120th N. Y.
Cyrus Hanks, G, 120th N. Y.
Henry G. Long, E, 40th N. Y.
Geo. Gainer, I, 57th Pennsylvania.
Simeon Weiler, H, 8th New Jersey.
Narris Blamondow, K, 8th New Jersey.

John Burns, C, 8th New Jersey.
Albert Phelps, K, 141st Pennsylvania.
H. B. Walker, H, 20th Michigan.

Yard near the last.

Jas. Cole, A, 77th N. Y.
Jas. Long, F, 61st P. V.
J. B. Grow, E, 3d Vt.
Jos. Titus, F, 4th Vt.
T. Prizzee, C. 93d P. V.
H. C. Libby, —— 1st Maine.
J. Holriggle, G, 61st P. V.
H. Kramer, K, 98th P. V.
S. Bernheim, B, 5th Vt.
N. W. Lemmon, A, 61st P. V.
G. Fairbanks, D, 2d Vt.
W. S. Kraft, A, 102d P. V.
A. Wingrove, I, 102d P. V.
Samuel Stall, E, 93d P. V.
H. C. Hadly, D, 11th Vt.
Corp. J. F. Brandon, A, 139th P. V.
Alfred Chase, B, 77th N. Y.
A. Halhorn, I, 2d Vt.
R. C. Cannon, C, 93d Pennsylvania.
Edward Farrel, E, 1st Me.
J. Kauffmann, G, 61st P. V.
W. H. Gould, C, 102d P. V.
Corp. H. G. Fillebrown, C, 4th Vt.
Sergt. Francis E. Kelley, D, 62d N. Y.
Lawrence Macdonald, D, 62d N. Y.
Sergt. Chas. Plummer, K, 1st Me.
Horace G. Barnes, I, 1st Vt. Art.
E. G. Sullivan, G, 1st R. I. Art.
Wm. N. Carpenter, E, 5th N. Y. Art.
Luther Search, H, 1st Ohio Art.
Michael Munster, 3d N. Y. Indep't Batt'y.
John A. Shay, A, 1st N. J.
H. Gove, —— 3d Vt.
Chas. Veislette, H, 1st R. I.
S. Hill.
F. O. Kearney, B, 1st N. J. Art.
Clark Lord, C, 179th N. Y.
C. W. Hartwell, I, 17th Vt.
Chris. P. Pratt, I, 179th N. Y.
W. H. Ham, I, 31st Maine.
J. Harnes, D, 186th N. Y.
L. G. Peagant, B, 1st N. J. Art.
Jas. Jowler, L, 4th N. Y. H. A.
David Fanc——

Yard near the R. R., at Patrick Station.

Thos. M. Jackson, I, 10th N. J.

L. C. Parsons, G, 1st Maine.
Chas. E. Cranmer, G, 11th N. J.
S. A. Bennett, G, 129th N. Y.
I. Walker, B, 8th N. J.
H. I. Duke, K, 87th Pennsylvania.
Calvin Ingerson, K, 8th N. J.
Jacob Kohl, F, 73d N. Y.
Wm. Kubler, H, 8th N. J.
Jos. Fulton, C, 57th Pennsylvania.
Geo. W. Kemmell, C, 57th Pennsylvania.
Fletcher Russell, I, 93d N. Y.
Preston Pempers, B, 11th Mass.
Wm. S. Butler, C, 1st Maine H. A.
Wm. Curtis, B, 7th N. J.
Jas. Owins, A, 1st Maine H. A.
John Rosh, G, 7th N. J.
Thos. Ulric, A, 8th N. J.
Wm. Hoffman, I, 8th N. J.
Fred. Christ, Batt. F, 5th U. S. Art.
Nathaniel Chambers, A, 1st Maine.
Abiel Farrows, M, 1st Mass.
Lewis Thompson, B, 1st Maine H. A.
John W. Johnson, I, 8th N. J.
Geo. H. Mason, A, 124th N. Y.
Jonathan Eckart, H, 141st Pennsylvania.
Jos. Reynolds, G, 120th N. Y.
Matthew Esglison, D, 105th Pennsylvania.
Carter Nelson, (colored servant at Head-quarters.)
Jas. Woodcock, G, 93d N. Y.
Martin Covell, F, 124th N. Y.
Edward N. Lahn, B, 11th N. J.
John B. Miles, A, 17th Maine.
Wm. A. Chapman, F, 20th Ind.
Gustav Davison, D, 11th N. J.
Henry Schultz, K, 8th N. J.
Jas. Morris, I, 8th N. J.
Augustus Keaney, C, 8th N. J.
Jacob Bauer, K, 8th N. J.
John De Crow, A, 8th N. J.

Yard east of last.

Geo. Frick, C, 93d Pennsylvania.
S. Carpenter, A, 2d Vt.
I. T Tripp, I, 1st Maine.
J. Smith, C, 43d N. Y.
L. Richardson, C, 122d N. Y.
I. Cronan, C, 43d N. Y.
Sergt. A. D. Spaulding, E, 2d Vt.
Peter Philips, F, 1st Maine.
Dennis Sullivan, F, 3d Del.
Corp. N. Flanders, G, 12th U. S. Inft'y.
Corp. I. Barbur, H, 12th U. S. Inft'y.

W. Stutic, F, 1st Md.
John Cartel, F, 4th Del.
Arthur Steele, C, 118th Pennsylvania.
M. Cullen, K, 155th N. Y.
Nelson Southworth, G, 95th N. Y.
W. H. Slawter, I, 4th Del.
I. Liddell, D. 1st Md.
Henry Burns, D, 8th Md
Jonas Kime, G, 11th U. S. Inft'y.
Jas. Fow.
Chas. Fleet, B, 5th N. Y.
Thos. Corcoran, A, 10th U. S. I.
Wm. Berger, D, 8th Md.
Geo. Harris, A, 10th U. S. I.
Herman Bohne, D, 8th Md.

Near Mrs. Comming's house, Hatcher's Run.
Jas. O. Abbott, L, 8th N. Y. A.
R. Savage, H, 198th Pennsylvania.
Geo. Lewis, B, 32d Mass.
Frank Izen, H, 187th N. Y.
C. F. Cady, D, 198th Pennsylvania.
B. F. Kelley, I, 20th Maine.
Hiram Hewitt, I, 189th N. Y.
Col. Wyatt. Near Hatcher's Run.
Wm. E. Foster, H, 1st Maine Cav.

In Mrs. Comming's garden.
Thos. Hornly, 11th Pennsylvania.
E. B. Hadley, E, 39th Mass.
—— Pollock, C, 95th N. Y.
C. McNulty, B, 88th Pennsylvania.
S. Stevens, F, 56th Pennsylvania.
Wm. Gilbert, —— 16th Maine.
Geo. Wallace, I, 22d Mich.

Near R. R. bridge, Hatcher's Rnn.
Sergt. Danl. Meaghr, —— 10th N. Y. Ca
Sergt. J. P. Morgan, C, —— O. V.
H. A. McCantry, A, 4th Ohio.
T. O. Brien.

West of Comming's house.
D. Stevens, G, 11th Maine.
D. McLaughlin, B, 10th W. Va.
J. Reynolds, D, 12th W. Va.
A. Bowley, E, 11th Maine.
J. Core, I, 55th Pennsylvania.
J. Smith, E, 116th Ohio.
A. Mock, — 55th Pennsylvania.
E. A. Morgan, H, 39th Ill.
J. Bartlett, E. 11th Maine.
H. W. Ryon, D 11th Maine.

On Vaughn road, south of Comming's house.

Lieut. S. Patterson, — 7th Mich.
Lieut. Chas. E. Nugent, — 4th Pa. Cav.
G. Wallace, E, 1st Del.

Cemetery at Hatcher's Run.

Auther.
Thos. Elder, F, 191st Pennsylvania.
Matthew Doyle, H, 140th N. Y.
Franklin Stewart, — 191st Pennsylvania.
Samuel Fitch, A, 146th N. Y.
Wm. Stornes, A, 94th N. Y.
Geo. McClernan, D, 146th N. Y.
Jas. Gillen, F, 140th N. Y.
John W. Ellis, H, 1st Md.
C. G. Smith, G, 140th N. Y.
Jas. Horan, — 5th N. Y.
John Tracy, G, 4th N. Y.

Near Sergt. Daniel Meagher, G, 10th N. Y. Cav.

Near Spain house.

———— Sink, D, 198th Pennsylvania.
Geo. Stephens, D, 198th Pennsylvania.
Wm. T. Homer, L, 198th Pennsylvania.
Chas. Rogers, K, 185th N. Y.
Stephen Finnegan, F, 91st N. Y.
Corp. Philip Wyand, G, 91st N. Y.
Sidney Margnet, D, 91st N. Y.
Wm. Richardson, C, 12th S. C.
Peter Delong, G, 11th N. Y.
Edward Contle, F, 11th Pennsylvania.
Wm. Robinson, F, 11th Pennsylvania.
Wm. (or Josiah) Brown, B, 11th Pennsylvania.
John Farrell, F, 91st N. Y.
Andrew Bordon, C, 91st N. Y.
Frank D. Wood, F, 91st N. Y.
August Festi, H, 95th N. Y.
John Rogers, L, 11th Pennsylvania.
Andrew Morrison, G, 147th N. Y.
I. E. Parker, G, 147th N. Y.
Christopher Woodbeck, H, 91st N. Y.
———— Baunters.
Milton Vauneler.
J. H. Harmer, F, 198th Pennsylvania.
J. Kimball, F, 189th N. Y.
H. B. Davis, F, 189th N. Y.
F. Emery, F, 189th N. Y.
John L. Brewer, G, 198th Pennsylvania
Lieut. J. Strong, F, 155th P. V. Res.

South-west of above

C. B. Biser, G, 7th Md.

J. W. Hall, E, 210th Pennsylvania
Christian Shultz, B, 15th N. Y. H. A.
Geo. Strael, C, 15th N. Y. H. A.
Jas. McGrady, E, 3d Del.
Enos Wanfield, K, 15th N. Y. H. A
John W. Bartlett, A, 1st Mass. Batt.
John R. Beach, F, 56th Va.
Wm. H. Wilson, B, 171st Pennsylvania.

Near Bosevill's House; North of Lookout, Patrick's Station.
Corp. John Best, B, 2d Conn. H. A.

At and near Fort Gregg.
Henry Ohlhues, E, 39th Illinois.
Sergt. W. W. Lamb, F, 39th Illinois.
S. F. Proud, A, 39th Illinois.
W. McLean, C, 39th Illinois.
— Vahn, D, 39th Illinois.
R. N. Hurnell, D, 39th Illinois.
Peter Sowers, K, 39th Illinois.
P. Diviney, F, 39th Illinois.
— Steelhamer, F, 39th Illinois.
Thos. W. Shinkle, I, 39th Illinois.
Corp. David Bailey, I, 39th Illinois.
R. Babcock, E, 39th Illinois.
G. W. Gurton, E, 39th Illinois.
Thos. Dewey, F , 39th Illinois.
Hugh Rorke, A, 39th Illinois.
Lieut. R. McMillin, I, 199th Pennsylvania.
I. W. Tewksberry, I, 199th Pennsylvania.
—— Kinny, I, 199th Pennsylvania.
John J. Moreland, D, 199th Pennsylvania.
Caleb Hagenbaugh, D, 199th Pennsylvania.
Henry Moyer, F, 199th Pennsylvania.
Jos. Roger, C, 199th Pennsylvania.
J. Martin, A, 199th Pennsylvania.
N. Hess, B, 199th Pennsylvania.
David Ensley, G, 199th Pennsylvania.
Jos. Vance, H, 199th Pennsylvania.
John Shaughnecy, E, 34th Mass.
Harvey B. Stone, I, 34th Mass.
Noah Connel, K, 67th Ohio.
Jeremiah Gusford, — 67th Ohio.
Thos. Guff, K, 67th Ohio.
Adam Sivarnel, K, 67th Ohio.
— Ashem, K. 67th Ohio.
Chas. D. Long, K, 67th Ohio.
Henry C. Whitman, G, 34th Mass.
I. I. Ropes, H, 110th N. Y.
Corp. I. M. Hartley, B, 116th Ohio.
Sergt. H. E. Humphrey, B, 116th Ohio.
Lieut. Wm. H. Bush, H, 116th Ohio.

Sergt. John G. Riethmiller, E, 116th Ohio.
Martin Hysell, G, 116th Ohio.
Henry Michaels, B, 158th N. Y.
C. Bridert, E, 23d Illinois.
Jas. Kennedy, H, 58th N. Y.

South-west of Sidney's House.

Chas. V. Chase, B, 20th Maine.
Gideon Stoudt, G, 198th Pennsylvania.

Near Sidney's House; near "Five Forks."

Thos. Gilmore, A, 157th Pennsylvania.
— O. Field, — 5th Corps.
Henry James, B, 94th N. Y.
Jas. Pilcher, — 94th N. Y.
Barney Cush, E, 4th Delaware.

On Road to Five Forks; W. Dinwiddie C. H.

J. L. Scott, M, 20th Pennsylvania Cav.
Sergt. John H. Charles, G, N. Y. Drag.

Near Five Forks.

Sergt. Henry Weber, B, 185th N. Y.
S. W. Bryan, E, 155th Pennsylvania.
Corp. T. McCust, I, 155th Pennsylvania.
T. M. Areny, I, 97th N. Y.
Robt. Brewster, K, 155th Pennsylvania.

Jas. Boissean's House; Five Forks.

Theodore Tenny, — 2d Ohio Cav.
I. H. Wall, C, 2d N. Y. Cav.
John Corcon, D, 2d N. Y. Cav.
A. R. Ely, L, 1st Connecticut Cav.
Sergt. J. B. Flickinger, G, 17th Pennsylvania.

Mrs. Gillun's House, Five Forks.

Wm. E. Hunt, D, 15th N. Y. Cav.
R. Amidon, B, 15th N. Y.
Capt. U. N. Parmelee, I, 1st Conn. Cav.
Nathan Bowen, D, 8th N. Y. Cav.
W. Hoag, B, 3d N. Y. Cav.

B. G. Boiscan's House; Five Forks

F. Pettit, — 32d Virginia.
F. Young, 30th Virginia.
R. Boyne, C, 94th N. Y.

Near Mrs. Wallace's House.

Lieut. C. C. Croxton, K, 4th Va. Cav.

Sutherland's Tavern.

A. W. Hearin, G, 20th Maine.
E. Gutheridge, I, 11th Virginia.
Porter Crawford, D, 94th N. Y.

Wm. H. Howard, H, 22d South Carolina.
Adam Grosgelose, A, 1st Virginia.
Daniel Conway, — A, 1st Virginia.
J. B. Maylin, H, 53d Virginia.
Daniel B. Williamson, E, 47th North Carolina.
John H. Stanton, C, 23d South Carolina.
Geo. Gonburn, D, 9th N. Y.
Jonathan Henderson, H, 44th North Carolina.
B. F. McGillberry, — 23d South Carolina.
N. T. Norwood, — South Carolina V.
Sergt. Math. Creamer, B, 10th New Jersey.
Sergt. Jas. Haskins, M, 17th Mich. Cav.

Near *our Forts* on "Boydton Plank Road."
Capt. E. Comuck, F, 124th N. Y.

Hospital House in our lines near "Boydton Plank Road."
Wm. K. Crant, L, 198th Pennsylvania.
John Kimler, C, 198th Pennsylvania.
Corp. Robt. Hadden, C, 198th Pennsylvania.
Jas. Givens, C, 198th Pennsylvania.
E. A. Hill, E, 188th N. Y.
Erastus Rosenburg, C, 185th N. Y.
John Hoath, A, 185th N. Y.
E. Marshall, I, 185th N. Y.
P. Parker, H, 185th N. Y.
Theo. Walk, B, 195th Pennsylvania.
Thos. H. Berry, N, 198th Pennsylvania.
Geo. Bowman, N, 198th Pennsylvania.
Wm. Forner, N, 198th Pennsylvania.
Sergt. John May, N, 198th Pennsylvania.
Corp. J. Smith, N, 198th Pennsylvania.
S. D. Labar, A, 198th Pennsylvania.
Matthew Russell, H, 198th Pennsylvania.
Francis Diehel, M, 198th Pennsylvania.
Jos. Derhamer, H, 198th Pennsylvania.
Wm. Heist, G, 198th Pennsylvania.
David Smith, G, 198th Pennsylvania.
Sergt. Henry Smith, G, 198th Pennsylvania.
John Thompson, F, 88th N. Y.

Dinwiddie Court House, near Church.
Lieut. I. O. King, —— 10th Va. Cav.
H. P. Cook, —— 17th Ga. Cav.
Major Robt. S. Munroe, —— 11th Pa. Cav.
Rufus Halston, H, 1st N. C. Cav.
F. A. Finch, —— 20th Va. Cav.

East Hancock Station, near Jones' House.
Daniel Nash, B, 1st N. J. Bat.
Edward Rowe, C, 179th N. Y.
Daniel Smith, C, 179th N. Y.
Waterman Thornton, C, 179th N. Y.

One mile East H's Station, Timble's House.

Sergt. C. H. Howard, H, U. S. S. S.
J. Riley, E, 57th N. Y.
C. Leach, I, 116th Pennsylvania.
I. Bartlett, K, 33d North Carolina.
Marcus Van ——, C, 38th North Carolina.
Edward Simons, E, 4th N. Y. A.
Chas. White, H, 7th N. Y.

Belcher's Farm, near "Timble's."

Sergt. — Halpin, —— 4th Pa. Cav.
Lieut. J. F. Newman, K, 2d N. Y. M. R.
Corp. W. T. Andrews, B, 10th N. Y. Cav.
Wm. Keefouver, B, 21st Pennsylvania.
Levi Tracy, M, 1st Maine Cav.
E. Reynolds, H, 10th N. Y. Cav.
John Chesly, I, 24th N. Y. Cav.
Jacob Ringler I, 1st Pa. Cav.
Nathan Perden, G, 16th Pa. Cav.
Chas. Brown, A, 24th N. Y. Cav.

Hospital yard, South Timble's House.

Wm. McKenna, E, 1st N. J. Cav.
Chas. Danone, H, 1st N. J. Cav.
Benjamin Haxton, K, 10th N. Y. Cav.
I. W. Fisher, M, 10th N. Y. Cav.
Jos. Dushane, M, 2d N. Y. M. R.
J. Blass, E, 24th N. Y. Cav.
Jas. Bacon, C, 24th N. Y. Cav.
H. Bisbron, D, 24th N. Y. Cav.
Wm. Wright, G, 24th N. Y. Cav.
Wm. Warner, L, 16th Pa. Cav.
Thos. Harpster, C, 13th Pa. Cav.
Andrew Temple, H, 13th Pa. Cav.
Jeremiah Hettuck, D, 13th Pa. Cav.
Michael Thomas, K, 4th Pa. Cav.
G. H. Smith, H, 4th Pa. Cav.
John Decker, D, 4th Pa. Cav.
Isaac Steller, L, 6th Ohio Cav.
Chas. F. Shaw, C, 1st Maine Cav.
John Esbern, G, 21st Pa. Cav.
Henry Winck, G, 21st Pa. Cav.
Lewis Allen, I, 21st Pa. Cav.
Geo. Hiner, G, 21st Pa. Cav.
I. N. Green, I, 13th Ohio.

Small yard near by.

Corp. I. Hall, K, 8th Pa. Cav.
Jas Keer, I, 8th Pa. Cav.

Near Westbrook House.

Daniel Ward, —— 1st N. J. Cav.

Back of Wood's House.

Andrew Madison, G, 1st Mass. H. A.
Joel W. Gardner, B, 3d Michigan.

¼ mile south west "Fort Stevenson."

I. K. Marsh, D, 87th Pennsylvania.
Sergt. M. Riter, E, 87th Pennsylvania.
Corp. Isa Hoff, —— 87th Pennsylvania.

Near Aiken's House east, under apple tree.

N. Paine, K, — Va. Volunteer.

Yard near *apple tree*.

—— Thomas, K, 11th Pennsylvania.
Henry Typkie, E, 104th N. Y.
Detric Dantz, I, 88th Pennsylvania.
John Coulter, A, 11th Pennsylvania.
A. P. Atkinson, C, 16th North Carolina.
Albert Rusco, A, 104th N. Y.
W. Glifford, H, 94th N. Y.
E. Wilcox, G, 104th N. Y.
Andrew I. More, G, 107th Pennsylvania.
Gon. Haahn, K, 6th Wisconsin.
Richard Libby, B, 16th Maine,
Wm. Brallier, G, 197th Pennsylvania.

At Fort Wadsworth.

David Ferguson, H, 1st N. Y. A.

Little south of Fort Davis.

Corp. A. J. Gillsey, Bat., B, 1st Pa. Art.

At Ream's Station, in grove, near Church.

Conrad Theisel, K, 2d Pennsylvania Cav.
John King, L, 16th Pennsylvania Cav.
Jos. Hall, B, 16th Pennsylvania Cav.

Near Perkin's House.

A. C. Stone, C, 198th Pennsylvania.
Henry Minke, Col. Spear's Regt., Pennsylvania.
Ames, (Mrs. Caroline Ames, Hartford, Conn.,—wife.)
J. Tanner, —— 7th Wisconsin.

On Peeble's Farm.

O. Flinx, C, 6th New Hampshire.
Cyrus A. Munjer, E. 38th Wisconsin.
Stephen A. Clark, K, 7th R. I.
All. Robbins, A, 155th Pennsylvania.
Wm. Davis, A, 155th Pennsylvania.
S. J. Denny, I, 155th Pennsylvania.
Corp. Robt. F. Webb, A, 36th Wisconsin.
Albert Little, B, 2d N. Y. M. R.
Sergt. Robt. McCulloch, C, 35th Mass.
Daniel Boyes, — 48th Pennsylvania.

W. H. Newhouse, F, 13th Ohio.
E. M. Beneamp, H. 80th Pennsylvania.
Smith Dennington, E, 83d Pennsylvania.
Sergt. Chas. W. Trumbull, B, 2d Michigan.
A. Baker, C, 91st Pennsylvania.

Little south of above, *between two Corduroy Roads.*

Theo. Bodley, F, 30th U. S. C. T.

Graves in edge of woods about one hundred rods south of Drucy's House, near Richmond Virginia.

T. Ulrick, I, 6th Iowa V. V., killed May, 11th 1865.
T. Coffman, D, 30th Iowa V. V.

FIELDS BEFORE RICHMOND AND PETERSBURG.

The following lists were prepared by Messrs. Clark'c and Charters, who, immediately after the close of the last campaign, went over the fields before Petersburg and Richmond, copying the names from the head-boards with great care. The parts of the field not thus catalogued here, will be found elswhere. Probably many names are yet unrecorded in these lists.

Graves at Bermuda Hundred.
>I. Perry.

Between Bermuda Hundred and Jones' Landing: North of Road.
>Charles White.

Jones' Landing: Near the Neck.
>John Ramsden.

At James' Farm, one and a half miles west of Jones' Landing.
>John Merrit.

Near Turner's House: Near Butler's Head Quarters.
>I. Oad——.
>H. Curry.

Cox's House, two miles from Dutch Gap.
>Levi Adams.

Graves at Field Hospital of 24th Army Corps, one mile east of Fort Burnham.
>William Gillen.
>Arthur Smith.

List of graves at Point Rocks Cemetery.
>I. Van Martin.
>I. Windson.
>I. Creft.
>A. Fisher.
>Henry Harvey.

Charles E. Horton.
Joseph Jones.
List of Graves, on line of City Point Rail-Road.
L. Berberi.
S. H. Linpuk.
Francis Hartman.
Edward Barnes.
John Gilroy.
Hubert Sactchel.
Mosier Mascar.
David Cochre.
James Anderson.
Charles F. Green.
Sergt. E. Curtis.
Isaac Edmond.
John Seippe.
John F. Miller, (unassigned.)
Wm. Heise, (unassigned.)
Jas. Mummert, (unassigned.)
S. Beal, (unassigned.)
James Green.
List of graves in cemetery of Field Depot-Hospital at City Point.
J. Fields.
J. Walker.
C. Benson.
A. Rhodes.
C. Miller.
A. Keller.
John Noyes.
J. Treville, D, Hampton Legion.
N. Stanton.
W. Dewitt.
S. Emphy.
G. Brooks.
Michael Welch.
Charles Siebert.
G. H. Robinson.
W. Smith, 1st Engineers.
E. Joslyn.
W. H. Hawkins.
J. Berghaus.
J. Leonard.
Ira Audley, Dixon's Light Artillery.
J. Shoemaker.
E. Lamb.
J. Adams, C, ———
S. H. Wright.
D. Arnold, D, Dunell Battery.
W. Hitner, 5th Excelsior.
D. Wheeler.

S. R. T. (on left arm.)
N. J. Kein.
W. A. Hood.

List of graves at Cavalry Corps Cemetery, City Point.

Richard Ansel, B, 5th U. S. Cav.
John Metcalf, F, 5th U. S. Cav.
F. Kramer, C, 3d U. S. Cav.
J. W. White, L, 2d U. S. Cav.
I. Brownsaugh.
J. Auger, (citizen.)
E. Comstock, E, 1st U. S. Cav.
G. Tracy, 2d U. S. Battery.
Major G. M. Crawford.
D. McCarty, K, 5th U. S. Cav.

List of graves near Thos. Lepsey's House, near City Point.

John C. E. Benudetz.
Jacob Winfield, F, ——
Daniel Goward.
Samuel Street, A, 19th ——
Charles Sportes, A, ——
Geo. L. McCorison, — 1st Delaware Cav.
Ezra Ayers, — 1st U. S. Artillery.

In the enclosure near Hospital of 2d Div., 9th A. C., at Meade Station.

D. Lapham.

In Cemetery 3d Div., 9th A. C., Hospital, Meade Station,

Geo. L. Putman.
Lieut. Sharks, 106th ——

In adjoining ground of 3d Div.

Crutipher Fry.
Jos. Reifer, K, ——
Albion O. Page.

In Cemetery of 1st Div., 9th A. C., near same Station.

A. Arrent.
David Leonhart.
H. H. Peck.
D. Huver.
Richardson.
Henry H. Howe.
S. Pearson, E, 109th ——
M. Mulfar.
Corp. W. H. Bruce, G, 1st Rifles.
Sannuay Maddis.
Corp. Wallace Litcher, Independent S. S.
I. Schlosser.
Alexander Barber.
John O. Fanfield, ⎫
Miron Westcott, ⎬ On one board
Geo. Wags, ⎭

Royal C. Griffis.
George Metz.
James Reed.
Henry Roberson.

In enclosure on Prince George Road, half a mile east of Meade Station
— Linsley.
Sergt. J. E. George.
Daniel Flemming.

To the left of Prince George Road, nearly opposite the "enclosed ground," on the hill-side towards road.
J. Fitzgerald, — 11th U. S.
Patrick Cartland, F, 12th U. S.
Albert Ankerson, G, 11th U. S.
G. D. Bailey, K, 4th U. S.
Oliver P. Stewart, A, 10th U. S.
James McDonald, — 10th U. S.
Jos. W. Warrenco, — —— Cav.
James S. Sipe, — 10th U. S.
Charles Myers, — 10th U. S.

Fair Ground Hospital, Petersburg, Va.
Charles Logan, F, 14th U. S.
Daniel Thomas, ——

In Fort Hell.
A. R. Bixby, F, 2d U. S.

Between Forts Hell and Davis.
James Idel.

Near the Avery House.
John Thorp, D, 5th U. S. Art.

Half mile north west of Avery House.
Edward Harris, — 11th Mass. Bat.
George M. Grath, ——

Half mile east of Avery House near the Grove.
Sergt. George H. Coffin, D, 2d U. S. S. S.

Yard fifty rods south west Pitkins Station, near Rail-Road.
H. Wolffer, L, 4th U. S. Art.

South of Friend House, near the Run.
Alexander Dunlap.
Fred. Shandeum.

At Fort Rice.
Lewis Poolex, K, 146th ——
E. Boothe, C, —— Cav.

Back of Fort Rice.
I. Stork, F, U. S. Infantry.
I. T. Myers, D, 11th U. S. Infantry.
Hurbut Stone, 11th U. S. Infantry.
10

Back of Meade Station, west.

A. J. Locke, F, ———

Between Picket Lines front of Fort Steadman.

I. C. Gray, ———

Near Meade Station.

J. T. Johnson.
Lewis Poole, K, 146th ———
E. Boothe, Purnell Cav.
Fred. Miller, D, 10th U. S Infantry.
Last three at Fort Steadman,

Half mile west of Parke Station.

George Rosisons, D, ———
Joshua T. Copper, ———
John Stenner, A, Purnell Legion.

Large yard west of Parke Station.

M. I. Moss.

Near the House of Mr. Kane.

H. Murphy.

Near Warren Station, on Weldon Rail-Road.

Alonzo Hetchum, ———

Near Patrick Station, to the south east.

Wm Huffman.
Lieut. H. G. Maclavish.

Yard near the last.

S. Hill.
David Fane ———.

Yard near the R. R., at Patrick Station.

Fred Christ, Bat. F, 5th U. S. Art.

Yard east of last.

Corp. M. Flanders, G, 12th U. S. Infantry.
Corp. I. Barbur, H, 12th U. S. Infantry.
James Fow.
Jonas Kime, G, 11th U. S. Infantry.
Thos. Corcoran, A, 10th U. S. Infantry.
George Harris, A. 10th U. S. Infantry.

Near R. R. Bridge, Hatcher's Run.

T. O. Brien.

Near Spain House.

Milton Vauneler.

Near Sidney's House, near Five Forks.

— O. Field, 5th Corps.

One mile East of Hancock's Station ; Timble's House.

Sergt C. H Howard, H, — U. S. S. S.

Burksville Junction, Va.
    Samuel T. Read, Orderlies Staff.
    John M. Moore.
Buried, between Middletown and Strasburg, near Sperry's House.
    Harvey Winters, B, 2d Conn. Art.
Buried between Kernstown and Newton, one and a half miles from Kernstown, near woods.
    Patrick Delany, B, 2d Conn. Art.
Buried in Hospital burying-ground, near Patrick's Station.
    Allen W. Barnet, A, 82d Pennsylvania.
    Wm. Fransher, C, 82d Pennsylvania.
    John Southmaid, E, 5th Wisconsin.
    Wm. H. Averill, H, 37th Massachusetts.
    Corp. Edward Vallette, D, 2d Rhode Island.
    Joshua Gordon, E, 10th New Jersey.
    S. Smith, E, 4th New Jersey.
    Henry A. Strange, F, 2d Rhode Island.
    Henry Cooker, A, 2d Pennsylvania Cav.
    Alfred Tompkins, C, 1st New Jersey.
    Quinton Bliss, B, 37th Massachusetts.
    Jas. C. Carpenter, B, 95th N. Y.
    David Kemper, I, 82d Pennsylvania.

Buried about three miles east of Burksville Junction, south of R. R, twenty rods from house used as 1st Div., Hd. Qrs., 6th A. C.
    James Murray, C, 40th New Jersey.
Buried near Middletown.
    John McGunnigle, K, 1st Maine.
    Jas. W. Davis, K, 1st Maine.
Buried in Kernstown.
    Carl. Busche, B, 43d N. Y.
    Wm. A. Dow, F, 5th Vermont.
    B. F. Whitney, K, 11th Vermont.
    Jas. F. Toland, F, 102d Pennsylvania.
Buried in 2d Div. Hospital grounds, near Patrick's Station.
    Jacob Hebrilge, G, 61st Pennsylvania.
    Jos. Zihes, K, 4th Vermont.
    Henry Cramer, K, 98th Pennsylvania.
    Henry C. Libby, C, 1st Maine.
    Jas. Cole, A, 77th N. Y.
    Corp. Jos. Grow, E, 11th Vermont.
    John Brazee, C, 93d Pennsylvania.
    Henry C. Hadley, D, 11th Vermont.
    Wm. S. Craft, A, 102d Pennsylvania.
    Nathan W. Lemmon, A, 61st Pennsylvania.
    —— Winegrove, — 102d Pennsylvania.

Geo. Fairbanks, D, 2d Vermont.
Sergt. A. D. Spaulding, E, 2d Vermont.
Frank Raber, F. 93d Pennsylvania.
Lieut. Jos. Whelpley, D, 1st Maine.
Capt. Samuel Oakley, I, 77th N. Y.
John Cronin, D, 43d N. Y.
Patrick Callahan, K, 122d N. Y.
Wm. Oliver, C, 5th Vermont.
Jas. Golth, A, 1st Maine.

Buried in 3d Div. Burying-ground, near Patrick's Station.
Corp. Henry O. Wing, K, 9th N Y.
Joshua Liuier, G, 67th Pennsylvania.
Corp. G. L. Britton, F, 9th N. Y.
Jacob R. Wolcott, B, 14th New Jersey
Wm. Birch, H, 151st N. Y.
Nelson Valentine, E, 9th N. Y.
Erastus Griswold, G, 9th N. Y.
Lieut. David H. Stone, F, 9th N. Y.
Amos Herns, F, 6th Maryland.
John Stine, I, 6th Maryland.
Jos. Roger, G, 126th Ohio.
Oliver Casler, E, 9th N. Y.
Wm. I. Merritt, G, 10th Vermont.
Godfrey Engle, D, 67th Pennsylvania.
David Gruber, A, 9th N. Y.
Denton Linehart, — 67th Pennsylvania.
Solomon Pencil, E, 67th Pennsylvania.
David L. Compt, A, 14th New Jersey.
Lucian Searle, A, 9th N. Y.
Wm. Williams, F, 122d Ohio.
O. Sergt. Michael Halloran, E, 6th Maryland.
Corp. Minor Marland, E, 122d Ohio.
Henry Henry, E, 67th Pennsylvania.
Michael Dwyer, C, 110th Ohio.
Jacob Schmidt. D, 110th Ohio.
Corp. W. W. Rand, C, 9th N. Y,
John H. Armstrong, H, 110th Ohio.
Avery Griffeth, E, 110th Ohio.
Jas. Easter, H, 67th Pennsylvania.
Jos. A. Smith, H, 10th Vermont.
John Smith, H, 10th Vermont.
Lieut. Kassey, — 87th Pennsylvania.
Corp. Christopher Kastler, I, 138th Pennsylvania.
Jos. J. Wallace, I, 9th N. Y.
Isaac N. Shoemaker, F, 9th N. Y.
Louis Teeter, A, 9th N. Y.

Buried about seven miles west of Burkesville, five rods west of John T. Branch's.
Lieut. C. Jackson, I, 148th N. Y.

Buried on Major Watson's Farm, four miles from Farmville.
Lieut. Cyrus Patton, G, 54th Pennsylvania.
David Cringle, G, 54th Pennsylvania.
Lieut. Geo. T. Davis, L, 4th Mass. Cav.

We repaired sixty-two graves, covering the graves deeper, and marking the graves thus repaired.

About three hundred and forty skeletons were buried in seven common graves. Nos. one and seven being to the left of Cold Harbor Road. Nos. two, three and four, between Cold Harbor and Quaker Roads. No. five, at the right of Quaker Road, and near the point where it turns to go to Kidd's Mills. No. six, to the right of Quaker Road, on the Gaines' Mills Battle-field, about half a mile from Stewart's house.

We have the following, which may furnish some clue to the identification of a few persons:

A number of envelopes, a few of each directed as follows.

> Andrew Acker, Tonawanda, Erie Co., N. Y.
> Gregory Kerberger, East Amherst, Erie Co., N. Y.
> Peter Pauley, East Amherst, Erie Co., N. Y.
> Thos. Cook, East Carlton, Orleans Co., N. Y.

Graves at Bermuda Hundred.

> John Wyegle, A, 1st Mass. Cav.
> Col. Boston Martin, — 2d Maryland
> I. Weaver, A, 39th U. S. C.
> I. Perry, ———
> I. Harold, Col'd., died Feb. 5th.
> C. Zimmers, ——— 4th U. S. C. T.
> John Furgerson, E, 8th North Carolina.
> Chas. Bedee, C, 118th N. Y.
> Daniel Lovejoy, D, 9th Vermont.
> Samuel Graff, K, 76th Pennsylvania.
> Julius L. Parsons, A, 1st Conn. Bat.
> Jos. Robinson, — 11th Conn. Bat.
> Benj. P. Jones, — 40th Massachusetts.
> Fernando Nichols, Col'd., 2d M. Dept.
> Isaac Balm.
> Gabriel Banbria, 2d M. Dept.
> W. Wiggins, ——— 2d M. Dept.
> W. Hammond, D, 29th Conn.
> D. White, ——— 2d M. Dept.
> Thos. Williams, G, 45th U. S. C. T.
> Major Jacocks, ——— 2d M. Dept.
> Jim Edwards, 2d M. Dept.
> Doctor Mullen, 2d M. Dept.
> Corp. R. Offord, — 30th U. S. C. T.
> Harry Stanton, 2d M. Dept.
> I. H. Jones, (colored.)
> W. M. Golden, ———

Lieut. Chas G. Ward, 29th Mass.
Lieut. Edgar Clough, 24th Mass.
Asa G. Merrill, C, 9th Maine.
C. H. Harrington, A, 30th Maine.
John Sheckles, A, 1st Md. Cav.
Sergt. Cornelius Hill, B, 149th Ohio.
Wm. Saston, I, 98th N. Y.
John Jobbs, — 148th Ohio.
Lieut. S. C. Scott, E, 149th Ohio.
Eli W. Hall, G, 148th Ohio.
Geo. Tyson, 1st Md. Cav.
H. S. Simmons, D, 9th Maine.
Wm, Taylor, H, 142d N. Y.
A. I. Huff, — 203d Pennsylvania.
C. Hill, 148th Ohio.
Wm. Atkinson, 148th Ohio.

Between Bermuda Hundred and Jones' Landing, north of Road.
Wm. Warren, D, 10th Conn.
Chas. White, ——
Daniel Anderson, A, 116th U. S. C. T.
Henry Mattox, G, 116th U. S. C. T.
Edward Porter, Bangor, Maine.
Jas. B. Norton, D, 2d Pa. Art.
Jas. Coffee, C, 118th U. S. C. T.
Hawkins Whetzel, B, 118th U. S. C. T.
I. Whetzel, B, 118th U. S. C. T.
Thos. Williams, — 45th U. S. C. T.

South of Road.
I. Fishbey, G, 27th U. S. C. T.
Thos. Henry, C, 6th U. S. C. T.
I. Monroe, G, 45th U. S. C. T.
A. Owens, — 107th U. S. C. T.
E. Wabbs, — 114th U. S. C. T.
M. Wadhams, C, 39th Illinois.
I. Black, — 17th N. Y. Art.

Jones' Landing, Kautz Cav. Hospital.
David Hart, E, 11th Pa. Cav.
S. Hawkenberry, E, 11th Pa. Cav.
Henry Ernet, D, 9th Md. Cav.
Jos. B. Wall, K, 11th Pa. Cav.
Warren Stearns, L, 20th N. Y. Cav.

Jones' Landing, Head of Neck.
Jas. E. Thayer, ——
Edwin Hillman, U. S. Steamer Mendota.
Archibald Sims, U. S. Steamer Mackinaw.
W. Coltman, H, 9th U. S. C. T.
Henry Thompson, A, 29th Conn.
W. H. Kinlow, — 41st U. S. C. T.
W Weller, C, 117th U. S. C. T.

Sergt. John Freeman, K, —— U. S. C. T.
Geo. Bigler, A, 41st U. S. C. T.
Robt. Cole, B, 29th Conn.
Hal. Perren, A, 117th U. S. C. T.
H. Brown, C, 117th U. S. C. T.
A. Arellianes, I, 118th U. S. C. T.
Moses Morse, I, 29th Conn.
Benj. Disham, K, 118th U. S. C. T.
Alex. Trout, D, 127th U. S. C. T.
Reaf. Dunn, E, 37th U. S. C. T.
Henry Floyd, B, 7th U. S. C. T.
Wm. Fowler, C, 29th U. S. C. T.
Jacob Davis, D, 37th U. S. C. T.
Chas. B. Starr, C, 29th Conn.
Henry Walker, F, 45th Ohio.
Still Mason, — 4th U. S. C. T.
John Deamy, I, 11th Pennsylvania Cav.
J. J. Mills, A, 29th Conn.
Frederick Griffin, E, 9th U. S. C. T.
Frank Doll, G, 16th N. Y. H. A.
Sigmud Stutell, L, 5th Pennsylvania Cav.
I. Deem, — 16th N. Y. H. A.
C. H. Stevens, D, 4th New Hampshire.
John Card, F, 16th N. Y. H. A.
Wm. Harnish, D, 203d Pennsylvania.
Morris Snill, K, 76th Pennsylvania.
John Shau, F, 16th N. Y. H. A.
Corp. W. Wilson, K, 112th N. Y.
Arthur I. Shau, F, 16th N. Y. H. A.
R. Munchmar, Bat. B, 1st U. S. Art.
Corp. Ephraim Lydeck, A, 2d Pennsylvania.
Jacob Maloney, A, 203d Pennsylvania.
Bernerd McGray, Bat. B, 4th New Jersey Art.
Fred'k Deuts, G, 203d Pennsylvania.
Jacob Eman, K, 199th Pennsylvania.
Saml. M. Howell, B, 1st South Carolina.
Smith Travis, E, 115th N. Y.
Thos. C. Colman, I, 11th Pennsylvania Cav.
Henry H. Kelley, E, 206th Pennsylvania.
Wm. Fosmire, F, 16th N. Y. H. A.
Franklin Doan, C, 11th Pennsylvania Cav.
John Reader, A, 127th U. S. C. T.
John McGill, H, 45th U. S. C. T.
Chas. Creoil, A, 4th U. S. C. T.
Wm. G. Nellus, B, 29th Connecticut.
Jas. Fitz Cimmons, A, 10th Connecticut.
Saml. Pace, A, 9th Maine.
Leonard Koenig, E, 199th Pennsylvania.
Lester Noble, D, 13th Indiana.
S. S. Gamble, C, 206th Pennsylvania.
Chas. H. Wooley, "Schooner O. H. Booth."

W. H. McHose, N, 16th N. Y. H. A.
W. Leville, D, 7th New Hampshire.
Jas. W. Long, F, 5th Pennsylvania Cav.
Thos. Welch, E, 3d N Y. Cav.
Jas. Wilson, I, 11th Maine.
Jos. E. Bunnell, E, 6th Connecticut.

Jones' Landing near the Neck.

Geo. Thomas, died April 9.
Wm. Robinson, —— 45th U. S. C. T.
R. Handerson, C, 116th U. S. C. T.
Edwd. Peters, C, 29th Connecticut.
Louis Tuck, D, 109th U. S. C. T.
Thos. Mauley, I, 7th U. S. C. T.
G. Dickson, K, 45th U. S. C. T.
Henry Morman, A, 117th U. S. C. T.
John Ramsden.
Geo. Sanders, K, 116th U. S. C. T.
Sergt. Jas. Smith, B, 29th Connecticut.
Eliza Bonnell (colored).
Corp. Bose Brooks, A, 109th U. S. C. T.
Chas. Bacon, K, 9th Maine.
Chas. Frances, A, 16th N. Y. H. A.
Jas. Yates, B, 16th N. Y. H. A.
Jas. Brown, M, 16th N. Y. H. A.
Benj. Johnson, D, 203d Pennsylvania.
Eli Thompson, B. 3d N. Y.
E. McEmory, E, 199th Pennsylvania.
Michael O'Brien, D, 3d New Hampshire.
Thos. G. Pease, B, 117th N. Y.
Corp. Thos. Polla—, G, 16th N. Y. Art.
Chas. E. Hevener, I, 117th N. Y.
Jas. Fountain, B, 16th N. Y. H. A.
Wesley Bennet, A, 112th N. Y.
John Rouser, A, 5th Pennsylvania Cav.
John C. Richards, G, 11th Pennsylvania.
Thos. Lynn, —— 9th Maine.
Jacob Hansom, E, 67th Ohio.
Silas Woodward, —— 9th Vermont.

At the James' Farm, 1½ miles W. Jones' Landing.

G. W. Hanrey, I, 4th New Hamphsire.
Sergt. Dougherty, H, 16th Pennsylvania.
Sergt. A. B. Nichols, D, 7th Connecticut.
Wm. Watson, ——, 75th Pennsylvania.
Jos. Lenosh, D, 169th N. Y.
H. Bromley, A, 142d N. Y.
H. C. Cleveland, F, 142d N. Y.
Saml. Chapman, E, 4th New Hampshire.
John Halleham, A, 43d N. Y.
Alf. Kellogg, G, 10th Connecticut.
Sergt. G. Edwards, G, 7th Connecticut.

Thos. Wishart, C, 17th N. Y.
John Merrit.
Jas. Orcutt, I, 117th N. Y.
John M. Gant, C, 13th Indiana. ⎫
Jonathan Gouser, B, 13th Indiana. ⎪
Wm. Kebathkey, H, 13th Indiana. ⎬ One grave.
John Gohan, B, 13th Indiana.   ⎪
Sergt. S. Martin, A, 3d Indiana. ⎭
Henry H. Homan, K, 40th Massachusetts.
Lieut. W. C. Casselman, C, 117th N. Y.
W. H. Davis, F, 117th N. Y.

Yard near Turner's House, East Butler's Hd. Qrs.

Peter Jones, I, 37th U. S. C. T.
Henry Myers, E, 117th U. S. C. T.
H. Johnson, C, 6th U. S. C. T.
Thos. Adams, G, 107th U. S. C. T.
I. McLane, G, 118th U. S. C. T.
C. H. Tickenor, A, 118th U. S. C. T.
Frank W. Barr, K, 31st U. S. C. T.
A. Vesne, I, 107th U. S. C. T.
W. Calvin, I, 43d U. S. C. T.
John Moore, I, 23d U. S. C. T.
Silas Slout, E, 109th U. S. C. T.
Thos. Parish, A, 117th U. S. C. T.
Thos. Clay, E, 116th U. S. C. T.
Chas. Clark, ——— U. S. C. T.
Jackson Rucker, E, 117th U. S. C. T.
Ben Merrill, E, 117th U. S. C. T.
John Tyler, — 30th U. S. C. T.
S. Glentry, — 116th U. S. C. T.
L. P. Mundy, I, 116th U S C T
John Hicks, I, ——— U S. C. T.
H. Lewis, ——— U. S. C. T.
Sergt. G. Griffin, K, 7th U. S. C. T.
B. W. Sewille, ——— U. S. C. T.
I. Hayden, — 38th U. S. C. T.
I. Trivet, B, 117th U. S. C. T.
I. Cugsby, C, 10th U. S. C. T.
John Woods, G. 118th U. S. C. T.
R. Kennedy, — 117th U. S. C. T.
Sergt. E. Graves, I, 116th U. S. C. T.
Wm. Moore, G, 30th U. S. C. T.
Fred Brown, I, 1st U. S. C. T.
Nathl. Smith, B, 39th U. S. C. T.
Saml. Cheatem, C, 107th U. S. C. T.
Stephen Posey, E, 118th U. S. C. T.
Cowell Moore, D, 43d U. S. C. T.
S. Nelson, K, 27th U. S. C. T.
Byron Cox, I, 37th U. S. C. T.
Corp. I. Wilson, E, 8th U. S. C. T.

Owen Holmes, H, 37th U. S. C. T.
Robt. Rawson, H, 37th U. S. C. T.

Near Turner's House: near Butler's Head Quarters.

Stephen Owens, F, 38th U. S. C. T.
H. F. Brown, F, 2d U. S. C. T.
Jas. Procter, C, 118th U. S. C. T.
B. Mag——te, K, 107th U. S. C. T.
G. Shackle, B, 118th U. S. C. T.
H. Taylor, B, 2d U. S. C. T.
S. Brimmer, K, 16th N. Y. H. A.
Wm. Stratton, D, 158th N. Y.
Edmund Williams, G, 36th U. S. C. T.
Thos. Burns, C, 158th N. Y.
John Gear, — 19th Virginia.
A. Erwin, G, 8th Maine.
Rudolph Warner, G, 8th Connecticut.
I. Oad——, ——
Thos. Fox, — 8th N. Y.
H. Curry, ——
Geo. Sawyer, A, 118th U. S. C. T.
—— Brooker, —, 107th U. S. C. T.
Chas. Edino, D, 148th N. Y.

Aiken's Landing ——

A. Gilmon, — 2d Maryland Cav.

Cox's House, two miles from Dutch Gap.

I. C. C. Jones, Bat. A, 1st Pa. Art., Sept. 29th, 1864.
Levi Adams, ——

At Dutch Gap.

Thos. McDonald, Iron Clad "Onondaga," May 22d, 1864.

Deep Bottom.

Albert Baker, M, 37th N. Y.
Henry Mader, A, 1st Maryland Cav.
Sergt. Wm. Pelton, H, 1st Maryland Cav.
Corp. W. E. Darcy, — 48th N. Y.
Jas. Griffing, A, 10th Connecticut.
Michael Fitzgerald, K, 158th N. Y.
Wraham, —— I, ——
Corp. Timothy I. Sullivan, H, 24th Massachusetts.
Wm. Michael, I, 158th ——
Capt. W. W. McB. Houston, I, 1st U S. C. T.
I. T. Bowley, I, 38th U. S. C. T.
Lewis Payne, I, 115th U. S. C. T.
Jerry Morse, G, 23d U. S. C. T.
J. M. Pepper, K, 97th Pennsylvania.
Nathaniel Gaspel, I, 116th U. S. C. T.
Henry Brown, F, 45th U. S. C. T.
Noble Hanson, H, 7th U. S. C. T.
Jack Meiley, E, 115th U. S. C. T.

Peter Dorus, G, 127th U. S. C. T.
Hudson K. Dyer, D, 11th Maine.
Phineas Jersey, F, 114th U. S. C. T.
Jos. Phœnix, K, 117th U. S. C. T.
Alfred Dudley, D, 119th U. S. C. T.
Sergt. Jas. Dewy, I, 142d N. Y.

On road from Pt. Rocks, to Richmond and Petersburg Pike.
Wm. C. McBride, 3d U. S. Infantry.

Near Friend's House, at Drury's Bluff.
Sergt. G. P., K, 118th N. Y.
—— Shaw, B, 76th Pennsylvania.
Wm. Denning, E, 76th Pennsylvania.

Back of New Market Station.
Jas. Gilmore, B, 1st U. S. Art.
Robt. C. Harden, died March 16th, 1865.
Saml. A. Simmons, K, 7th New Hampshire.
—— Holstein, A, 7th New Hampshire.
Geo. P. Hoyt, C, 7th New Hampshire.
Jas. Dinger, N, 16th N. Y. H. A.

Clapin's Farm Burying-ground.
W. Dawry, G, 117th U. S. C. T.
H. F. Bevans, I, 2d U. S. C. T.
J. Smith, died December 5th.

Two hundred rods east Fort Burnham, or Harrison.
B. J. Anderson, C, 23d, U. S. C. T.
Jas. Bigot, R, 96th N. Y.

Two hundred rods N. E. Fort Burnham, or Harrison.
Saml. Van Auken, C, 21st C. V.
Cyrus Johnson, D, 41st U. S. C. T.
Jas. Loper, E, 41st U. S. C. T.

Three quarters of a mile east Fort Burnham, at Henry's Station.
Sergt. W. H. Sipe, I, 188th Pennsylvania.
John A. Carson, H, 188th Pennsylvania.

One mile east Fort Burnham, Field Hospital, 24th A. C.
Robt. Van Fleming, E. 67th Ohio.
L. F. Farnsworth, F, 10th New Hampshire.
Jas. Yougher, G, 158th N. Y.
Chas. Kerr, A, 199th Pennsylvania.
J. Grant, A, 7th New Hampshire.
J. F. Randall, F, 142d N. Y.
L. Woodruff, I, 7th Connecticut.
Richard Fite, A, 199th Pennsylvania.
L. Heffinn, H, 5th Maryland.
Geo. Golden, G, 123d Ohio.
Daniel Smith, I, 9th Maine.
Benj. Aney, H, 199th Pennsylvania.

John R. Strong, — 62d Ohio.
Jas. W. Wilkins, D, 206th Pennsylvania.
L. Bachelor, H, 127th U. S. C. T.
A. Burroughs, E, 41st U. S. C. T.
Richard Gerrard, F, 116th U. S. C. T.
Corp. F. Parslow, I, 3d N. Y.
Corp. W. I. Hart, B, 112th N. Y.
Corp. W. Lock, C, 3d N. Y.
Wm. Gillen, ———
Philetus Park, E, 142d N. Y.
Chas. A. Burr, A, 67th Ohio.
Arthur Smith, — 7th ——
Sergt. D. A. Fletcher, B, 12th W. Va.
John Dennis, I, 116th Ohio.
S. Maxin, K, 9th Maine.
F. Dwyer, C, 9th Vermont.
I. Fink, I, 9th Vermont.
A. Smith, G, 7th Connecticut.

SAILOR'S CREEK LIST

The following list of graves in this part of the field—S. W. of Richmond, has been furnished by Rev. J. B. Perry, Chaplain 10th Vt. Regt.

Dead at Sailor's Creek.

Thos. J. Partridge, H, 37th Mass.
Chas. A. Wade, B, 2d R. I.
Chas. C. Vanalstein, G, 5th Wis.
Edwd. Merley, A, 37th Mass.
Henry Luce, E, 37th Mass.
Chas. Spellman, K, 37th Mass.
Geo. Shay, G, 121st N. Y.
Jas. R. Gaily, F, 67th Pa.
John McElroy, G, 2d R. I.
Gideon Beard, G, 93d Pa.
Chas. M. Bailey, E, 1st Maine Cav.
D. E. Wise, I, 4th Pa. Cav.
John Keas, I, 4th Pa. Cav.
Corp. Norris ——, H, 121st N. Y.
Edwin Lewis, I, 121st N. Y.
Jas. Sherman, G, 121st N. Y.
Wm F. Leggett, F, 37th Mass.
Timothy Muller, K, 37th Mass.
[Henry] Messenger, B, 47th Mass.
Geo. Swab, D, 67th Pa.
Jos. Shyenberger, K, 87th Pa.
L. Wm. Myers, K, 87th Pa.
Lieut. Wm. Perry, F, 2d R. I.
Corp. Morris E. Hinkle, A, 138th Pa.
Sergt. Calvin Cain, C, 49th Pa.
Saml Wolf, G, 49th Pa.
Jas. Ambrose, C, 49th Pa.
Sgt. Maj. Jas. R. Hackenburg, —— 49th Pa.
C. Vanalstine, G, 5th Wis.
John McElroy, A, 2d R. I.
Corp. A. Johnson, C, 5th Wis.
Danl. H. May, H, 82d Pa.
G. Beards, G, 95th Pa.
Geo. Shay, 121st N. Y.
J. D. Gurnee, E, 5th Wis.
Chas. Blakeslee, C, 37th Mass.
Sergt. G. Purdy, D, 5th Wis.
T. J. Cartridge, D, 10th Ga.

The following are buried at New Grounds, *Danville*.

John Heller, —— 95th P. V. D. May 5th, '65.
Jos. Richardson, B, 4th N. Y. D. May 6th, '65.
Isaiah Shultz, C, 98th P. V. D. May 6th, '65.
Jos. Erman, A, 102d P. V. D. May 5th, '65.
Adam Ost, D, 77th N. Y. D. April 30th, '65.
W. H. Cook, —— 9th N. Y. H. A. D. May 7th, '65.
Michael Madigan, —— 110th Ohio D. May 3d, '65.
Johnston Harless, H, 110th Ohio D. May 3d, '65.
Corp. Sylv. B. Ball, K, 10th Vt. D, May 5th, '65.

Buried at Burkesville Junction, Va.

G. Seeman, H, 155th N. Y. D. April 7th, '65.
D. R. White, K, 8th P. V. D. April 11th, '65.
Lieut. Finney, —— 6th Mich. Cav. ——
Saml. T. Read, Ord's Staff, —— D, April 6th, '65.
Corp. D. Keecher, B, 54th P. V. D. April 9th, '65.
W. H. Ribbans, I, 1st N. J. Cav. D. April 11th, '65.
Pat Sullivan, D, 10th N. Y. D. April 13th, '65.
Capt. — Hodges, —— 4th Mich. Cav. K. April 6th, '65.
W. J. Parrish, E, 25th Va. Bat. D. April 13th, '65.
Sergt. Saml. Freer, E, 2d N. Y. H. A.'——
Henry A. Evans, E, 1st Maine H. A. ——
Saml. Berry, F, 9th P. V. D. April 7th, '65.
Capt. H. H. Darby, E, 64th N. Y. ——
Sergt. Wm. B. Osman, G, 49th P. V. ——
Jas. Jerville, I, 86th P. V. ——
Wm. Sculley, K, 188th N. Y. ——
Capt. — Harris, C. S. A. *Philip's Legion*, D. April 13th, '65.
Eugene Lawson, F, 5th N. Y. D. April 9th, '65.
Capt. John Bond, B, 81st P. V. D. April 7th, '65.
Capt. Chas. Wilson, A, 81st P. V. D. April 7th, '65.
Josiah Minie, B, 26th Mich. D. April 7th, '65.
Saml. Ross, B, 82d P. V. D. April 7th, '65.
Corp. Harvey Cuberson, F, 57th P. V. D. April 7th, '65
L. C. Brigham, C, 35th Mich. ——
John M. Moore, Chapin's Bluff, Va. April.
Corp. Jas. Mansall, E, 2d R. I. D. April 8th, '65.
Chas. Jupper, F, 2d R. I. D. April 8th, 65.
Jas. E. Wade, B, 2d R. I. D, April 8th, '65.
Sergt. E. P. Cowles, D, 37th Mass. D. April 9th, '65.
Sergt. D. B. Miller, A, 37th Mass. D. April 9th, '65
Erastus Smart, A, 82d P. V. D. April 8th, '65.
John Griffeth, C, 49th P. V. D. April 8th, '65.
J. Reardon, B, 5th Wis. D. April 9th, '65.
Corp. J. Dewey, C, 49th P. V. D. April 10th, '65.
E. W. Carver, D, 2d Conn. H. A. D. April 5th, '65
—— Hinkleman, K, 7th N. Y. ——
J. H. Comins, K, 30th N. C. ——

Register of Deaths at Camp Lawton, Millin, Ga.

1864-5.

In the hasty evacuation of Savannah by the rebels in Dec., 1864, there was left behind a small box of blank books connected with the Medical Department of Camp Lawton. One of these books contained the "Death Register" of the Rebel Prison above named. A Presbyterian Clergyman cut out the leaves containing the list of the dead and brought them to the Christian Commission. This valuable MS. has since been deposited by the Commission in the national archives at Washington.

The numbers given probably refer to the order in which the graves were dug. If so the bodies may be identified by the corresponding number marked upon the graves at Millin.

1. Unknown.
2. Chas. Garlock 117th N. Y.
3. William Rice, T, 6th Reg. Maine.
4. R. Rankin, D, 10th Reg. Vermont.
5. Chas. Seigel, I, 74th Reg. Pennsylvania.
6. Chas. Seigel, D, 64th Reg. N. Y.
7. Loven Cox, G, 24th Reg. N. Y. Cav.
8. Unknown.
9. Amount Day, A, 9th Reg. Minnesota.
10. Unknown.
11. Amos Brown. (Unknown.)
12. J. Mayor, K, 2d N. Y. Cav.
13. A. L. M. Claun, I, 118th Pennsylvania.
14. T. Kenon, ——, 164th N. Y.
15. Frederick Haker, C, 19th Massachusetts.
16. Unknown.
17. A. Atfield, C, 11th Kentucky.
18. J. Saxmen, F, 13th Vermont.
19. H. Carver, E, 184th Pennsylvania.
20. C. Hathfield, D, 11th Kentucky.
21. Francis Daily, B, 11th Connecticut.
22. G. Grech, D, 11th Massachusetts.
23. C. Crumford. (Unknown.)
24. Denis Doeld, A, 11th U. S. I.

25. J. Day, C, 4th U. S. I.
26. W. Cathcart, H, 4th Pennsylvania Cav.
27. P. Fergurson, K, 4th Vermont.
28. J. Navilligan, K, 122d N. Y.
29. G. Chapman, I, 27th Massachusetts.
30. I. Humell, F, 95th Reg. Ohio.
31. Levi Geahart, T, 113th Reg. Illinois.
32. I. Brow, H, 11th Heavy Art.
33. T. Martingale, C, 11th Vermont.
34. J. Beam, E, 35th New Jersey.
35. Unknown.
36. Barnard Donohue, A, 90th Illinois.
37. C. Danen, D, 9th Minnesota.
38. W. H. Grinder, G, 14th Pennsylvania Cav.
39. J. J. Monks, M, 16th N. Y. Cav.
40. John Ringold, B, 93d Indiana.
41. J. Sullivan, M, 16th Illinois Cav.
42. E. Meachan, K, 27th Massachusetts.
43. Unknown.
44. Wm. Ridneer, F, 118th Pennsylvania.
45. A. Mayer, A, 27th Massachusetts.
46. D. Reed, A, 16th Ohio.
47. W. H. Goff, G, 76th N. Y.
48. C. Cechum, G, 81st Illinois.
49. C. Evans, B, 5th Connecticut.
50. James Wilson, H, 3d N. Y. Cav.
51. C. F. Riley, F, 1st Massachusetts H. Art.
52. Unknown.
53. L. Mason, D, 4th N. Y. H. Art.
54. G. W. Cochran, B, 16th Ohio.
55. Thos. Armitage, H, 9th Minnesota.
56. B. Gardner, H, 2d Pennsylvania.
57. M. Dunn, D, 4th Ohio.
58. R. Dufer, A, 55th Pennsylvania.
59. C. S. Smith, C, 57th Massachusetts.
60. G. D. Jordan, B, 17th Connecticut.
61. W. H. Ehrit, F, 49th Pennsylvania.
62. Ingersoll, I, 1st Massachusetts H. A.
63. I. Day, H, 27th Massachusetts.
64. N. S. Clarke, G, 1st Rhode Island Cav.
65. G. H. Arnold, K, 95th N. Y.
66. Wm. H. Stockman, K, 11th Vermont.
67. F. Powers, D, 1st Vermont Cav.
68. T. Flood, I, 4th New Hampshire.
69. Sergt. And. Galvin, H, 42d N. Y.
70. Corp. Wm. J. Thompson, M, 7th Tenn. Cav.
71. F. Allen, I, 2d Tenn. Cav.
72. John Hanley, I, 14th Connecticut.
73. T. Filben, F, 7th Connecticut.
74. R. S. Joiner, F, 18th Massachusetts.
75. D. Irvingpower, 11th Pennsylvania Cav.

76. D. S. Slausan, B, 7th Connecticut.
77. C. Wirtchood, M, 13th Pennsylvania.
78. Corp. Chas. Reed, E, 24th N. Y.
79. A. Collins, I, 27th Massachusetts.
80. John Straney, H, 113th Illinois.
81. Wm. Fitzgerald, A, 1st Michigan Cav.
82. John O'Neal, A, 4th U. S. Infantry.
83. John Donnell, F, 14th Connecticut.
84. J. Ferguson, E, 15th Wisconsin.
85. A. Curry, B, 140th Pennsylvania.
86. B. Potts, D, 140th Pennsylvania.
87. Corp. A. Johnson, I, 54th N. Y.
88. R. Kantanel, 18th U. S.
89. T. C. Devit, F, 4th U. S.
90. J. V. M'Kown, F, 1st Massachusetts H. A.
91. G. Murray, F, 83d Indiana Infantry.
92. W. D. Rossett, C, 7th Tenn. Cav.
93. J. W. Coleman, F, 124th Indiana Infantry.
94. Jos. Albrin, I, 7th N. Y. H. A.
95. Sangas Donald, G, 33d New Jersey Infantry.
96. A. Harst, I, 140th N. Y. Infantry.
97. A. Ames, C, 9th Minnesota Infantry.
98. G. Marshall, I, 55th Pennsylvania Infantry.
99. S. Spiker, B, 16th Ohio Infantry.
100. J. Widdigar, I, 71st Pennsylvania.
101. Edward Moony, A, 1st Indiana Art.
102. P. Fink, A, 110th Pennsylvania Infantry.
103. Unknown.
104. Unknown.
105. Unknown.
106. Neil Boyd, E, 7th Missouri Infantry.
107. W. F. Mooney, F, 103d Pennsylvania Infantry.
108. —— Dernont, 72d Michigan Infantry.
109. N. Meisinhelder, H, 8th Ohio Infantry.
110. L. Baxter, A, 22d N. Y. Cav.
111. I. S. Ward, I, 7th Tenn. Infantry.
112. J. Johnson, C, 11th Connecticut Infantry.
113. D. Strouse, B, 69th Pennsylvania Infantry.
114. W. Smith, C, 19th Minnesota Infantry.
115. A. J. Brower, E, 7th N. Y. Art.
116. Jesse Elkins, D, 31st Illinois Infantry.
117. E. F. Randall, K, 1st Massachusetts Cav.
118. J. E. Jewett, E, 6th Ohio Infantry.
119. Thomas Smith, G, 6th Wisconsin Infantry.
120. S. Dawson, E, 93d Indiana Infantry.
121. Unknown.
122. P. Hanbey. K, 72d Ohio Inf.
123. E. P. Phillips, I, 3d Maine Inf.
124. C. J. Williams, D, 2d Indiana Inf.
125. John Kenney, C, 93d N. Y. Inf.
126. J. R. Rogers, F, 2d Pennsylvania Art.

11

127. J. Rowe, G, 69th Pennsylvania Inf.
128. M. Abbott, C, 4th N. Y. Art.
129. I. Flyn, C, 73d Pennsylvania Inf.
130. T. Patton, E, 55th Pennsylvania Inf.
131. P. Dolan, G, 9th N. Y. Cav.
132. C. Moulard, B, 140th Pennsylvania Inf.
133. J. Roth, H, 9th Minnesota Inf.
134. F. Kemp, C, 33d Massachusetts Inf.
135. A. Tribby, B, 7th Ohio Cav.
136. Corp. J. C. Hemming, F, 16th Iowa Inf.
137. H. Blatz.
138. John T. Shepard, A, 10th Connecticut Inf.
139. Sergt. J. Cowls, E, 27th Massachusetts Inf.
140. Wm. Pasmer, K, 1st N. Y. Drag.
141. R. L. Preston, B, 7th Tennessee Cav.
142. I. P. Myracle, C, 7th Tennessee Cav.
143. Wm. Seely, B, 100d N. Y. Inf.
144. H. Feenig, B, 7th Connecticut Inf.
145. Unknown.
146. H. Druery, E, 56th Massachusetts Inf.
147. J. Rodman, H, 146th N. Y. Inf.
148. D. Fultersmith, B, 135th Ohio Inf.
149. Unknown.
150. Unknown.
151. W. Shambers, A, 5th U. S. Cav.
152. H. Dunn, B, 147th N. Y. Inf.
153. Chas. Stuart, C, 9th Minnesota Inf.
154. G. Fritz, A, 11th Connecticut Inf.
155. Adam Sibert, G, 15th Kentucky Inf.
156. R. Brady, D, 11th Tennessee Inf.
157. J. Sterling, A, 15th N. Y. Inf.
158. A. Mintzer, A, 72d Pennsylvania Inf.
159. David Elliott, A, 98th Ohio Inf.

October 26th.

160. Wm. Stump, F, 6th Kentucky Cav.
161. Corp. J. C. Irvin, H, 93d Pennsylvania Inf.
162. C. Tampeied, C, 7th Michigan Inf.
163. I. H. Baughman, E, 118th Pennsylvania Inf.
164. A. Risinger, E, 32d Indiana Inf.
165. Wm. H. Gherfelt, K, 111th Illinois Inf.
166. A. Engerman, C, 4th Kentucky Inf.
167. C. P. Bush, G, 91st Indiana Inf.
168. J. Gross, B, 11th Tennessee Cav.
169. Unknown.
170. J. H. Courtney, G, 111th Illinois Inf.
171. Abner Hungerford, D, 7th N. Y. H. A.
172. Sergt. Thompson Alexander, B, 5th Indiana Cav.
173. J. Brode, B, 110th Pennsylvania Inf.
174. M. E. Baird, E, 13th Tennessee Cav.
175. Sergt. Geo. Thompson, H, 1st N. Y. Cav.
176. Unknown.
177. Sergt. C. B. Kephart, D, 13th Tennessee Inf.

178. Unknown.
179. F. Siler, C, 15th N. Y. Inf.
180. A. M'Farlin, C, 89th Illinois Inf.
181. R. Dearbro, K, 51st Pennsylvania.
182. Unknown.
183. Unknown.
184. W. Q. White, G, 27th Massachusetts Inf.
185. M. Gilbert, K, 20th Connecticut Inf.
186. L. Bradon, C, 11th Tenn. Inf.
187. L. Martin, G, 53d Ohio Inf.
188. Geo. Patterson, C, 2d N. Y. Inf.
189. Thos. Clover, D, 42d N. Y. Inf.
190. G. M. Phelp, G, 3d New Hampshire Inf.
191. Geo. Stoly, A, 4th Kentucky Inf.
192. H. J. Kennedy, L, 6th Pennsylania Cav.
193. Unknown.
194. Corp. J. Berk, K, 1st U. S. Art.
195. W. A. Hessington, D, 111th N. Y. Inf.
196. H. C. Tidaback, G, 7th N. Y. Art.
197. Sergt. Saldon P. Quay, K, 7th U. S. Art.
198. A. Ameron, B, 7th Connecticut Inf.
199. S. H. Phelps, I, 27th Massachusetts.
200. H. Hilland, B, 86th N. Y. Inf.
201. P. Wasser, D, 59th N. Y. Inf.
202. Corp. L. A. Colman, B, 2d Maryland Inf.
203. Corp. John F. Day, L, 4th Massachusetts Cav.
204. W. I. Miller, K, 81st Illinois Inf.
205. Sergt. T. Wallace, G, 164th Inf.
206. Corp. V. D. Daly, L, 2d Pennsylvania Cav
207. M. Bishop, K, 24th Michigan Inf.
208. C. Nixon, A, 15th U. S. Inf.
209. Sergt. O. P. Nelson, I, 39th Illinois Inf.
210. Chas. Shoorod, A, 9th Minnesota Inf.
211. Jas. Miller, F, 113th Illinois Inf.
212. Peter M. Miller, D, —— Minnesota Inf.
213. I. Davis, D, 7th Connecticut Inf.
214. Unknown.
215. H. Slesser, C, 21th Pennsylvania.
216. E. Rudis, E, 9th Minnesota Inf.
217. C. A. Warren, F, 16th Maine Inf.
218. J. Hancock, D, 13th Tenn. Inf.
219. E. Knowse, F, 119th Pennsylvania Inf.
220. Thos. Lynch, D, 5th N. Y. Cav.
221. Unknown.
222. W. E. Owen, L, 1st Vermont Art.
223. G. W. Porter, H, 4th Ohio Inf.
224. C. F. Wilmont, D, 113th Illinois Inf.
225. P. Backer, B, 93d N. Y. Inf.
226. Unknown.
227. Corp. N. Walker, H, 7th Connecticut Inf.
228. D. Holly, K, 48th Illinois Inf.

229. J. Boyle, G, 26th Pennsylvania Inf.
230. Wm. Pendleton, C. 99th Illinois.
231. Unknown.
232. Corp. I. R. Thacker, B, 6th Tenn. Cav.
233. Unknown.
234. C. C. Besse, D, 7th Massachusetts Inf.
235. Unknown.
236. J. Brown, L, 13th Pennsylvania Cav.
237. E. Keech, I, 152d N. Y. Inf.
238. E. Nash, A, 9th N. Y. H. A.
239. J. M. Dennison, B, 1st N. Y. Drag.
240. Nelson Loveless, A, 111th Pennsylvania Inf.
241. Benj. Bowen, E, 128th Indiana Inf.
242. Unknown.
243. Sergt. A. Hersog, G, 9th Minnesota Inf.
244. J. Shutsman, C, 74th N. Y. Inf.
245. William Colvin, L, 1st U. S. Art.
246. Sergt. William Dunham, E, 8th Iowa Cav.
247. S. B. Drul, I, 1st New Hampshire Cav.
248. Orderly Sergt. Nathan Smith, K, 73d Pennsylvania Inf.
249. Stephen Richards. F, 7th Connecticut Inf.
250. B. Bruner, B, 72d Ohio Inf.
251. G. Hart, K, 7th Tennessee Inf.
252. G. P. Hoyt, C, 19th N. Y. Inf.
253. Wm. Gitchouse. K, 53d Illinois Inf.
254. H. Mansfield, A, 67th Ohio Inf.
255. J. Hooley, G, 2d Virginia Cav.
256. Adam Weeker, F, 37th Ohio Inf.
257. J. B. Northroup. G, 111th N, Y. Inf.
258. M. A. Stewart, E, 9th Minnesota Inf.
259. L. Twick.
260. M. G. Roberte, E, 89th Illinois Inf.
261. Orville Merrihew, D, 7th N Y. H. Art.
262. W. Watson, E, 6th N. Y. Cav.
263. W. Shutt, B, 135th Ohio Inf.
264. Unknown.
265. J. Arnald, D, 13th Indiana Inf.
266. Unknown.
267. W. T. Thayer, G, 24th Massachusetts Inf.
268. A. T. Brown, ——, 5th N. Y. Cav.
269. D. M. Oakley, D, 16th Kentucky Cav.
270. Peter Amey, H, 120th N. Y. Inf.
271. Corp. George E. Ganby, D, 4th Kentucky Inf.
272. W. H. Sweeny, ——— Tennessee Citizen.
273. A. Greealy, H, 2d U. S. Inf.
274. E. C. Moor, B, 100d N. Y. Inf.
275. Joshua Keller, F, 142d Pennsylvania Inf.
276. Charles F. Hurols, C, 118th Pennsylvania Inf.
277. Unknown.
278. L. Bender, F, 113th Illinois Inf.
279. W. F. Cline, G, 11th Pennsylvania Res.
280. W. R. Rick, C, 6th U. S. Cav.

281. J. Bassett, A, 12th U. S. Cav.
282. Unknown.
283. W. F. Sherman, C, 31st Maine Inf.
284. Sergt. J. Johnson, F, 14th West Virginia Inf.
285. William Deeren, G, 5th Indiana Cav.
286. A. Knouse, F, 149th Pennsylvania Inf
287. Unknown.
288. R. Condon, F, 2d N. Y. Cav.
289. P. Cromer, A, 55th Pennsylvania Inf.
290. Horace E. Wallace, D, 9th Minnesota Inf.
291. George H. Snivley, D, 16th Iowa Inf.
292. J. Hanafer, Bridger's Illinois Batt.
293. Lewis Bergman, E, 113th Illinois Inf.
294. R. C. Adams, E, 9th Virginia Inf.
295. Unknown.
296. John Auston, G, 36th Wisconsin Inf. .
297. Robert McLoughlin, B, 170th N. Y. Inf.
298. Jerm. Ackey, E, 51st Pennsylvania Inf.
299. Henry Parris, K, 9th Tennessee Cav.
300. Unknown.
301. Edward Rhodes, ——, 24th Massachusetts.
302. Unknown.
303. H. Gross, F, 1st Pennsylvania Cav.
304. Peter S. Halverson, D, 9th Minnesota Inf.
305. John McKey, D, 9th Minnesota Inf.
306. L. Graw, C, 61st Pennsylvania Inf.
307. P. Kurchner, D, 146th N. Y. Inf.
308. F. O. Webster, E, 9th Minnesota Inf.
309. Unknown.
310. Corp. A. Patton, B, 140th Pennsylvania Inf.
311. J. C. Roberts, F, 1st Pennsylvania Inf.
312. Jesse R. Flora, E, 45th Pennsylvania Inf.
313. James Colter, K, 20th Connecticut Inf.
314. J. H. Weater, L, 15th N. Y. Cav.
315. G. Ross, Citizen, Teamster.
316. Sergt. B. W. Cadwell, E, 113th Illinois Inf.
317. J. Holmes, A, 2d Pennsylvania H. Art.
318. J. Megent, B, 146th N. Y. Inf.
319. Thomas West, K, 2d Virginia Cav.
320. Augustus Wilbert, E, 113th Illinois Inf.
321. Thomas Lamont, H, 1st N. Y. Cav.
322. Uriah S. King, M, 1st Massachusetts H. Art.
323. Unknown.
324. Unknown.
325. R. Waits, E, 3d Tennessee Inf.
326. James Sirels, C, 30th Illinois Inf.
327. J. Crosby, I, 27th Massachusetts Inf.
328. W. C. Chapman, H, 7th N. Y. H. Art.
329. Unknown.
330. Sergt. I. S. Spear, F, 16th Iowa Inf.
331. W. Forest, D, 13th Indiana Inf.
332. G. Lolley, E, 5th New Hampshire Inf.

333. A. Summerville, D, 55th Pennsylvania Inf.
334. I. L. Purdy, G, 7th N. Y. H. Art.
335. J. Lewis, G, 2d Maryland Inf.
336. Unknown.
337. A. Knapp, ——, 12th Wisconsin Inf.
338. I. Hanagan, B, 7th N. Y. H. Art.
339. Eugene Alar, ——, 11th Connecticut Inf.
340. Corp. Walter V. Rider, E, 6th N. Y. Cav.
341. I. Waldon, D, 14th N. Y. Art.
342. Wm. Henderson, H, 2d Massachusetts Cav.
343. R. Swan, M, 2d Delaware Inf.
344. G. Detling, ——, 3d Indiana Cav.
345. J. Taytler, E, 140th Pennsylvania Inf.
346. Corp. E. Newhall, C, 22d Massachusetts Inf.
347. Unknown.
348. C. Peck, B, 117th N. Y. Inf.
349. R. Crosby, ——, 8th N. J. Inf.
350. Unknown.
351. Unknown.
352. Unknown.
353. Unknown.
354. L. D. Green, K, 1st U. S. Art.
355. D. Chadwick, I, 3d Maine Inf.
356. S. N. Chandler, C, 9th Minnesota Inf.
357. Martin Dunn, B, 164th Minnesota Inf.
358. E. P. Morton, H, 27th Massachusetts Inf.
359. J. Humphreys, F, 3d Pennsylvania Cav.
360. Unknown.
361. Unknown.
362. W. Mullins, D, 113th Ill. Inf.
363. Unknown.
364. Unknown.
365. Unknown.
366. Albert Harrington, —— —— Maine Inf.
367. Unknown.
368. R. Allen, B, 1st Wisconsin Art.
369. I. Hille, F, 4th Kentucky Inf.
370. Jas. Goodrich, H, 11th Vermont Inf.
371. Elias Goff, K, 7th Tenn. Cav.
372. Unknown.
373. David Moore, H, 39th N. Y. Inf.
374. R. W. Lehman, E, 118th Pennsylvania Inf
375. Unknown.
376. Unknown.
377. J. S. Scrone, K, 14th Illinois Inf.
378. Unknown.
379. Unknown.
380. Corp. M. Keller, B, 60th Ohio Inf.
381. L. Sweaney, Signal Corps.
382. Unknown.
383. M. Horn, K, 7th Pennsylvania.
384. Corp. W. Shumichen, E, 4th Massachusetts

385. R. C. Sawyer, E, 138th Ohio.
386. Unknown.
387. Sergt. S. D. Boyer, D, 118th Tenn.
388. Wm. Snyder, 2d Pennsylvania H. Art.
389. E. S. Wessie, H, 24th Massachusetts.
390. J. Thompson, K, 84th Pennsylvania.
391. Unknown.
392. Sergt. A. Hardy, G, 123d Illinois.
393. Philip Mous, G, 72d Ohio Inf
394. Charles Habor, I, 15th N. Y. H. A.
395. Unknown.
396. W. H. Barrett, E, 120th N. Y. Inf.
397. Unknown.
398. C. Launsbury, E, 39th N. Y. H. A.
399. Joseph Hatfield, C, 54th Ohio Inf.
400. Wm. H. Harrison, B, 18th Pennsylvania Inf.
401. W. Brigg, K, 96th N. Y. Inf.
402. Sergt. H. E. Peck, E, 1st Connecticut Cav.
403. Mathew Hines, I, 14th Indiana Inf.
404. Unknown.
405. Unknown.
406. Unknown.
407. J. King, H, 108th N. Y. Inf.
408. Sergt. R. H. Morris, E, 7th Tenn. Cav.
409. Lyman L. Stewart, F, 8th Maine Inf.
410. T. Baker, H, 40th N. Y. Inf.
411. Unknown.
412. J. Gaghigan, A, 5th Massachusetts Inf.
413. Unknown.
414. Unknown.
415. Unknown.
416. Unknown.
417. B. Buckley,C, 17th U. S. Inf.
418. Unknown.
419. Albert Couse, H, 63d N. Y. Inf.
420. Solomon Dunn, C, 6th Va. Cav.
421. W. Hazelett, K, 107th Pennsylvania Inf.
422. Unknown.
423. Unknown.
424. Unknown.
425. Unknown.
426. Henry B. Tobias, Battery, K, 1st H. A.
427. W. H. Stout, B, McLocran's Squadron.
428. Perry G. Amos, H, 14th Va.
429. Unknown.
430. Unknown.
431. J. Foley, F, 28th Mass.
432. Corp. E. Evitt, L, 3d N. Y. Cav.
433. Corp. A. R. White, —, 12th Kentucky Cav.
434. John Slidell, G, 95th Ohio.
435. D. Everett, H, 75th Ohio.
436. Unknown.

437. W. Cunningham, —, 1st Vt. Cav.
438. Unknown.
439. M. Koffman, E, 72d N. Y.
440. Unknown.
441. R. Anderson, H, 106th Penn.
442 Unknown.
443. George E. Eddy, E, 1st Mass. Heavy Art.
444. J. Jones, B, 105th Ill.
445. Sergt. W. R. Cassell, II, 17th Conn.
446. J. M. Baker, C, 15th Tenn.
447. Sergt. John Kenedey, E, 146th N. Y.
448. A. R. Whiting, H, 1st N. Y. Drag..
449. Unknown.
450. Unknown.
451. Unknown.
452. Thos. II Barrett, E, 103d Ohio.
453. Henry Bain, H, 7th Tenn. Cav.
454. James B. Harvy, D, 8th N. Y.
455. Stephen Williams, B, 152d Heavy Art.
456. Unknown.
457. O. D. Rhodes, C, 9th Minn.
458. Unknown.
459. John Hedleen, L, 5th N. Y. Cav.
460. Unknown.
461. B. Branch, I, 3d Maine.
462. Unknown.
463. Unknown.
464. David C. Cemline, C, 72d O. V. I.
465. Unknown.
466. Michael Kinna, B, 9th Minn.
467. Henry Howard, D, 6th N. Y.
468. Michael Kavnagh, G, 27th Mass.
469. Unknown.
470. W. Davenport, L, 1st Wis. Cav.
471. Unknown.
472. Unknown.
473. Unknown.
474. Sidney Battleson, L, 13th Penn. Cav
475. Unknown.
476. Unknown.
477. Leonard Cowles, D, 2d O. V. C.
478. Unknown.
479. Thomas Parker, C, 63d N. Y.
480. Unknown.
481. D. Smith, I, 3d Va. Cav
482. Unknown.
483. R. Adams, M, 1st N. Y. Cav.
484. James Throp, —, 4th Penn. Cav.
485. J. Jones, I, 7th Tenn. Cav.
486. Unknown.
487. Pat. Fox, D, 6th Conn.
488. M. Brown, C, 4th U. S. Inf.

INDEX.

☞ Only the surname is given in the index. The figures mark the pages on which the name appears.

A.

A——, 125.
Abbott, 32, 64, 127, 134, 162.
Abraham, 62.
Acker, 149.
Ackerman, 75, 108.
Ackey, 165.
Ackland, 77.
Ackle, 68.
Ackley, 40, 129.
Adams, 13, 19, 36, 44, 45, 46, 49, 63, 67, 81, 85, 88, 102, 112, 118, 122, 128, 142, 143, 153, 165, 168.
Adcloser, 6.
Adder, 68.
Addis, 123.
Addison, 21, 91.
Addlespont, 40.
Adkins, 35.
Aeberle, 127.
Agan, 85.
Ageye, 67.
Ahein, 126.
Aiken, 86.
Aikens, 47.
Aker, 101.
Akin, 38.
Akins, 31.
Aklee, 36.
Akres, 128.
Alar, 166.
Albert, 20.
Albren, 161.
Albus, 88.
Aldred, 21.
Aldrich, 71, 85.
Alexander, 62, 97.
Alfred, 62.
Alison, 17.
Alkinson, 144.
Allbright, 81.

Allen, 7, 12, 17, 25, 26, 29, 30, 34, 44, 46, 50, 59, 74, 85, 88, 101, 101, 105, 112, 122, 129, 139, 160, 166.
Allenback, 100.
Allenmange, 21.
Alonzo, 79.
Althorp, 100.
Althoff, 100.
Alts, 5.
Alwine, 102.
Alwines, 72.
Ambrose, 157.
Ameron, 163.
Ames, 140, 161.
Amey, 164.
Amidon, 137.
Amie, 31.
Amob, 40.
Amos, 167.
Anderson, 21, 25, 26, 30, 41, 44, 45, 49, 51, 54, 55, 97, 131, 150, 155, 168.
Andrew, 37.
Andrews, 139.
Aney, 155.
Anes, 50.
Ankerson, 116.
Ansell, 93, 144.
Ant, 82.
Anthony, 8, 44, 114.
Anty, 57.
Apal, 128.
Aple, 62.
Applegate, 18.
Applin, 106.
Archer, 98, 105.
Arcry, 26.
Aremy, 137.
Arellianes, 151.
Armalar, 91.
Armitage, 160.
Armstrong, 9, 49, 67, 73, 92, 94, 112, 148.

Arnold, 16, 66, 72, 83, 84, 160, 164.
Arrance, 112.
Arrent, 108.
Arters, 51.
Arthurs, 20.
Artush, 110.
Asay, 32.
Ash, 64.
Ashbrook, 20, 26, 47.
Ashem, 136.
Asher, 7, 47.
Ashford, 5.
Ashley, 49.
Askey, 47.
Asnew, 9.
Asobson, 90.
Aspforth, 80.
Askinburg, 16.
Aspinal, 108.
Aspeler, 41.
Assar, 7.
Atfield, 159.
Atherton, 108, 114.
Atheson, 56.
Atkins, 101.
Atkinson, 44, 79, 140, 150.
Attick, 30.
Attrey, 64.
Atwater, 42.
Atwood, 90, 91, 105.
Auchler, 62.
Audley, 78.
Aurell, 85.
Austin, 21, 29, 48, 60, 88, 98, 165.
Aurand, 109.
Auther, 134.
Avery, 43, 66.
Average, 49.
Averil, 69.
Averill, 147.
Ayers, 73, 99.
Ayres, 34.

A

B.

Baatman, 119.
Babb, 74.
Babcock, 19, 38, 130, 136.
Babbitt, 36.
Baber, 98.
Bachelor, 156.
Backett, 88.
Bachman, 38.
Badenschaatz, 108.
Bailey, 33, 46, 46, 46, 54, 61, 69, 70, 72, 76, 100, 101.
Baird, 49, 102, 118, 162.
Baissey, 47.
Baker, 9, 32, 39, 42, 53, 59, 63, 73, 81, 107, 110, 131, 141.
Bakeman, 98, 110.
Ballard, 123.
Bain, 92, 168.
Balby, 86.
Baldwin, 28, 28, 74, 75.
Ballinger, 93.
Balcom, 60.
Balkett, 45.
Ballett, 46.
Ball, 11, 67, 153.
Ballieu, 29.
Balm, 149.
Banch, 58.
Bancroft, 77, 104.
Bankell, 47.
Banks, 48, 50, 52, 55.
Bande, 52, 58.
Banker, 105.
Banderson, 108.
Bangs, 81.
Bankhard, 80.
Bartlett, 6, 21, 26, 41, 134, 136, 139.
Barnard, 7.
Barnet, 21, 147, 38, 39.
Barber, 19, 113, 133.
Barnesley, 23.
Bartha, 22.
Barnhart, 26, 35.
Barden, 27.
Barston, 15.
Barnes, 18, 20, 32, 45, 48, 58, 65, 74, 80, 84, 87, 97, 118, 120, 125, 133, 143.
Barthick, 34.
Barney, 45, 55.
Barrett, 45, 57, 63, 102, 167, 168.
Barker, 49, 91, 105, 105, 114, 123, 127.

Barren, 56
Baring, 102.
Barich, 103.
Barton, 104, 64.
Barrington, 66.
Barpee, 70.
Barr, 72, 153.
Barry, 73, 88, 107.
Barrows, 121.
Bartholomew, 10.
Barskey, 43.
Barkholder, 82.
Bartsuff, 95.
Barver, 113.
Barlleman, 119.
Bass, 42.
Bassett, 36, 165.
Bascy, 54.
Bates, 33, 81.
Battleson, 168.
Baughman, 162.
Bauer, 133.
Baunters, 135.
Baxter, 54, 74, 100, 161.
Baynard, 55.
Bavser, 74.
Bealman, 66.
Beal, 92, 98.
Beardsley, 7.
Beach, 12, 111, 112, 136.
Beath, 17.
Beaty, 34.
Beasley, 43.
Beablehimer, 107.
Beacraft, 121.
Beaumont, 120.
Beard, 50, 110, 157.
Beards, 157.
Beam, 160.
Bean, 35, 57, 60, 68, 106.
Beckwith, 114.
Beck, 122, 123.
Beebe, 85.
Beem, 15.
Beech, 73.
Beekman, 97.
Beddick, 13.
Bedford, 43.
Beber, 92.
Bedee, 149.
Bedford, 43.
Befurt, 129.
Behm, 127.
Beirce, 70.
Bell, 9, 10, 47, 48, 50, 50, 56, 61, 61, 65, 76, 103, 109, 112, 123, 124.
Bellows, 9, 115.
Belty, 14.
Bellinger, 41.

Beller, 44.
Belcher, 83.
Belts, 107.
Belge, 111.
Bellis, 115.
Bellanger, 110.
Bencamp, 141.
Benner, 21.
Bennett, 22, 29, 48, 48, 56, 84, 133, 152.
Benjamin, 33, 121.
Benson, 48, 49, 66, 70, 100, 119, 143.
Benton, 58, 105, 112.
Bently, 62, 102, 109, 116.
Bender, 73, 164.
Benting, 79.
Benudetz, 90.
Benning, 118.
Beoins, 70.
Bergman, 165.
Perryman, 13.
Berry, 47, 49, 111, 121, 138, 158.
Berwick, 95.
Berbere, 97.
Berges, 133.
Besom, 13.
Bessy, 56.
Betta, 83.
Best, 136.
Besse, 162.
Better, 83.
Bevans, 155.
Bevins, 95.
Biard, 118.
Bier, 31.
Biery, 111.
Bigdy, 9.
Biggord, 5.
Bigot, 155.
Bilaston, 67.
Billings, 17.
Billis, 24.
Bingamin, 115.
Bingham, 131.
Birch, 131, 148.
Bird, 91.
Bisbron, 139.
Bishop, 32, 38, 44, 62, 166
Bisley, 59.
Bissell, 59.
Bissere, 57.
Bittles, 102.
Bitts, 67.
Bixby, 32.
Black, 59, 89, 150.
Blackall, 86.
Blackburn, 37.
Blackman, 11.

Blaig, 119.
Blair, 30, 52, 75, 113.
Blake, 54, 107, 116, 123.
Blakely, 35.
Blakeslee, 157.
Blamondow, 131.
Blan, 63.
Blanchard, 36, 50, 86, 99, 104.
Blaney, 48.
Blanped, 31.
Blass, 139.
Blatchley, 36.
Blatz, 152.
Blazor, 82.
Bledson, 43.
Blimmer, 22.
Bliss, 105, 146.
Blivins, 22.
Blockman, 28.
Blood. 124.
Bloom, 116.
Blunt, 46.
Blystone, 86.
Board, 51. 59.
Bodkin, 33.
Bodley, 141.
Body, 10.
Bogart, 121.
Bohne, 134.
Bollinger, 94.
Bolton, 14, 36, 55.
Bond. 48, 82, 158.
Boner, 61.
Bonnell, 152.
Bonner, 122.
Bonnester, 119.
Booker, 22.
Booland, 93.
Booley, 53.
Boon, 52, 82, 129.
Boothe, 147.
Booze, 49, 76.
Bordon, 135.
Bork, 36.
Borrus, 121.
Bosart, 109.
Bosher, 26.
Bossard, 94.
Boston, 19, 46.
Botham, 125.
Bothby, 18.
Bott, 139.
Bottom, 27.
Bourne, 65.
Boush, 25.
Bowen, 11, 102, 137, 164.
Bower, 11.
Bowers, 20, 27, 67, 74, 129, 130.

Bowey, 55.
Bowker, 121.
Bowle, 56.
Bowley, 60, 134, 151.
Bowls, 76.
Bowman, 7, 45, 128, 138.
Boxburgh, 72.
Boyd, 46, 57, 120, 161.
Boyer, 47, 52, 109, 112, 167.
Boyes, 140.
Boylan, 70.
Boyle, 29, 31, 115.
Boyne, 137.
Boyson, 83.
Brackett, 36, 71.
Braden, 106, 163.
Bradford, 21, 129.
Bradley, 52, 77, 80, 80.
Bradman, 93.
Brady, 42, 66, 96, 114, 119, 162.
Bragg, 86.
Brallier, 140.
Braman, 60.
Brame, 94.
Branch, 55, 163.
Brandon, 132.
Brandt, 16, 83.
Brangle, 34.
Branstetter, 107.
Brannen, 187.
Brannon, 17.
Braum, 34.
Bray, 18, 75.
Brayford, 50.
Brazee, 77, 147.
Breah, 91.
Breckerson, 45.
Bree, 89.
Brennan, 120, 130.
Brent, 50.
Brett, 22, 116.
Brew, 53.
Brewer, 28, 63, 63, 135.
Brice, 95.
Bricket, 115.
Brickford, 17.
Brickman, 52.
Brident, 137.
Brien, 59, 87, 89, 95, 134.
Brierly, 67.
Briggs 8, 27, 113, 167.
Brigham, 158.
Brink, 99.
Briner, 38.
Brinit, 80.
Brion, 53.
Brisell, 5.
Brissent, 79.

Bristol, 118.
Britton, 40, 148.
Broadrup, 27.
Brodo, 162.
Bromley, 51, 152.
Bronlingen, 69.
Bronson, 108.
Bronswell, 31.
Brooks, 18, 23, 35, 42, 64, 69, 74, 82, 112, 115, 143.
Brooker, 154.
Brooklyn, 35.
Brophy, 81.
Brothers, 62.
Brotschi, 6.
Brougham, 125.
Brow, 105, 160.
Brower, 161.
Browers, 48.
Brown, 12, 17, 21, 22, 27, 30, 31, 33, 34, 39, 45, 46, 48, 51, 52, 55, 57, 58, 58, 59, 59, 60, 60, 62, 64, 65, 74, 74, 74, 78, 78, 81, 82, 83, 86, 87, 87, 83, 88, 96, 99, 104, 105, 105, 106, 108, 110, 115, 118, 131, 135, 139, 151, 152, 153, 154, 154, 159, 164, 161, 168.
Brownman, 89.
Browning, 17.
Brownsaugh, 85, 94.
Bruce, 23, 44, 53, 63, 78, 110, 120.
Bruer, 84.
Bruner, 164.
Brunyan, 119.
Bryan, 137.
Bryant, 24, 61, 65, 77, 97, 98, 128.
Bu——, 9.
Buchanan, 47, 53, 65.
Buchard, 121.
Buck, 35, 141.
Buckett, 55.
Buckley, 123, 167, 27.
Buckingham, 79.
Buckle, 25.
Bucks, 65.
Buggs, 74.
Buga, 121.
Buise, 69.
Ballard, 109.
Ball-les, 59.
Barnn, 9.
Bumeranz, 95.
Bumgardner, 22, 25.

Bundy, 92.
Bunn, 116.
Bunnuell, 152.
Bunting, 75, 94.
Bunty, 131.
Burch, 77.
Burger, 81.
Burcher, 57.
Burgess, 81, 85, 126, 130.
Burke, 23, 59, 86, 119, 163.
Burket, 111.
Burkeal, 130.
Burkhart, 79.
Burnett, 80.
Burness, 86.
Burgmire, 127.
Burnheim, 132.
Burns, 6, 23, 32, 43, 46, 53, 55, 60, 97, 101, 111, 132, 134, 154.
Burncworth, 29.
Burroughs, 65, 156.
Burton, 19, 30, 44.
Burr, 19, 159.
Busche, 147.
Bush, 24, 49, 83, 91, 124, 136, 162.
Bushammer, 38.
Bustin, 24.
Bussker, 77.
Buster, 126.
Butcher, 6.
Buttran, 9.
Butler, 34, 46, 38, 39, 59, 91, 133.
Button, 66.
Buzzell, 66.
Byus, 13.
Bynum, 20.
Byerts, 25.
Byron, 90.
Byam, 113.

C.

Cable, 53.
Cadwell, 62, 99, 116, 165.
Cady, 100, 103, 134.
Cafuld, 129.
Cain, 34, 115, 157.
Calagher, 107.
Calhoun, 118.
Callaghan, 148.
Callingham, 64.
Calvin, 153.
Cambell, 43, 129.
Cammers, 56.
Camp, 20.
Campanus, 35.

Campbell, 27, 70, 82, 94, 103, 120, 126, 133.
Camper, 46.
Campfield, 85.
Cane, 104.
Canfield, 78.
Canford, 80.
Cann, 55.
Cannon, 132.
Cappell, 97.
Capern, 82.
Capron, 105.
Card, 151.
Careoltan, 63.
Carl, 77.
Carlon, 101.
Carly, 98, 105.
Carman, 165.
Carne, 25.
Carncross, 27.
Carnes, 108.
Carney, 75, 98.
Carnett, 47.
Carnhc, 106.
Carny, 96.
Carpenter, 19, 29, 49, 70, 80, 132, 133, 147.
Carr, 22, 37, 38, 54, 57, 70, 71, 122, 127.
Carrell, 46, 78.
Carroll, 17, 24, 59, 90.
Cars, 73.
Carson, 17, 48, 80, 81, 92, 155.
Cartel, 134.
Carter, 23, 37, 39, 48, 130.
Cartland, 110.
Cartler, 52.
Cartney, 24.
Cartridge, 102.
Cartrig, 108.
Cartwright, 121.
Carver, 158, 159.
Cary, 13, 69, 81, 102, 112.
Case, 16, 66.
Casey, 24, 30, 81, 103.
Cash, 76.
Casmer, 103.
Cass, 9.
Casmer, 103.
Casler, 148.
Cassell, 168.
Casselman, 153.
Castleman, 58.
Castoe, 34.
Catch, 83.
Cates, 59.
Cathcart, 160.
Cathen, 80.
Caton, 100.

Catton, 52.
Cau, 53.
Caul, 71.
Caulfield, 127
Cawdel, 63.
Ceahon, 86.
Cechum, 160.
Cecil, 59.
Cemline, 168.
Cesar, 89.
Chace, 88.
Chadwick, 166.
Chafman, 105.
Chambers, 51, 62, 83, 101, 110, 127, 133, 162.
Chamberlin, 61.
Chandler, 88.
Chapel, 81.
Chapin, 19.
Chaplin, 25.
Chapman, 24, 54, 79, 100, 107, 113, 133, 152, 160, 165.
Chappell, 19.
Charles, 29, 131, 137, 166.
Chase, 12, 17, 39, 108, 109, 121, 132, 137.
Chassen, 55.
Cheatem, 153.
Chelsey, 139.
Chester, 97.
Chew, 48.
Cheyney, 114
Chick, 9.
Childs, 59.
Chilly, 24.
Chillingworth, 73.
Chipman, 100.
Chiseltine, 129.
Christ, 31, 133.
Christian, 116.
Christinger, 24.
Christy, 29.
Chrysler, 77.
Church, 33, 78.
Churchas, 87.
Churchill, 62, 72, 110.
Churdell, 103.
Cigin, 21.
Cillengham, 7.
Claggaart, 59.
Clago, 110.
Clagrate, 57.
Clanden, 77.
Clare, 23, 118, 113, 112.
Clark, 6, 14, 19, 25, 42, 46, 61, 90, 116, 113, 106, 106, 106, 160, 153, 140, 120.
Clarkson, 69.

Clarkston, 59.
Clatter, 41.
Claun, 159.
Clay, 56, 83, 153.
Claypole, 48.
Clayton, 39, 40, 93, 119.
Cleary, 30.
Cleamond, 9.
Clegg, 33.
Clellum, 50.
Clement, 7, 105.
Clemihern, 85.
Clemments, 90, 93.
Clemmins, 112.
Cleveland, 152.
Clifford, 36.
Clift, 84.
Climan, 96.
Cline, 25, 164.
Close, 17.
Closeless, 73.
Closs, 112.
Closson, 17.
Cloud, 126.
Clough, 150.
Clover, 163.
Coaley, 113.
Coates, 57.
Cobb, 67, 72, 124.
Cobran, 9.
Coburn, 64.
Coch, 85.
Cocherell, 62.
Cochran, 19, 95, 122, 160.
Cochre, 97.
Cockran, 120.
Cockerman, 20.
Cocks, 95.
Cod, 59.
Codrag—, 8.
Cofeer, 82.
Coffee, 48, 150.
Coffin, 102, 120.
Coffine, 75.
Coffman, 141.
Coggins, 49.
Coil, 24.
Colbey, 20.
Cole, 14, 34, 34, 37, 84, 89,
    90, 101, 106, 109, 132,
    147, 151.
Coles, 53.
Coleman, 44, 51, 56, 36,
    79, 161.
Coley, 58.
Colflesh, 130.
Collins, 12, 14, 18, 20, 27,
    48, 62, 77, 87, 94, 98,
    99, 113, 129, 131, 161.
Colman, 151, 163.

Coltman, 150.
Colton, 65.
Colter, 165.
Colvin, 164.
Colwell, 48, 78.
Combs, 20.
Comby, 79.
Comins, 74, 158.
Comlow, 79.
Comfort, 27.
Comstook, 95.
Compton, 50, 85.
Cominger, 46.
Comuck, 138.
Compt, 148.
Connoy, 5.
Conray, 7.
Conner, 10, 77, 85.
Connor, 16, 85.
Conrad, 37, 68, 120.
Conklin, 33, 34, 72.
Connell, 62, 136.
Conaway, 63.
Cone, 4.
Coney, 83.
Condon, 71.
Conlard, 75.
Conamaa, 93.
Conners, 80.
Connard, 82.
Conden, 84, 165.
Concher, 89.
Conaver, 90.
Conart, 94.
Contras, 97.
Condo, 101.
Conevay, 107.
Conlon, 126.
Conahy, 122.
Conlay, 122.
Contle, 135.
Cooly, 9.
Cope, 17.
Cook, 15, 29, 38, 44, 52,
    53, 56, 67, 69, 70, 71,
    94, 96, 104, 124, 125,
    131, 138, 158.
Copus, 21.
Cooper, 44, 112.
Copeland, 36.
Coock, 85.
Coonts, 48.
Copp, 107.
Copper, 128.
Cooker, 147.
Corcoran, 6, 134.
Cortis, 27, 87.
Core, 39, 134.
Cornell, 31.
Corry, 31.

Cordelia, 52.
Cornish, 50.
Corville, 60.
Corney, 79.
Corier, 85.
Corben, 88.
Corham, 90.
Corby, 121.
Corson, 125.
Corcon, 137.
Cossin, 10.
Costerlough, 38.
Coston, 87.
Cosgrove, 100.
Costello, 121.
Cott, 128.
Coules, 14, 15.
Courtney, 45.
Couch, 38, 48, 60.
Courser, 56.
Coup, 94.
Coulter, 140.
Courtney, 162.
Couse, 167.
Covell, 133.
Cowden, 21.
Cowan, 22, 113.
Cowell, 45.
Cowles, 65, 111, 119, 158,
    168.
Coward, 90.
Cowes, 162.
Cox, 18, 22, 35, 35, 76, 82,
    153, 159.
Coyfort, 17.
Coyle, 82.
Cozzen, 106.
Crakl——, 9.
Craycroft, 24.
Cramer, 67, 147.
Crall, 26.
Crandall, 31.
Crampton, 38.
Crawford, 45, 94, 137.
Cracker, 52.
Crabb, 54.
Crawner, 66.
Craig, 56.
Cratton, 67.
Cray, 70.
Craigne, 71.
Crainer, 76.
Craighead, 84.
Craft, 53, 147.
Crambly, 123.
Craiger, 123.
Cramner, 128.
Cranmer, 133.
Crant, 138.
Creveling, 37.

Creft, 53.
Cressler, 56.
Crebbs, 56.
Creek, 33.
Crego, 62.
Cremonin, 113.
Creamer, 138.
Crevil, 151.
Crise, 81.
Crittenden, 94, 104.
Cringle, 149.
Cronk, 16, 116.
Cronmett, 12.
Crow, 5, 24, 28, 133.
Cross, 10, 20, 38, 69, 79.
Comwell, 50, 75.
Crosley, 51, 123.
Crowningshield, 61.
Crowell, 41, 67, 127.
Crowl, 69.
Crouch, 72.
Crocker, 78, 89, 89.
Croker, 87.
Cronin, 87, 148.
Crowley, 90.
Crooke, 97.
Cromer, 112.
Croff. 125.
Crozby, 126.
Crosson, 129.
Cromfar, 131.
Cronan, 133.
Croxton, 137.
Cromer, 165.
Crooks, 39.
Crumford, 159.
Cuberson, 158.
Cudworth, 82, 114.
Cuff, 55.
Cuffer, 45.
Cugsby, 153.
Cullen, 134.
Culins, 69.
Cullum, 44.
Cummings, 23, 91, 103.
Cuncam, 62.
Cunnines, 78.
Cunningham, 13, 17, 23, 24, 168.
Cupp, 12.
Curby, 47.
Curl, 34.
Curns. 116.
Curran, 7.
Curry, 21, 87.
Currey, 76.
Curtin, 103.
Curtis, 98, 118, 133
Cush, 137.
Cushman, 75.

Cusick, 102.
Custard, 102.
Cutter, 59.
Cutts, 39.
Cuvey, 142, 161.

D.

E. D., 12.
J. P. R. D., 14.
Dafferty, 67.
Daggett, 42, 124.
Daisey, 52.
Daily, 159.
Daker, 105.
Dale, 27.
Dalley, 45, 90.
Dalrymple, 39.
Dalton, 59, 60, 117.
Daly, 163.
Dan ——, 9.
Danenhower, 10.
Daniel, 27, 35.
Danley, 36.
Dandy, 45, 47.
Daniels, 50, 62.
Dany, 83.
Dance, 83.
Dana, 109.
Dane, 110.
Dend, 111.
Danouc, 139.
Dantz, 140.
Danen, 160.
Darrigh, 19.
Darrow, 31.
Darling, 80.
Darsey, 42.
Darha, 165.
Darnell, 124.
Darcy, 154.
Darby, 158.
Daubenmarkle, 27.
Daubenspach, 67.
Davis. 8, 14, 26, 26, 33, 37, 38, 40, 44, 45, 50, 51, 53, 54, 59, 74, 81, 85, 87. 98, 108, 116, 128, 129, 135, 140, 147, 149, 151, 153, 163.
David, 24, 71.
Davenport, 67, 99, 168.
Davidson, 78, 100.
Davison, 133.
Dawson, 65, 99, 161.
Dawsey, 83.
Dawry, 155.
Day, 40, 41, 113, 131, 159, 160, 163.
Deaton, 10.

Deabolt, 26.
Dean, 28, 37, 47, 86, 104.
Dearwood, 75.
Dearborn, 87, 95.
Dearbeau, 95.
Deans, 98.
Dearing, 113.
Deamy, 151.
Dearbro, 163.
Debrick, 24.
Debont, 91.
Debell, 109.
Decker, 9, 22, 62, 84, 87
96, 103, 104, 123, 139
Deeren, 165.
Degan,61.
Dehorne, 83.
De ito, 38.
Deity, 77.
Delph, 51.
Delmore, 92.
Delmore, 92.
Delensy, 99.
Deaney, 108, 147.
Delong, 135.
Demerest, 34.
De Morest, 75.
Demas, 89.
Dennis, 20, 83, 156.
Denson, 23, 95.
Den, 67.
Dennison, 83, 164.
Deuton, 91.
Denny, 140.
Dennington, 141.
Denning, 155.
Derrickson, 24.
Deruck, 63.
Dernuth, 71.
Derhan, 86.
Derschner, 90.
Dermoth, 108.
Derguett, 109.
Derwin, 122.
Derhamer, 138.
Dernout, 161.
Deseru, 21.
Des Mold, 23.
Desmona, 89.
Detling, 166.
Detrow, 7.
Deusemore, 13.
Deuts, 151.
Devolly, 42.
Devor, 42.
Dever, 102.
Develin, 107.
Devine, 107.
Devins, 116.

Devit, 161.
Dewes, 30.
Dewberry, 36.
Dewitt, 39, 74.
Deway, 73.
Dewyen, 87.
De Wolffe, 94.
Dewey, 136, 158.
Dewy, 155.
Deyo, 124.
Dexheimer, 131.
Dickerson, 27, 59.
Dickson, 45, 52, 55, 152.
Dick, 77.
Didler, 20.
Dierce, 116.
Diehl. 138.
Deem, 151.
Digman, 35.
Dihey, 5.
Dilkson, 9.
Dilley, 44.
Dillon, 54, 62.
Dillingham, 107.
Dim——, 9.
Dinsmore, 16.
Dingee, 97.
Dinger, 155.
Dippy, 78.
Disham, 151.
Ditch, 28.
Diving, 136.
Dixon, 136.
Doan, 151.
Dock, 110.
Docrathy. 41.
Dodson, 56, 119.
Doeld, 159.
Dohl, 23.
Dohart, 105.
Dolt, 75.
Doll, 151.
Dolan, 62.
Donnall, 25.
Donneyhue, 26.
Donald, 57, 57, 122, 161.
Donley, 75.
Donovan, 86.
Donahue, 89, 122, 160.
Donlon, 95.
Donnelly, 103, 104.
Donham, 121.
Donnell, 161.
Doremus, 12.
Doris, 13.
Dorrah, 20.
Dorsey, 46, 58, 73.
Dorsham, 67.
Dorce, 99.
Dorlander, 99.

Dority, 112.
Dorus, 155.
Doty, 64, 108.
Douler, 7.
Dougherty, 13, 14, 17, 22, 27, 30, 38, 91, 126, 152.
Douglas, 23.
Doughty, 128.
Dow, 15, 147.
Downs, 32, 95.
Dowdy, 45.
Dowell, 46, 103.
Doway, 105.
Dowen, 130.
Doxie, 121.
Doyle, 41, 79, 114, 135.
Dozier, 49.
Drake, 61, 61.
Drane, 64.
Drayer, 110.
Dreuds, 54.
Dreaish, 107.
Druig, 77.
Druery, 162.
Drul, 164.
Dubois, 102.
Duchtler, 81.
Ducat, 102.
Dudden, 22.
Dudley, 38, 53, 84, 155.
Duer, 104.
Duff, 55, 99, 103.
Duffey, 101.
Dufer, 160.
Duggan, 66.
Dugeon, 87, 131.
Duke, 133.
Dull, 125.
Dumpey, 114.
Dunn, 16, 110, 116, 151, 160, 162, 166, 167.
Dunivan, 32.
Duncan, 46, 95.
Dunham, 59, 65, 84, 85, 101, 106, 164.
Dungan, 86.
Dunninge, 96.
Dunton, 110.
Dunlap, 123.
Dunlan, 124.
Dunbar, 124.
Dupont, 76.
Duroll, 77.
Durtin, 78.
Dusenberry, 21.
Dustine, 104.
Dushane, 129.
Dutton, 62, 71, 130.
Dutcher, 68.

Duyer, 62, 66.
Dwinnel, 106.
Dwyer, 148, 156.
Dyer, 155.
Dyke, 69.
Dync, 7.
Dyson, 37.
Dyse, 53.

E.

Eager, 9.
Eagle, 22.
Eagan, 75.
Ealf, 127.
Eames, 92.
Earlel, 86.
Eastman, 105.
Easter, 149.
Eaton, 60, 102.
Ecker, 85.
Eckley, 85.
Eckerman, 109.
Eckart, 133,
Eddy, 168.
Edgarton, 13.
Edgard, 33.
Edenger, 84.
Edino, 154,
Edmister, 20.
Edmend, 98.
Edmunds, 122.
Edwards, 12, 14, 35, 30, 44, 57, 57, 101, 116, 149, 152.
Effreds, 98.
Ehenger, 31.
Ehrit, 160.
Eichencour, 79.
Eignor, 160.
Elder, 41, 135.
Eldred, 65, 105.
Elderkin, 72.
Eldrid, 75.
Eldridge, 84.
Elden, 104.
Elexson, 26.
Elkins, 61, 161.
Elliott, 10, 59, 60, 99, 122, 162.
Ellis, 31, 54, 129, 135.
Ellery, 51.
Ellison, 75.
Ellinwood, 113.
Elmer, 42, 48.
Elrah, 86.
Elridge, 61, 80.
Elsington, 93.
Elvers, 44.
Elwell, 130,

Ely, 137.
Emanuel, 105.
Eman, 151.
Emery, 43, 45, 135.
Emerson, 85.
Emilels, 103.
Emmons, 62, 95.
Emmett, 123.
Emory, 47.
Emphy, 74.
Ende, 127.
Enes, 82.
England, 11.
English, 26, 115.
Engler, 82.
Engle, 149.
Engerman, 162.
Enox, 120.
Ensilis, 73.
Ensley, 149.
Entwistle, 102.
Eppauline, 70.
Epp, 84.
Erginger, 81.
Erhart, 70.
Erion, 106.
Erline, 81.
Erman, 158.
Ernet, 150.
Erskin, 81.
Erwin, 86, 154.
Erwen, 129.
Esbern, 139.
Eschelman, 81.
Esglesin, 133.
Eslich, 11.
Esty, 64.
Estus, 80.
Eten, 65.
Etheridge, 123.
Evans, 7, 16, 17, 18, 37, 44, 82, 82, 100, 104, 109, 158, 160.
Everly, 19.
Everett, 46, 167.
Evens, 51.
Evers, 64, 115.
Evern, 65.
Everhart, 102.
Eveland, 128.
Evitt, 167.
Ewell, 61.
Ewing, 22.
Ewirett, 116.
Eyer (or Ezer,) 78.

F.

F——, 125.
Fadder, 61.

Fagian, 26.
Fagan, 97.
Fairweather, 64.
Fairbanks, 132, 143.
Fall, 17.
Fallman, 67.
Fanar, 41.
Fanen, 64.
Fanc——, 132.
Farrell, 11, 12, 62, 90, 132, 135.
Farley, 27, 57, 108.
Farnsworth, 40, 151.
Farthing, 82.
Farris, 93.
Fardell, 98.
Farrows, 133.
Fassett, 41.
Faurke, 28.
Fauver, 39.
Faulk, 52.
Faulkner, 88.
Fawkes, 111.
Fay, 73.
Fazen, 50.
Feathergill, 31.
Feagles, 122.
Fee, 12.
Feeley, 53.
Feenig, 162.
Felty, 12.
Felton, 55, 109.
Feltman, 83.
Felmly, 88.
Felio, 123.
Fenn, 13,
Ferguson, 46, 93, 140, 149, 160, 161.
Ferrill, 82.
Ferris, 122.
Fesler, 50, 67.
Festi, 135.
Fiery, 31.
Field, 49, 58, 86, 137.
Fields, 69, 45, 92.
Fillebrown, 132.
Filben, 160.
Finnegan, 14, 68, 88, 102, 135.
Finchum, 19.
Finley, 34, 87.
Finney, 43, 158.
Finman, 57.
Finch, 138.
Fink, 156, 161.
Fisthaner, 6.
Fisher, 30, 31, 40, 53, 55, 63, 77, 78, 85, 139.
Fisk, 103, 106.
Fish, 115, 127.

Fishbey, 150.
Fitzpatrick, 60, 77, 116.
Fitzsimmons, 70, 116, 179, 181.
Fitzgerald, 116, 154, 162.
Fitchett, 76, 118.
Fitch, 124, 135.
Fite, 155.
Fivetack, 72.
Flanigan, 64.
Flanders, 66, 133.
Flamburgh, 88.
Fletcher, 35, 40, 70, 156.
Fleck, 39.
Flemming, 67, 115, 155.
Flessining, 126.
Fleet, 134.
Flickinger, 137.
Flinx, 140.
Flower, 61.
Florence, 75, 110.
Floyd, 51, 98, 151.
Flood, 125, 160.
Flora, 165.
Flynn, 85, 113, 162.
Foders, 93.
Fogg, 78.
Foltz, 10.
Foley, 38, 88, 93, 167.
Folks, 36, 47.
Folay, 74.
Follbyer, 76.
Follansbe, 106.
Folley, 107.
Font, 77.
Foor, 34.
Foote, 100, 100, 103.
Forbes, 10.
Ford, 17, 35, 47, 55, 75, 77, 111, 123.
Fortune, 44, 61.
Forseman, 83.
Forney, 114.
Forrest, 130, 165.
Forner, 138.
Foster, 11, 39, 42, 43, 60, 69, 72, 91, 95, 106, 106, 109, 122, 134.
Fosmire, 151.
Fouler, 67.
Fountain, 152.
Fowell, 36.
Fowler, 105, 151.
Fow, 134.
Fox, 34, 50, 62, 66, 80, 91, 111, 119, 154, 168.
Frankl——, 8.
Frank, 10, 29.
Frayer, 17.
Frayry, 18.

Frazier, 39, 128.
Fraseer, 54.
Franklin, 8, 55.
Frances, 56, 152.
Frail, 75.
Francis, 103.
Frainer, 131.
Fransher, 147.
Freeman, 22, 81, 83, 116, 151.
Fredgill, 26.
Fresboure, 30,
French, 36, 77, 84, 97.
Freny, 58.
Fremble, 92.
Fretby, 92.
Freadmore, 131.
Freer, 158.
Friday, 9.
Frinkham, 33.
Frizbie, 49.
Fritch, 75.
Fritz, 112, 162.
Frick, 133.
Froego, 14.
Fromard, 33.
Frost, 64, 65, 66, 76, 105.
Froggett, 74.
Frothingham, 89.
Fruitman, 109.
Fry, 18, 48, 67, 97, 104.
Fryer, 127.
Fuchs, 119.
Fultz, 16, 72, 111.
Fuller, 23, 128.
Fulton, 88, 133.
Fulkerson, 120.
Fullersmith, 162.
Funnell, 63.
Furguson, 46, 149.
Furman, 121.
Fuze, 49.
Fyer, 81.

G.

Gabbetts, 6.
Gabriel, 49.
Gage, 106.
Gaghigan, 167.
Gailey, 25, 117, 157.
Gainer, 131.
Gallagher, 14, 83, 108, 123.
Galfilland, 37.
Gale, 50.
Galliger, 83.
Gallaway, 102, 129.
Galvin, 160.
Gambol, 17, 120.
Gamell, 23.

Gamble, 32, 168, 157.
Gammon, 124.
Gannagle, 75.
Ganer, 109.
Gant, 153.
Ganby, 164.
Garrith, 10.
Garner, 17, 54, 54.
Garnes, 30.
Garnett, 43, 48.
Garrison, 54.
Gay, 59.
Garrow, 70.
Gardner, 80, 83, 85, 111, 140, 160.
Garett, 82.
Garvine, 99.
Garting, 103.
Garlock, 159.
Gastim, 74.
Gaspell, 154.
Gates, 18.
Gaunt, 29.
Gavron, 70.
Gawyer, 73.
Gear, 154.
Geahart, 160.
Gedrick, 70.
Gee, 36, 105.
Gehr, 118.
Gentry, 40.
George, 19, 27, 115, 121.
Gerstung, 16.
German, 18.
Gerritt, 32.
Geriosh, 85.
Gevica, 114.
Gerrard, 156.
Getschell, 95.
Getler, 111.
Ghe, 105.
Gherfelt, 162.
Gearraro, 108.
Gibbs, 17, 35, 46.
Gibson, 26, 30, 109, 109.
Gibney, 128.
Gifford, 31.
Gillingham, 5, 102.
Giles, 18, 50, 118.
Gillespie, 19, 59, 65, 109.
Gilbert, 25, 52, 81, 134, 163.
Gilmer, 39.
Gilbough, 58.
Gilland, 58.
Gilletts, 64.
Gilson, 64.
Gilroy, 97.
Gillett, 97.
Gilbraith, 102.

Gill, 105.
Gillan, 106.
Gilman, 108, 154.
Gillen, 135, 142, 156.
Gilmore, 137, 155.
Gillsey, 140.
Ginkin, 116.
Girt, 95.
Gitchhouse, 164.
Givens, 57, 138.
Givesiez, 124.
Glauphlin, 14.
Glasscott, 34.
Glasco, 39.
Glace, 71.
Glassen, 73.
Glading, 75.
Glass, 88, 125.
Glancy, 94.
Glem, 33.
Gleason, 73.
Glentry, 157.
Gliddin, 127.
Glifford, 140.
Glossuer, 17.
Gloner, 42.
Gloughlin, 70.
Glover, 91.
Gloze, 95.
Godfren, 99.
Godsey, 125.
Goeding, 91.
Goeder, 130,
Goff, 160, 166.
Goheen, 120.
Gohan, 153.
Goldsboro', 76.
Gold, 71.
Golth, 148.
Golden, 149, 155.
Gond, 34.
Gonburn, 138.
Goodrich, 9, 14, 75, 166
Coodhue, 16.
Gooch, 25.
Goodlow, 30.
Goodall, 31.
Goodfellow, 38.
Goodyear, 71.
Goodwin, 71, 122.
Good, 80.
Gorten, 6.
Gordon, 26, 69, 73, 147.
Goss, 107.
Gotham, 123.
Gothan, 28.
Gould, 42, 76, 93, 110, 132.
Gough, 58.
Gout, 58.

Gouser, 153.
Gove, 132.
Gow, 25.
Goward, 90.
Gozney, 82.
Graham, 5, 7, 27, 34, 93, 127.
Gracee, 6.
Gray, 18, 33, 35, 73, 84, 99, 107, 110, 113, 127.
Graves, 28, 54, 84, 153.
Grath, 33, 120.
Granger, 78.
Grant, 83, 85, 99, 155
Grasett, 99.
Grases, 114.
Grayler, 118.
Gratten, 130.
Granley, 131.
Graff, 149.
Graw, 165.
Gregory, 5, 84, 67.
Greller, 10.
Green, 15, 19, 21, 32, 40, 45, 47, 51, 52, 58, 60, 77, 83, 88, 94, 98, 99, 102, 109, 116, 123, 125.
Grey, 29.
Greenwood, 32.
Greer, 40.
Greyson, 56.
Greneger, 85.
Geenfield, 86, 94.
Greenhouse, 109.
Gretton, 111.
Grech, 159.
Greely, 122, 164.
Grider, 48.
Grinnell, 16.
Griffin, 19, 38, 52, 63, 65, 100, 151, 153, 154.
Grimes, 49.
Griffith, 26, 31, 148, 158,
Griggs, 84, 131.
Grimm, 36.
Grise, 40.
Griffiths, 62.
Grizzle, 63.
Griswold, 100, 148.
Griffis, 114.
Grinder, 120, 160.
Grove, 6.
Groffh, 21.
Grossthwait, 49.
Grout, 24.
Gross, 51, 59, 162, 165.
Groves, 60.
Groan, 74.
Grobis, 84.

Groff, 94.
Groser, 99.
Grommett, 106.
Grosvenor, 113
Gronter, 115.
Grotten, 130.
Grow, 132, 147.
Grosclose, 138.
Gruin, 29.
Grucyr, 95.
Gruber, 148.
Grubb, 20.
Guest, 126.
Guff, 136.
Guinin, 115.
Gumes, 14.
Gun, 56.
Gunner, 56, 87.
Gunmer, 61.
Gunnier, 83.
Gurnsey, 71.
Gurney, 113, 157.
Gurrens, 115.
Gurlon, 136.
Gustin, 37.
Gusford, 136.
Guthrie, 108.
Guthridge, 137.
Guyld, 61.
Guyyer, 79.
Gwin, 22.

H.

Hasse, 114.
Habald, 81.
Haber, 167.
Hach, 9.
Hacy, 28.
Hackenburg, 157.
Hadsell, 12, 122.
Hadly, 132, 134, 147.
Hadden, 138.
Haffeman, 54
Haft, 79.
Hagoith, 31.
Hager, 69.
Hagadern, 74.
Hagon, 91.
Hagerty, 126.
Hagenbaugh, 136
Hahn, 18, 140.
Hainist, 24.
Haines, 66, 109.
Haight, 78, 93.
Hair, 90.
Haish, 125.
Haker, 159.
Hale, 5, 19, 23, 38.
Hall, 14, 15, 28, 30, 37,

40, 43, 43, 45, 46, 57, 58, 59, 64, 64, 65, 76, 87, 88, 194, 112, 120, 121, 128, 136, 139, 140, 150.
Halman, 45.
Halligan, 32.
Halloway, 51.
Hallus, 72.
Haley, 111.
Hallinger, 115.
Halhorn, 132.
Halston, 138.
Halpin, 139.
Halloran, 148.
Halleham, 152.
Halverson, 165.
Hammachet, 7.
Hammond, 11, 23, 30, 31, 47, 104, 149.
Hamner, 24.
Ham, 27, 132.
Hampton, 50.
Hamlin, 55, 116.
Hamilton, 60, 60, 61, 78, 83, 84, 89.
Hamm, 65.
Hanagan, 166.
Hang, 11, 14.
Hand, 25, 31, 47.
Handford, 42.
Hankley, 51.
Hannan, 83.
Hanno, 91.
Handslan, 91.
Hance, 94.
Hane, 101.
Hanson, 105, 154.
Hancock, 59, 105, 163.
Hannah, 122.
Hanks, 131.
Hanrey, 152.
Hansom, 152.
Hanley, 160.
Hanbey, 161.
Hanafer, 167.
Hapel, 88.
Harden, 43.
Hart, 8, 94, 113, 150, 156, 164.
Hardien, 9.
Harman, 9, 44.
Harris, 10, 14, 21, 37, 37, 42, 43, 47, 49, 55, 84, 91, 94, 99, 115, 120, 131, 134, 158.
Harrison, 44, 46, 56, 115, 167.
Hartbrock, 45.
Harper, 19, 131.

Harmon, 20, 21, 40, 60, 83.
Harmell, 23.
Harrin, 46.
Harlow, 24, 31, 33, 77, 141.
Hardy, 26, 100, 167.
Harvy, 29, 76, 168.
Harrington, 32, 49, 87, 121, 150, 166.
Harnasy, 39.
Hartman, 27.
Harley, 63.
Harding, 71, 72, 92.
Hartwell, 77, 132.
Hartung, 80.
Harpster, 89, 139.
Harvey, 90.
Haruret, 95.
Harlan, 96.
Hartman, 71, 97.
Harning, 103.
Harland, 104.
Harrigan, 107.
Harget, 126.
Harder, 128.
Harnes, 132.
Harmer, 135.
Hartley, 136.
Harold, 149.
Harnish, 151.
Harden, 155.
Harless, 156.
Harst, 161.
Hastings, 26, 29.
Hass, 66.
Hascall, 69.
Hassiage, 72.
Haskell, 104.
Haskins, 138.
Hatter, 22.
Hathaway, 48, 87.
Hatchell, 129.
Hatfield, 159, 167.
Haunser, 29.
Hauber, 107.
Havis, 25.
Havens, 30, 67.
Havvey, 53.
Haven, 30.
Haverill, 128.
Hawsey, 7.
Hawkins, 45, 50, 54.
Hawes, 45, 53, 54.
Hawker, 57, 97.
Hawley, 111.
Hawkenberry, 150.
Haxton, 139.
Hayes, 10, 39, 53, 58.
Hay, 32, 44, 46, 52, 88, 115, 127.
Haywood, 39.

Haynesworth, 28.
Haynes, 89.
Hazzard, 15, 55.
Hazel, 102.
Hazelett, 157.
Healy, 26, 67.
Heard, 33.
Heath, 57, 118.
Heal, 60.
Heastley, 88.
Heasy, 113.
Heafy, 124.
Hearin, 137.
Heburn, 84.
Hebrilge, 147.
Heck, 76.
Heckathorn, 78.
Hecter, 114.
Hedrick, 81.
Hedloy, 100.
Headleen, 168.
Hefner, 86.
Heffinn, 155.
Hegeman, 116.
Heggekjar, 128.
Heimstead, 92.
Heise, 98.
Heiss, 108.
Heintze, 116.
Heidy, 124.
Heist, 138.
Heltzel, 35.
Hellry, 15.
Hellishar, 105,
Helberg, 126.
Heller, 158.
Hemphill, 85, 103.
Hemmenger, 119.
Hemitaran, 120.
Hemming, 162.
Hendri, 7.
Hendershott, 12, 37.
Henderson, 13, 138, 152, 166.
Henry, 17, 27, 45, 47, 51, 56, 66, 67, 86, 89, 98, 107, 122, 148, 150.
Hendrick, 33.
Henson, 35, 82, 83,
Henzman, 64.
Henmon, 83.
Hendig, 91.
Henklegury, 121.
Herkness, 5.
Herrick, 18.
Herrin, 23.
Herbert, 63.
Hersh, 76.
Herington, 85.
Herman, 111.

Herns, 148.
Hersog. 164.
Hess, 21, 22, 25, 41, 136.
Hester, 40.
Heskel, 65.
Heseldon, 57.
Hessington, 163.
Hettinger, 79.
Hettuck, 139.
Hevener, 152.
Hewes, 53.
Hewitt, 134.
Hibbard, 128.
Hickhman, 37.
Hicks, 54, 109, 153.
Hickey, 103.
Higgins, 18, 30, 39, 92.
Hignet, 88.
Higden, 128.
Hilber, 5.
Hill, 6, 13, 20, 27, 32, 40, 56, 60, 64, 69, 88, 95, 99, 132, 138, 150, 150.
Hillegars, 14.
Hillman, 39, 150.
Hillery, 38.
Hills, 40, 60.
Hilland, 163.
Hille, 160.
Himes, 23.
Himtoon, 110.
Hin——, 9.
Hines, 22, 167.
Hinsinger, 28.
Hinton, 57.
Hinds, 81, 113.
Hinty, 90.
Hiner, 139.
Hinkle, 157.
Hinkleman, 158.
Hires, 83.
Hite, 43, 104.
Hitch, 23.
Hitchcock, 65.
Hitner, 84.
Hittstead, 110.
Hixon, 23.
Hoard, 23.
Hoag, 137.
Hoath, 138.
Hobson, 28, 37.
Hockman, 72.
Hocum, 123.
Hodges, 24, 54, 111, 158.
Hodson, 37.
Hodgson, 115.
Hoffman, 6, 13, 36, 64, 65, 65, 103, 133
Hogerson, 10.
Hogi, 116

Hoghan, 123.
Hofferand, 130.
Hoff, 140.
Holcombe, 20, 21.
Hollensworth, 22.
Holmes, 22, 114, 118, 154, 165.
Holden, 31.
Holliday, 43, 108.
Holt, 58.
Holland, 61, 82, 116.
Holman, 66.
Holders, 66.
Hollenbach, 78.
Hollinger, 78.
Holler, 115.
Holbrook, 126.
Holriggel, 132.
Holstein, 155.
Holly, 163.
Homer, 33, 100, 109, 135.
Homan, 153.
Hooper, 23, 51.
Hood, 38, 67, 88, 115.
Hooder, 65.
Hoofman, 103.
Hooley, 164.
Hopwood, 27.
Hopkins, 49, 130.
Hope, 57.
Horey, 22.
Horner, 35, 81.
Horton, 53, 53, 129.
Horns, 63.
Horn, 67, 81, 160.
Horsley, 75.
Horr, 120.
Hornley, 134.
Horan, 135.
Hosmer, 13, 15.
Houston, 122, 154.
Houghton, 37, 108.
Houghtaling, 84.
Houk, 100.
Hovey, 71.
Howlett, 17, 29.
Howell, 13, 151.
Howard, 17, 18, 33, 40, 51, 59, 60, 72, 87, 93, 130, 138, 139, 168.
Howser, 38, 85.
Howerton, 48.
Howland, 78.
Howe, 107, 109, 126, 130.
Hoyet, 62.
Hoyt, 155, 164.
Hoys, 74.
Hozon, 104.
Hubbard, 45, 93, 96, 97, 105.

Huck, 116.
Hudson, 111, 112.
Huff, 76, 150.
Huffman, 38, 130, 87.
Hughnorline, 20.
Hughes, 37, 46, 51, 54, 67, 82, 112, 120.
Hulloway, 23.
Hull, 32, 111.
Hulbert, 61, 120.
Hulshisher, 76.
Humphreys, 13, 166.
Humphrey, 92, 136.
Hummer, 103.
Hummison, 108.
Humell, 160.
Hunter, 10, 19, 32, 46, 64, 69, 77, 99, 103.
Huney, 10.
Hunston, 21.
Huntington, 23, 61.
Hunt, 31, 32, 40, 64, 75, 121, 137.
Huntoon, 64.
Huntly, 100.
Huntress, 123.
Hungerford, 162.
Hurd, 27, 85.
Hurley, 61.
Hurst, 77.
Hurlburd, 129.
Hurnell, 136.
Hurols, 164.
Huston, 28.
Hussey, 110.
Hutchins, 10, 77, 119, 122.
Hutchinson, 13, 86, 92, 106.
Huttenhoun, 102.
Huvor, 109.
Huzzy, 124.
Hyatt, 65, 82.
Hyde, 68, 75, 75, 126.
Hyland, 37.
Hyler, 74.
Hyman, 63.
Hynn, 89.
Hysell, 137.

I.

Ialus, 48.
Ice, 12.
Idel, 119.
Ides, 115.
Idol, 119.
Inell, 112.
Ingalsbe, 85.
Ingersoll, 20, 116.
Ingerson, 133.

Ingraham, 44.
Inglo, 85.
Inhoff, 8.
Inman, 39.
Ireland, 20, 84.
Iris, 10.
Irvin, 162.
Irvingpower, 162.
Isaacs, 114.
Isaacold, 76.
Ischi, 119.
Ives, 71.
Izen, 134.

J.

Jackson, 18, 30, 33, 35, 45, 48, 49, 51, 52, 57, 58, 63, 89, 90, 97, 120, 124, 132, 148.
Jacobson, 19, 22.
Jacobs, 25, 28, 49, 81, 84, 93.
Jackwell, 84.
Jacocks, 149.
Jago, 43.
Jamerson, 24, 84.
James, 32, 57, 79, 124.
Jameson, 55, 89.
Janes, 48, 50, 76, 110, 137.
Janvrin, 93.
Japl——, 8.
Jarvis, 29.
Jaring, 116.
Jasslyn, 40.
Jaynes, 61.
Jefferson, 38, 56.
Jeffry, 76.
Jeffers, 86.
Jemmins, 8.
Jentees, 6.
Jenkins, 10, 33, 46, 48, 75, 79, 90, 94.
Jennings, 17.
Jennison, 89.
Jepperson, 38.
Jersey, 155.
Jerville, 158.
Jessup, 24.
Jestive, 77.
Jevine, 121.
Jewett, 161.
Jimerson, 84.
Jin——, 9.
Jinical, 8.
Jobbs, 150.
Joe, 44.
Johnston, 7, 64, 81, 123, 128, 129.

Johnson, 10, 17, 20, 21,
28, 32, 35, 42, 42, 44,
45, 46, 46, 47, 47, 47,
48, 49, 51, 51, 51, 54,
54, 55, 55, 55, 56, 58,
58, 59, 63, 63, 69, 72,
74, 80, 82, 83, 87, 96,
100, 104, 105, 106,
107, 119, 119, 125,
127, 130, 131, 152,
153, 155, 157, 161,
161, 165.
John, 14.
Johns, 29, 52.
Johnes, 101.
Joice, 12.
Joiner, 79, 160.
Jolly, 36.
Jones, 8, 11, 14, 17, 20,
22, 31, 33, 37, 37, 42,
44, 45, 47, 50, 51, 52,
53, 53, 54, 54, 54, 57,
58, 59, 69, 79, 83, 86,
88, 91, 97, 101, 103,
112, 115, 118, 118,
123, 125, 133, 149,
149, 152, 154, 168,
168.
Joneles, 10.
Jordan, 21, 51, 119, 160.
Joslyn, 76, 113, 127.
Jowler, 132.
Judd, 122.
Judson, 121.
Juggell, 103.
Jupper, 158.
Justice, 86.

K.

Kall, 86.
Kalloway, 129
Kane, 58.
Kantanel, 161.
Kaske, 103.
Kassey, 148.
Kastler, 148.
Kathan, 26.
Katterman. 124.
Kauffman, 76, 132, 168.
Kavanah, 168.
Kayhill, 38.
Kearns, 73.
Kearney, 132.
Keaney, 133.
Keas, 157.
Kebol, 130.
Kebathkey, 153.
Keefouver, 139.
Kedont, 92.

Keen, 64, 115.
Keecher, 87, 158.
Keeler, 98.
Xeer, 139.
Keech, 164.
Keggs, 20.
Kegan, 62.
Keily, 36.
Kein, 87.
Kelley, 39, 46, 65, 101,
122, 132, 134, 151.
Kellum, 42, 44.
Kelle, 65.
Keller, 70, 120, 164, 166.
Kelsey, 81.
Kelly, 85, 90, 100, 168,
119.
Kelty, 114.
Kellogg, 152.
Kemple, 5.
Kemney, 27.
Kemp, 110, 122, 162.
Kemmell, 133.
Kemper, 147.
Kent, 5, 85.
Kennedy, 13, 72, 110, 137,
153, 163, 168.
Kendell, 43.
Kenyon, 63.
Kendrick, 67, 96.
Kending, 77.
Kensey, 80.
Keny, 89.
Kendig, 94.
Kenned, 109.
Kendrickson, 110.
Kenon, 159.
Kenny, 161.
Kepner, 32.
Kephart, 162.
Kern, 93, 130.
Kerr, 155.
Kestry, 121.
Ketcham, 121, 130.
Keys, 115.
Kidd, 6.
Kiein, 125.
Kifford, 68.
Kiger, 94.
Kilear, 8.
Kileneed, 9.
Kilgore, 29.
Kilburn, 54.
Kilbun, 74.
Killink, 78.
Kilroy, 107.
Killer, 111.
Kimbol, 18.
Kimberlain, 29.
Kimball, 32, 135.

Kime, 134.
Kimer, 138.
King, 10, 13, 31, 45, 47,
91, 94, 104, 106, 113,
119, 138, 140, 165,
167.
Kinaman, 28.
Kinsey, 43.
Kinter, 66.
Kinney, 74, 84, 136.
Kinsel, 126.
Kinlow, 150.
Kinna, 168.
Kirwin, 19.
Kirby, 19.
Kirkpatrick, 32, 66.
Kirker, 35.
Kirk, 82, 86, 121.
Kitchen, 10, 103.
Kite, 31.
Klander, 98.
Klenheen, 111.
Klice, 61.
Klingensmith, 72.
Knapp, 17, 107, 166.
Knight, 27, 29, 44, 66, 90.
Knightlonge, 74.
Knoble, 71.
Knoid, 74.
Knowles, 97, 102.
Knox, 106.
Knowse, 163, 165.
Koering, 10.
Koenig, 151.
Koffman, 168.
Kohler, 111.
Kohl, 133.
Koil, 28.
Koomtz, 13.
Koothman, 37.
Kooker, 109.
Koothe, 111.
Korn, 37.
Krantz, 32.
Kratz, 39.
Kramer, 69, 93, 126, 132.
Kraft, 74, 132.
Kremer, 29, 94.
Krill, 20.
Kright, 44.
Krizer, 41.
Krieg, 111.
Krisel, 126.
Kubler, 133.
Kubn, 59, 75.
Kulefish, 123.
Kunkle, 33, 34, 35.
Kupferschum, 120.
Kurchner, 165.
Kutz, 6.

L.

L——, 123.
L——ll, 9.
Laaman, 122.
Labar, 138.
Labdcy, 9.
Laclaid, 19.
Lachard, 35.
Lacber, 77.
Lacttchell, 97.
Ladin, 5.
Ladd, 6, 20.
Ladoo, 66.
La Duke, 91.
Laguay, 62.
La Grange, 118.
Lahn, 133.
Laird, 72, 81, 118.
Lakeman, 64.
Lake, 86.
Lamoreau, 6, 20.
Laman, 22.
La Motte, 30.
Lambert, 36.
Lamney, 77.
Lamance, 78.
Lamb, 77, 79, 104, 123, 126, 136.
Lamer, 87.
Lamklerer, 90.
Lambrecht, 100.
Lamont, 165.
Lane, 23, 58, 62, 65, 71, 95, 102.
Lansey, 24.
Lander, 43.
Lananly, 80.
Lang, 100.
Lantz, 111.
Lanser, 116.
Lapham, 102.
Laplant, 130.
Lassing, 47.
Laskin, 54.
Lashine, 116.
Lattin, 28.
Lathrope, 30.
Latenhouse, 57.
Later, 78.
Laughbaugh, 104.
Launsbury, 167.
Laven, 58.
Lawson, 18, 118, 158.
Lawless, 21, 88.
Lawrence, 22, 30, 33, 33, 78, 112, 131.
Laws, 48, 56.
Lawner, 81.
Layfield, 17.

Leach, 13, 96, 139
Lear, 39.
Leavall, 51.
Leathers, 64.
Leahman, 103.
Lcabey, 131.
Lebold, 104.
Lecompt, 34.
Leddis, 122.
Lee, 17, 45, 50, 56, 59, 72, 74, 85, 87, 98, 117, 125, 131.
Leech, 89.
Leemgruber, 130.
Lefler, 28.
Lefever, 52.
Leffingwell, 123.
Leggite, 13.
Leggett, 157.
Lehman, 166.
Leidsinger, 7.
Leic——, 9.
Leith, 17.
Leiby, 18.
Leitey, 19.
Leithon, 28.
Leippe, 98.
Leinhart, 108.
Leissener, 108.
Leicester, 109.
Lellage, 62.
Lemons, 118.
Lemmon, 132.
Lent, 42, 96, 116.
Lenry, 84.
Lennen, 125.
Lenosb, 152.
Leonard, 28, 78.
Leop, 97.
Leo, 121.
Leroy, 78.
Lester, 17.
Lessley, 79.
Letes, 46.
Letchard, 49.
Lever, 32.
Leve, 97.
Leville, 152.
Lewis, 5, 7, 11, 15, 18, 45, 46, 49, 52, 58, 73, 95, 107, 111, 122, 128, 134, 153, 157, 166.
Lews, 111.
Liberty, 101.
Libby, 132, 140, 147.
Licester, 109.
Lidenster, 66.
Liddell, 134.
Lilly, 31.
Lillard, 57.

Lilliestein, 88.
Limbartar, 6.
Limpner, 64.
Limbach, 129.
Ling, 8.
Linsey, 9.
Line, 9.
Linton, 39, 130.
Linger, 71.
Lindler, 76.
Linpuk, 97.
Linn, 99.
Lincoln, 104.
Lindsley, 166.
Linsley, 115.
Linburger, 123.
Linier, 148.
Linchart, 148.
Lipe, 31, 117.
Lipp, 36.
Lippy, 39.
Lisley, 73.
Little, 20, 68, 91, 96, 122, 140.
Littlefield, 60.
Litcher, 111.
Livingston, 17, 72, 108.
Lockran, 7.
Lockett, 51.
Lockey, 52.
Lockwood, 72.
Lockington, 118.
Locke, 125, 156.
Loflin, 112.
Lofteet, 118.
Logan, 14, 25, 40, 88, 99, 118.
Logherman, 66.
Logue, 103, 130.
Lolley, 165.
Lombard, 60.
Long, 40, 41, 58, 87, 93, 102, 131, 132, 136, 152.
Lonnon, 67.
Lonefield, 88.
Longhouse, 105.
Lonwry, 114.
Looker, 21.
Loop, 23.
Loomis, 91.
Loper, 155.
Lorman, 29.
Lord, 87, 132.
Losaga, 19.
Lossee, 61.
Loth, 71.
Louis, 26, 111.
Loudon, 35.
Love, 43.

Loveall, 78.
Lovell, 9, 125
Lovejoy, 149.
Lovett, 56.
Lovellen, 164.
Lowe, 24.
Lowry, 27.
Lucian, 14.
Lucas, 22, 50, 75, 114.
Luce, 157.
Lueny, 80.
Luff, 105.
Lumazette, 27.
Lunt, 119.
Lund, 124.
Lutton, 91.
Lutman, 113.
Luther, 128.
Lydeck, 151.
Lyick, 99.
Lyke, 101.
Lymons, 61.
Lyman, 68, 89.
Lynch, 38, 54, 66, 75, 85,
    122, 123, 163.
Lynn, 152.
Lyon, 92, 100.

M.

Mabenc, 22.
Mabb, 59.
Mack, 29.
Machentrutz, 87
Macky, 59.
Maclem, 67.
Maclavish, 131.
Maddron, 34.
Madrid, 58.
Maddill, 45.
Madney, 54.
Maddis, 112.
Madden, 130.
Maddison, 140.
Mader, 154.
Madigan, 157.
Magruder, 43.
Maguire, 89.
Maguany, 53.
May—te, 154.
Mahoney, 6, 119
Mahen, 37.
Mahar, 102, 131.
Main, 25.
Maine, 116.
Major, 39, 79, 108.
Maltson, 12.
Maloney, 32, 121, 151.
Malcolm, 91.

Malloy, 100, 119.
Mallin, 59.
Malsed, 64.
Malone, 71.
Manck, 83.
Mangus, 26.
Mannie, 32.
Manderville; 40.
Manning, 39, 105.
Manley, 52.
Mansfield, 106, 164.
Mansey, 64.
Manderback, 67.
Mann, 72.
Manie, 78.
Mansall, 158.
Marsh, 6, 40, 121, 140.
Martin, 6, 12, 21, 22, 23,
    25, 27, 29, 31, 32, 32,
    38, 39, 40, 41, 52, 66,
    70, 75, 79, 81, 104,
    107, 113, 114, 124,
    127, 136, 149, 153,
    163.
Marchesess, 11.
Marston, 15.
Marshall, 17, 26, 46, 56,
    58, 87, 138, 161.
Mark, 39.
Marcellus, 40.
Mary, 44.
Maraldock, 47.
Markle, 109.
Marls, 63.
Marten, 66.
Marcteller, 67.
Maril, 113.
Mars, 114.
Marquis, 122.
Marvin, 127.
Margnet, 135.
Marland, 148.
Martingale, 160.
Mason, 10, 40, 59, 63, 74,
    99, 113, 133, 151, 160.
Mastaden, 35.
Masher, 40.
Maston, 62.
Mascar, 97.
Mattleber, 82.
Matthews, 14, 50, 95, 101.
Matt, 84.
Mattree, 87.
Matson, 36.
Mattis, 37.
Matncy, 47.
Mattix, 56.
Mattixin, 66.
Matton, 118.
Matteson, 129.

Mattox, 150.
Manley, 152.
Maxfield, 7.
Maxwell, 58, 61.
Max, 116.
Maxin, 156.
May, 12, 138, 157.
Maynader, 22.
Mayhan, 25.
Mays, 25, 111, 118.
Maynard, 87.
Mayor, 44, 50, 159.
Mayhuc, 111.
Mayle, 80.
Maylin, 138.
Mayer, 160.
McAllester, 64, 115, 115.
McAuliffe, 88.
McArdle, 96.
McAvoy, 113.
McBride, 42, 52, 155.
McConnanckel, 5.
McCluncy, 10.
McClure, 13, 42.
McCay, 18.
McClintock, 20.
McCarthy, 24, 24, 78, 102.
McCaully, 29, 102.
McClausland, 88.
McClain, 216.
McCombs, 50.
McCoy, 44, 130.
McCarey, 48.
McCann, 52.
McCarty, 63, 93, 96, 100.
McCorson, 72.
McClintic, 74.
McCaffery, 77.
McCannon, 79.
McClarry, 82.
McCloskey, 83.
McCaffarty, 87.
McCallister, 94.
McConskin, 99.
McClintock, 99.
McCorison, 99.
McCormick, 100.
McClore, 101.
McCall, 109.
McCauley, 112.
McCaubey, 125.
McCornish, 67.
McConnell, 120.
McConkey, 127.
McCantry, 134
McClernan, 135.
McCust, 137.
McCulloch, 140.
McDewell, 8.
McDaniels, 12, 14.

P INDEX.

McDonald, 17, 22, 79, 107, 116, 132, 154.
McDaniel, 22, 109.
McDowell, 25, 55.
McDonnell, 53, 122.
McDade, 123.
McElfresh, 25.
McEty, 52.
McElwee, 67.
McElvey, 111.
McElhenny, 123.
McEmory, 152.
McElroy, 157, 157.
McFerrin, 21.
McFarland, 23, 101, 163.
McFaller, 25.
McFall, 110.
McGinnes, 5.
McGlathray, 11.
McGlathing, 14.
McGee, 19, 28, 55, 121.
McGrew, 23.
McGill, 25, 151.
McGowan, 30.
McGray, 54, 151.
McGuire, 70, 100, 106.
McGown, 76.
McGinnis, 86.
McGlannel, 86.
McGratn, 86.
McGlaughlin, 89.
McGrady, 136.
McGilberry, 138.
McGunnigle, 147.
McHarry, 110.
McHose, 152.
McIntire, 51, 53, 63, 129.
McIntosh, 123.
McKinsey, 6.
McKussick, 39.
McKiffe, 66.
McKenney, 73, 127.
McKinney, 77.
McKissick, 83.
McKeen, 102, 120.
McKuhn, 107.
McKee, 112.
McKeil, 123.
McKenna, 127, 139.
McKinstry, 129.
McKown, 161.
McKey, 165.
McLean, 33, 136.
McLaughlin, 33, 134, 165.
McLane, 48, 51, 52, 153.
McLaughern, 67.
McLuerr, 75.
McMullen, 13, 73.
McManey, 25.
McMara, 35.

McMann, 88, 113.
McMillan, 102, 136.
McManus, 103, 105.
McMinen, 128.
McNeal, 19.
McNamara, 71, 129.
McNasby, 94.
McNulty, 134.
McOrmick, 81.
McPown, 65.
McPhetridge, 113.
McQuistian, 95.
McSherler, 78.
McSam, 73.
McTaggart, 112.
McWilliams, 65.
Mead, 12, 14, 37, 39, 57, 71, 98.
Meagher, 134, 135.
Meachan, 160.
Meckley, 109.
Medley, 46.
Medowes, 101.
Meghan, 24.
Megent, 165.
Meier, 34.
Meiley, 154.
Meisenhelder, 161.
Meng, 6.
Menedill, 28.
Menger, 26.
Meneker, 48.
Mentor, 76.
Merrick, 28, 43.
Merson, 74.
Merritt, 75, 142, 148, 153.
Mercer, 82.
Merchant, 85.
Mertin, 88.
Mercey, 107.
Merrill, 150, 153.
Merley, 157.
Merrihew, 164.
Messer, 38, 70, 71, 88, 92.
Messick, 72, 130.
Messenger, 157.
Metcalf, 93, 102, 123.
Metz, 114.
Meure, 97.
Meyers, 71, 73, 75.
Meyon, 73.
Meyer, 83, 84.
Michel, 8, 56.
Mickerson, 38.
Michals, 29, 137.
Michels, 22.
Michael, 73, 154.
Michelfelder, 75.
Mickey, 78.
Middleton, 21.

Midget, 126.
Miller, 5, 7, 13, 18, 20, 22, 22, 31, 32, 34, 37, 38, 39, 42, 49, 52, 58, 65, 70, 72, 73, 80, 89, 93, 98, 104, 105, 109, 110, 111, 115, 118, 121, 121, 124, 131, 146, 158, 163, 163, 163.
Mills, 12, 14, 28, 151.
Milcham, 32.
Miles, 52, 88, 153.
Milburn, 58.
Millard, 62.
Milford, 71.
Milton, 93.
Millinger, 95.
Millingan, 100.
Minor, 24.
Miner, 49.
Mines, 92.
Minton, 113.
Minick, 115.
Minke, 140.
Minie, 158.
Mintzer, 162.
Mirim, 91.
Misinger, 37.
Mitchell, 30, 33, 44, 49, 54, 55, 59, 70, 75, 79, 84, 88, 122.
Mitterman, 78.
Mites, 87.
Moat, 24.
Mock, 134.
Modesett, 38.
Moden, 76.
Moise 66.
Moman, 48.
Montrison, 6.
Mongee, 13.
Monroe, 18, 38, 52, 76, 98.
Mongomery, 20, 98.
Monks, 160.
Moores, 18.
Mooney, 26, 161, 161.
Mooler. 80.
Moon, 129.
Moore, 20, 29, 33, 35, 36, 42, 45, 53, 59, 73, 78, 111, 114, 118, 131, 147, 153, 153, 158, 164, 166.
Morgan, 18, 41, 47, 57, 66, 74, 125, 129, 134, 134.
Morehead, 18, 116.
Morrison, 21, 89, 106, 135.
Moriarty, 29.

Morey, 30, 107.
Morris, 31, 81, 104, 123, 133, 167.
Morton, 32, 49, 60, 84, 166.
Moriarery, 35.
Morman, 54, 152.
Morse, 59, 71, 80, 151, 154.
Morte, 60.
Morely, 73.
Morehouse, 85, 86.
More, 97, 140.
Morrill, 126.
Moreland, 136.
Moss, 5, 56, 129.
Mosier, 18.
Mosby, 48.
Mostshler, 12.
Moulard, 162.
Mous, 167.
Mower, 66, 79.
Mowry, 72.
Moyer, 103, 136
Muckel, 20.
Muchman, 36.
Muddy, 106.
Mugan, 63.
Mulky, 9.
Mullican, 23.
Mullins, 24, 166.
Mullory, 58. .
Mulfar, 110.
Mulligan, 113, 120.
Mulless, 127.
Mullen, 149.
Mumford, 56.
Mummert, 98.
Munch, 53.
Munson, 95.
Munster, 132.
Munroe, 138.
Munjer, 40.
Munchman, 151.
Mundy, 153.
Murphy, 25, 27, 32, 60, 74, 80, 89, 97, 101, 129, 131.
Murduff, 40.
Murray, 60, 76, 112, 120, 147, 161.
Mushlee, 89.
Musgrave, 101.
Myers, 6, 12, 35, 39, 44, 58, 61, 70, 72, 92, 95, 98, 102, 103, 105, 117, 125, 125, 153, 157.
Myrick, 107.
Myres, 124.
Myrdale, 162.

N.

Nailom, 83.
Nally, 17.
Nalls, 40.
Nandy, 80.
Nangle, 94.
Narberger, 110.
Nashot, 77.
Nash, 81, 101, 138, 164.
Nathans, 78.
Navilligan, 160.
Nay, 27.
Neal, 19, 25, 45, 55, 128.
Nealy, 20, 53.
Neely, 21.
Neff, 127.
Negley, 26.
Neiw, 29.
Neich, 65.
Neigenfind, 91.
Neidell, 107.
Nelson, 26, 49, 50, 106, 119, 133, 153, 163.
Nelovis, 70.
Nellus, 151.
Nellis, 119.
Nephry, 82.
Neppem, 102.
Nesbern, 123.
Nethers, 13.
Nevins, 125.
Newton, 17, 108.
Newcomb, 30, 110.
Newmau, 36, 47, 66, 106, 139.
Newbert, 88.
Newell, 37, 111.
Newhall, 166.
Niblet, 48.
Nicholson, 66.
Nichols, 66.
Nichols, 95, 110, 149, 152.
Nicholy, 95.
Nicholas, 12.
Nickerson, 35.
Nickolson, 18.
Nickols, 33, 47, 54, 81.
Nie, 130.
Niles, 131.
Nixon, 133.
Noble, 28, 151.
Node, 67.
Noggle, 130.
Noise, 77.
Nolenger, 10.
Nolan, 17, 26.
Noland, 86.
North, 7, 52, 53, 57, 69, 124.

Norris, 36, 63, 157.
Nordike, 59.
Northway, 71.
Norton, 62, 84, 105, 150.
Northrop, 164.
Norwood, 138.
Noyes, 70.
Nuby, 97.
Nudham, 5.
Nugent, 135.
Nulf, 103.
Nuller, 122.
Nun, 54.
Nunumaker, 108.
Nutt, 74.
Nutter, 105.

O.

Oad——, 142.
Oaks, 20, 21, 107.
Oakey, 56.
Oakley, 148, 164.
O'Brien, 15, 33.
Oberly, 76.
Ocherlin, 20.
O'Connor, 33.
O'Connell, 101.
O'Donnell, 31, 120.
Odum, 45.
Odurgee, 51.
Offort, 50.
Offord, 149.
Ogden, 24, 64.
Ogburn, 40.
Ohlhues, 136.
Oipper, 5.
Oloden, 6.
O'Lury, 8.
Oliver, 18, 70, 114, 148.
Olsien, 30.
Omiston, 62.
Oman, 64.
Onder, 46.
O'Neill, 63, 128, 161.
Oniveller, 93.
Orcutt, 153.
Ormby, 34.
Ormsby, 112.
Orne, 86.
Orr, 53, 79.
Ortell, 69.
Os——, 9.
Osborne, 38, 41, 63, 70, 88, 88, 91, 104.
Osgood, 107.
Osterman, 23.
Ostrander, 73.
Ost, 158.
Osman, 158.

Otterson, 74.
Ousley, 48.
Owins, 133.
Owens, 150, 154.
Owen, 163.

P.

P——, 155.
Pace, 151.
Pack, 39.
Packard, 107.
Padgers, 76.
Page, 25, 54, 108, 110.
Paine, 79, 140.
Palemtory, 129.
Palmer, 6, 11, 43, 84.
Palmerston, 86.
Pankers, 67.
Panstle, 108.
Parey, 118.
Parish, 153, 158.
Park, 25, 36, 114, 156.
Parker, 17, 29, 32, 34, 40, 44, 48, 51, 56, 57, 66, 79, 95, 135, 138, 168.
Parkerson, 60.
Parkins, 66.
Parks, 43.
Parmelee, 137.
Parmer, 57.
Parmeter, 14.
Parrent, 121.
Parris, 165.
Parsage, 106.
Parslon, 156.
Parsner, 81.
Parsons, 35, 105, 130, 133, 149.
Parter, 46.
Partlen, 103.
Partridge, 70, 157.
Pasmer, 162.
Passmore, 125.
Paterman, 30.
Patterson, 27, 43, 55, 127, 135, 163.
Pattison, 40.
Pattet, 80.
Patton, 10, 34, 55, 91, 149, 162, 165.
Patrick, 25, 57.
Paul, 5, 39.
Paulson, 55.
Payne, 19, 154.
Paynter, 129.
Peabody, 90.
Peacher, 109.
Peack, 31.
Peacock, 92.

Peagant, 132.
Peakring, 8.
Pearcy, 121.
Peard, 111.
Pearson, 26, 83, 86, 110.
Pease, 71, 75, 104, 152.
Peassall, 123.
Peck, 38, 94, 101, 108, 125, 166, 167.
Pedrick, 52.
Peer, 85.
Peet, 67.
Pegt, 70.
Pell, 115.
Pelton, 73, 98, 153.
Pempers, 133.
Pencill, 148.
Pendleton, 60, 164.
Pennell, 101.
Pentland, 40.
Pepper, 154.
Perden, 139.
Pergh, 72.
Perkins, 27, 86, 90, 99, 105, 127.
Pero, 106.
Perriga, 110.
Perrine, 71.
Perry, 50, 79, 109, 142, 149, 157.
Persales, 89.
Person, 28.
Pessley, 78.
Peters, 51, 102, 152.
Peterson, 22.
Petffer, 51.
Pethord, 112.
Petollo, 91.
Pettibone, 24.
Pettijilu, 6.
Pettis, 33.
Pettit, 137.
Peulis, 99.
Phaler, 99.
Phelp, 163.
Phelps, 27, 132, 163.
Phile, 33.
Philbrick, 127.
Phillips, 19, 24, 29, 30, 41, 55, 57, 82, 84, 88, 115, 131, 133, 161.
Philipson, 94.
Philpit, 113.
Phiney, 71.
Phippen, 79.
Phipps, 76.
Phœnex, 165.
Phonax, 62.
Pibbles, 22.
Pien, 99.

Pierce, 8, 24, 74, 107, 109, 112.
Pierkerson, 63.
Pierson, 21, 92, 115.
Piggeny, 107.
Pigman, 39.
Pike, 95.
Pilcher, 137.
Pickney, 61.
Pinkham, 64, 90.
Pinson, 63.
Pinter, 125.
Pipkins, 83.
Pitt, 55.
Platt, 96.
Plrugh, 82.
Plum, 22.
Plummer, 47, 132.
Plump, 24.
Plunkett, 23, 120.
Plyly, 20.
Pocket, 84.
Poke, 119.
Poleman, 29.
Palla——, 152.
Pollard, 100, 128.
Pollock, 134.
Polston, 55.
Pomeroy, 104.
Ponstler, 33.
Pool, 18, 127, 131.
Poolex, 124.
Pope, 96.
Porney, 85.
Port, 127.
Porter, 28, 76, 82, 100, 123, 150, 163.
Posey, 153.
Possey, 47.
Post, 121.
Poster, 39.
Potsgrove, 113.
Potter, 8, 12, 38, 60, 62, 69, 84, 112.
Pottit, 113.
Potts, 122, 161.
Powell, 18, 52, 77, 119.
Powers, 32, 78, 113, 160.
Poyles, 115.
Prafest, 83.
Pratcliff, 24.
Pratt, 130, 132.
Preble, 27.
Presby, 127.
Prescott, 60, 89, 106.
Presley, 17, 18, 40, 41.
Prestley, 24.
Preston, 162.
Price, 47, 50, 82, 99, 116.
Pridea, 55.

Priest, 17.
Pritchard, 71.
Prithen, 74.
Prizzce, 132.
Proctor, 41, 52, 154.
Prooser, 74.
Proud, 30, 136.
Prout, 128.
Pryor, 73.
Pugh, 72.
Purdy, 35, 157, 166.
Purnell, 97.
Pursell, 26.
Purval, 80.
Putnam, 13, 14, 51, 83, 104, 123.
Putney, 120, 130.
Putt, 14.
Puttin, 62.
Pye, 107.
Pyersin, 8.
Pyle, 72.

Q.

Quackenbush, 66.
Quay, 163.
Queen, 43.
Quigley, 93, 128.
Quillian, 26.
Quinn, 38, 95.
Quinby, 28.
Quindar, 100.

R.

Raap, 28.
Rabb, 9.
Raber, 148.
Racey, 109.
Rachner, 126.
Radsell, 12.
Rafferty, 107.
Raines, 110.
Ralmstine, 124.
Ramer, 24.
Ramson, 37.
Ramsden, 152.
Rancliff, 22.
Randall, 54, 96, 155, 161.
Rankin, 125, 159.
Rand, 148.
Rarick, 103.
Rasbeck, 63.
Rattiff, 63.
Ratwell, 94.
Ravelle, 79.
Rawden, 32.
Rawlston, 34.
Rawson, 106, 113, 153.

Ray, 20, 31, 65, 79, 107.
Raymond, 31, 55, 57, 61, 80, 106.
Raynor, 112.
Read, 22, 147, 158.
Reames, 65.
Readingler, 70.
Reasure, 118.
Reader, 151.
Rearden, 158.
Recom, 6.
Redlich, 15.
Reder, 17.
Reddicke, 47.'
Redmond, 99, 130.
Rees, 42.
Reed, 22, 46, 48, 49, 50, 54, 61, 65, 66, 72, 86, 86, 94, 95, 96, 114, 160, 161.
Reeghard, 70.
Reeves, 35, 55.
Reedy, 95.
Reid, 25, 104.
Reicor, 79.
Reich, 81.
Reiman, 78.
Reihsnider, 91.
Reifer, 104.
Remine, 89.
Renklid, 43.
Rendell, 52.
Renter, 114.
Reortburn, 6.
Repler, 82.
Repel, 112.
Rese, 70.
Restolick, 71.
Respick, 113.
Reul, 97.
Reynolds, 25, 26, 62, 78, 100, 120, 128, 133, 134, 139.
Rhedan, 113.
Rhodes, 40, 63, 70, 95, 165, 168.
Rhudy, 50.
Rhyne, 25.
Ribbans, 158.
Ricket, 7, 92.
Richards, 7, 22, 61, 67, 114, 114, 120, 152, 164.
Rice, 49, 67, 94, 159.
Rickey, 27.
Richardson, 31, 49, 49, 63, 87, 100, 109, 121, 133, 135, 158.
Rickelson, 62.
Richwen, 104.

Rich, 107, 125.
Richmond, 126.
Ricthmiller, 137.
Rick, 164.
Ridg—, 6.
Rider, 50, 166.
Ridneer, 160.
Riggs, 31, 46.
Riggle, 34.
Rigers, 44.
Rikard, 87.
Riley, 55, 70, 85, 139, 160.
Rimpell, 128.
Rincheart, 18.
Rinhart, 30, 71.
Ringer, 33.
Riner, 104.
Rinkler, 114.
Ringler, 139.
Ringold, 160.
Ripley, 115, 123.
Risling, 6.
Risley, 50.
Risinger, 68, 162.
Rittenhouse, 24.
Ritchey, 28.
Ritz, 67.
Ritter, 72, 140.
Ritchie, 89, 129.
Rix, 10.
Roach, 40, 48, 61, 64, 99.
Robe, 8.
Robertson, 19, 20, 21, 28, 73.
Robinson, 24, 27, 30, 35, 43, 45, 49, 49, 56, 60, 76, 91, 94, 99, 112, 118, 122, 135, 149, 152.
Roberts, 46, 47, 54, 57, 76, 91, 165.
Robbins, 60.
Roberson, 114.
Robison, 126.
Roberte, 164.
Rockford, 37.
Rock, 51.
Rockwell, 116.
Rodman, 162.
Roe, 32, 36, 122.
Roff, 65.
Rogers, 35, 38, 43, 54, 64, 91, 106, 114, 135, 135, 161.
Roger, 54, 136, 148.
Rogan, 122.
Rohle, 110.
Rohr, 125.
Rollardson, 41.
Rollinson, 66, 67.

Rolleston, 100.
Romey, 37.
Ronan, 109.
Roots, 47.
Root, 65.
Rood, 94, 108.
Rooney, 116.
Ropes, 136.
Rorke, 136.
Ross, 11, 55, 65, 91, 158, 165.
Roswell, 44.
Rose, 88, 100.
Rosby, 98.
Rosenstron, 117.
Rosison, 128.
Rosh, 133.
Rosenburgh, 138.
Rossett, 161.
Roth, 162.
Routt, 21.
Routh, 66.
Roubleman, 130.
Rouser, 152.
Rowe, 10, 22, 23, 83, 99, 111, 138, 162.
Rowen, 53.
Rowlins, 87.
Rowley, 87.
Rowne, 112.
Rubley, 20.
Rucker, 153.
Rudar, 65.
Rudwick, 125.
Rudis, 163.
Ruggles, 39.
Rugg, 70.
Rullman, 83.
Rumble, 29.
Rummell, 33.
Rungin, 23, 111.
Runnington, 130.
Rupert, 68, 80.
Rupell, 71.
Russell, 26, 82, 85, 107, 124, 127, 127, 128, 133, 138.
Russ, 36, 105.
Russells, 45.
Rusk, 81.
Ruse, 97.
Rusco, 140.
Rutter, 41.
Ruth, 59.
Ruttle, 86.
Rutley, 90.
Ryan, 6, 12, 32, 87.
Ryder, 60, 124.
Ryeson, 90.
Ryerson, 120.

Ryon, 134.
Ryther, 126.

S.

Sailor, 22.
Sally, 34.
Sales, 53.
Sammer, 85.
Sams, 93.
Sampler, 129.
Sanders, 6, 23, 43, 58, 88, 152.
Sands, 49.
Sandass, 86.
Sankoff, 108.
Sandford, 121.
Sapp, 43.
Sargent, 60, 93, 122.
Sa-si-ka, 109.
Saston, 150.
Satvenson, 107.
Saunders, 11, 13, 126.
Saulbrig, 70.
Savage, 31, 89, 134.
Savley, 105.
Saville, 126.
Sawyer, 154, 157.
Saxman, 159.
Sayle, 79.
Scarr, 12.
Scandlon, 113.
Scanlan, 115.
Schaeffer, 30, 110, 122.
Schaap, 74.
Schemerhorn, 70.
Schenk, 112.
Schiefer, 35.
Schirmer, 111.
Schlotman, 9.
Schlieff, 77.
Schlosser, 113.
Schmiltz, 75.
Schmidt, 80, 148.
Schneider, 5.
Schnarel, 108.
Schoppe, 32.
Schoofs, 42.
Schonmaker, 112.
Scott, 10, 20, 24, 61, 62, 64, 68, 69, 74, 109, 109, 110, 129, 137, 150.
Scoflat, 53.
Scofield, 67.
Scotia, 68.
Scoff, 79.
Scrogan, 55.
Scrone, 166.
Scudder, 61.

Scully, 123, 158,
Sears, 64.
Seaman, 77, 112, 158.
Search, 132.
Searle, 148.
Sebastian, 50.
Sebold, 66.
Sedore, 42.
Seeler, 7.
Seebach, 94.
Seely, 162.
Seister, 7.
Seinder, 77.
Seiger, 80.
Seigel, 96, 159, 159.
Seippe, 143.
Selorick, 8.
Seley, 36.
Sellers, 75.
Sellen, 105.
Sembly, 128.
Sentance, 24.
Senay, 61.
Senn, 130.
Sepper, 82.
Setch, 98.
Setzer, 110.
Sevanders, 9.
Seville, 153.
Sewell, 106.
Seyfort, 67.
Seymour, 126.
Sharp, 5, 26, 30, 52, 81, 83, 120.
Shay, 12, 132, 157.
Shaffer, 18, 34, 72, 72, 100, 167.
Shankin, 28.
Shape, 56.
Shawgr, 65.
Sharps, 70.
Shaw, 72, 85, 139, 155
Shann, 75.
Sharo, 88.
Shafer, 94.
Shan, 95.
Shattuck, 97.
Shackles, 99.
Sharks, 104, 113.
Shantro, 121.
Shatock, 123.
Shandeum, 124.
Shaughnessy, 136.
Shau, 151, 151.
Shackle, 154.
Sheneler, 5.
Shelton, 9.
Shepperd, 13, 28, 58, 84.
Sheppard, 17, 64, 80, 86, 98, 118, 162.

Sherwood, 22, 65, 65, 105, 115.
Shemngsburg, 23
Shell, 25.
Sheetz, 29.
Shepley, 35.
Sheldon, 36, 73.
Shewell, 48.
Sheffield, 52.
Sheppston, 59.
Sherman, 61, 70, 92, 157, 165.
Sheshler, 64.
Shelly, 74.
Sherry, 75, 121.
Sheable, 87.
Sheridan, 101, 101.
Sheets, 109.
Sheckles, 150.
Shindler, 6.
Shill—, 8.
Shind, 8.
Shiltz, 26.
Shipley, 39, 124.
Shiffer, 85.
Shider, 90.
Shilling, 91.
Shields, 92.
Shillinly, 129.
Shinkle, 136.
Shlaffer, 81.
Shock, 23.
Shoper, 27.
Shove, 40, 88, 88.
Showell, 45.
Short, 47.
Shockton, 62.
Shoemaker, 78, 148.
Shoff, 91.
Shoop, 108.
Shores, 120.
Shoorod, 163.
Shriver, 23.
Shrine, 62.
Shult, 9.
Shultz, 19, 62, 79, 102, 108, 132, 136, 158.
Shumway, 33, 79, 110.
Shushell, 90.
Shupe, 103.
Shuter, 125.
Shutsman, 164.
Shutt, 164.
Shumichen, 166.
Shyenberger, 157.
Sickler, 98.
Sick, 119.
Sidler, 16.
Sidner, 29, 51.
Sidney, 43.

Sides, 95.
Siebert, 75, 162.
Siebricht, 92.
Siff, 57.
Sigler, 30.
Signal, 131.
Silverman, 87.
Silvers, 92.
Silver, 128.
Siler, 103.
Simpson, 28, 61, 71, 77, 107.
Simms, 65.
Simmers, 71.
Simmonds, 72.
Sims, 73, 150.
Simmons, 75, 77, 111, 155.
Simes, 100.
Simcox, 114.
Simons, 116, 139.
Sinniman, 81.
Sink, 133.
Sipe, 155.
Sirgent, 20.
Sirels, 165.
Sisco, 94.
Sivan, 49.
Sivens, 56.
Siarnel, 136.
Shank, 108.
Skinner, 20, 29, 64, 99.
Slater, 114.
Slade, 45, 76.
Slack, 68.
Slatterley, 78, 130.
Slayter, 98.
Slawter, 134.
Slausan, 161.
Slemond, 6.
Sledd, 48.
Sleckner, 116.
Slesser, 163.
Slim, 31.
Slidell, 167.
Slory, 6.
Sloan, 27, 110, 130.
Slout, 153.
Sly, 71.
Smallford, 37.
Small, 39, 60, 99.
Smaley, 47.
Smallon, 131.
Smart, 158.
Smith, 7, 9, 12, 14, 17, 19, 21, 25, 25, 27, 26, 28, 29, 30, 30, 31, 32, 37, 38, 38, 38, 41, 41, 45, 45, 49, 51, 52, 53, 55, 58, 61, 63, 64, 65, 66, 67, 70, 71, 71, 73, 73,

73, 75, 76, 78, 79, 80, 80, 82, 83, 83, 84, 86, 88, 90, 91, 92, 92, 94, 98, 99, 99, 100, 101, 102, 104, 105, 109, 110, 114, 123, 125, 126, 126, 126, 128, 128, 129, 131, 131, 133, 134, 135, 138, 138, 133, 138, 139, 142, 148, 148, 152, 153, 155, 155, 156, 156, 160, 161, 161, 164, 167.
Smither, 112.
Smidt, 80.
Snathel, 127.
Sneud, 92.
Snider, 19, 23
Snill, 131.
Sniveley, 165.
Snowden, 12, 47, 76.
Snooke, 18, 104.
Snow, 32, 32, 114.
Snodgrass, 73.
Soble, 98.
Somers, 36.
Somerwell, 49.
Sommermuir, 94.
Soper, 42, 59.
Sopher, 82, 87.
Sorbear, 115.
Southard, 31.
Souper, 57.
Sourwine, 93.
Southwick, 99.
Southmayde, 128.
Southworth, 134.
Soves, 58.
Sowers, 136.
Spankey, 24.
Spalding, 51, 55, 133, 148
Sparrow, 71.
Spantler, 131.
Spees, 7.
Speer, 13.
Spencer, 19, 63, 69, 81, 126.
Sperry, 26.
Speel, 80.
Speays, 46.
Speen, 57.
Spence, 67.
Spells, 77.
Spellman, 157.
Spear, 165.
Spiller, 43.
Spioney, 28.
Spingteen, 63.
Spiker, 161.

Spoteathe, 82.
Sportes, 92.
Sprague, 6, 29, 33, 34, 60, 61.
Spraight, 41.
Springsloyer, 83.
Sprecker, 84.
Sprowl, 86.
Sprouts, 90.
Springstead, 110.
Squeers, 114.
Starkweather, 6, 62.
Stackhouse, 22.
Starkson, 25.
Stanley, 28, 55, 104.
Staples, 34.
Starks, 58.
Stack, 65.
Stafford, 70.
Stahl, 70.
Stanton, 74, 102, 138, 149.
Stark, 83.
Stallman, 96.
Staysa, 101.
Stanchfield, 104.
Statea, 119.
Stacy, 126.
Stackpole, 130.
Stall, 132.
Starr, 151.
Stephens, 5, 43, 123, 135.
Stephenson, 11.
Stewart, 19, 72, 82, 85, 89, 91, 113, 116, 120, 135, 164, 167.
Steward, 21, 43, 51, 91.
Stevens, 25, 48, 72, 98, 111, 118, 122, 124, 134, 134, 151.
Steele, 31, 134.
Stedding, 36.
Stevenson, 56, 76, 82, 92, 95, 103, 108.
Sterling, 57, 162.
Steadings, 63.
Steepy, 68.
Steeles, 81.
Stearns, 95, 110, 150.
Steinbach, 98.
Stein, 98.
Steadman, 103.
Steingingle, 112.
Stenner, 128.
Steelhamer, 136.
Steller, 139.
Stiles, 9, 21.
Stilton, 40.
Stickert, 28.
Stickle, 68.
Stillwell, 71.

Stines, 122.
Stininger, 124.
Stine, 148.
Stone, 26, 44, 52, 78, 93, 120, 124, 135, 140, 148.
Stonifer, 29.
Stowell, 35, 55.
Stovell, 49.
Stoller, 63.
Stockwell, 64.
Stoddart, 71.
Stockley, 77.
Stoutfer, 79.
Stout, 79, 137, 167.
Stoplin, 91.
Stonebraker, 103.
Stolte, 107.
Stork, 124.
Stockton, 131.
Stornes, 135.
Stockman, 160.
Stoly, 163.
Strange, 18, 147.
Strand, 31.
Straser, 80.
Stratton, 90, 154.
Straka, 111.
Strahan, 130.
Strall, 136.
Straney, 161.
Strectinwater, 16.
Street, 91.
Streeter, 112, 113.
Strickland, 21, 85.
Strickfield, 47.
Stringwood, 58.
Strout, 27.
Strong, 62, 78, 135, 156.
Strohn, 111.
Strouse, 161.
Strutts, 25.
Struler, 111.
Strunk, 122.
Stryker, 103.
Stump, 138, 162.
Studt, 77.
Sturtevean, 86.
Stull, 103.
Studtman, 124.
Stutie, 134.
Stutdell, 151.
Stuart, 162.
Styes, 5.
Suffridge, 19.
Sufferage, 20.
Sullivan, 60, 70, 73, 85, 121, 123, 132, 133, 154, 158, 166.
Sulud, 92.

Summer, 10, 39.
Sumkins, 63.
Sumner, 97.
Summerville, 166.
Surface, 24.
Surtyam, 71.
Sutherlin, 23.
Sutton, 41, 47.
Sutter, 41.
Swan, 24, 46, 166.
Swaize, 41.
Swartz, 63, 113.
Swasey. 78.
Swab, 157.
Sweaney, 17.
Sweeney, 40, 98, 164, 166.
Sweet, 63.
Swede, 86.
Swift, 79, 103, 103, 106.
Sykes, 103.
Syme, 131.
Sympson, 20.

T.

T, 10, 86.
Taber, 27.
Tackeling, 77.
Tainter, 120.
Talley, 30.
Talmson, 43.
Tales, 58.
Talmadge, 100.
Tampied, 162.
Tankerly, 21.
Tanner, 37, 43, 140.
Tannings, 53.
Tann, 83.
Tapman, 21.
Tarbox, 13.
Tarham, 21.
Tart, 91.
Tasco, 29.
Tatter, 6.
Tate, 26, 32, 51.
Taylor, 6, 7, 22, 26, 28, 36, 40, 40, 41, 43, 44, 47, 55, 57, 59, 69, 91, 94, 98, 103, 108, 150, 154.
Taytler, 166.
Teeter, 148.
Teft, 123.
Tellman, 43,
Telyea, 93.
Temple, 139.
Tenny, 137.
Terleson, 111.
Terry, 16, 37, 47, 59.
Terrill, 27.
Terchman, 127.

Tester, 40.
Tewksberry, 136.
Thatcher, 19.
Thayes, 150, 164.
Thacker, 164.
Theller, 20.
Theisel, 140.
Thim—, 9.
Thiebold, 80.
Thorp, 7, 66, 119, 168.
Thompston, 11.
Thorn, 18, 66.
Thomas, 21, 26, 28, 30,
 33, 35, 36, 40, 41, 43,
 44, 45, 49, 49, 49, 49,
 50, 52, 54, 54, 57, 74,
 87, 90, 94, 94, 98, 98,
 105, 105, 106, 115,
 118, 119, 121, 131,
 139, 440, 152.
Thompson, 43, 46, 47, 50,
 50, 54, 60, 65, 72, 73.
 74, 75, 81, 93, 112,
 133, 138, 150.
Thomberg, 53
Tholkeim, 108.
Thurlow, 29.
Thurston, 60.
Tibbit, 7.
Tibbits, 18.
Tibbets, 94, 104.
Tibos, 129.
Tiche, 113.
Tickenor, 153.
Tidmarsh, 88.
Tidabach, 163.
Tifreld, 60.
Tiff, 87
Tifl, 106.
Tiffany, 123.
Tighe, 112.
Tilley, 44.
Tilford, 61.
Tillman, 83.
Tinkpunner, 6.
Tinker, 18, 81.
Tines, 44.
Titus, 132.
Tobias, 105, 111, 167.
Tobs, 129.
Todd, 30, 33, 46.
Tolby, 86.
Toland, 147.
Tomsen, 9.
Tomkins, 89, 128.
Tonsay, 130.
Toole, 35.
Toothaker, 60.
Tooney, 62.
Toomey, 121.

Torfe, 100.
Townsend, 14, 32, 53, 100,
 131.
Town, 84.
Travers, 42.
Travis, 25, 151.
Trask, 53, 60.
Trahern, 73.
Tracy, 95, 105, 136, 139.
Trail, 22.
Tres—, 10.
Trent, 28.
Treville, 73.
Trees, 88.
Tremper, 98.
Trimpert, 8.
Tripp, 35, 62, 133.
Trivet, 133.
Tribby, 162.
Troxel, 103.
Troy, 109.
Trout, 121, 151.
Truelock, 20.
Trun, 29.
Trusler, 36.
Trumbull, 141.
Tryon, 79.
Trym, 99.
Tubbs, 77.
Tucker, 19, 35, 38, 56, 56.
 57, 84, 100, 100.
Tuck, 151.
Tuestay, 88.
Tuick, 93.
Tully, 42, 94.
Tupper, 106.
Turner, 19, 30, 48, 48, 52.
 55, 56, 65, 76, 112.
Turgan, 75.
Tuskin, 24.
Tuttle, 71.
Tutler, 81.
Twines, 59.
Twick, 164.
Twyford, 128.
Tyler, 124, 153.
Typkie, 140.
Tyson, 150.

U.

Ulric, 133.
Ulster, 116.
Ultz, 42.
Undershover, 27.
Upclier, 55.
Updike, 33.
Upton, 53, 114.
Upwright, 86.

Urshler, 81.
Usher, 52.

V.

Vacht, 69.
Vahn, 136.
Vallette, 128.
Valentine, 8, 56, 58, 118.
 148.
Vamer, 50.
Van——, 139.
Vanarsdale, 26.
Van Auken, 155.
Van Alstine, 157, 157.
Van Buren, 54, 65.
Van Buskirk, 128.
Van Canborough, 19.
Vance, 136.
Van der Bing, 34.
Van der Grome, 57.
Van der Hird, 69.
Van der Poole, 87.
Van Driver, 127.
Van Dike, 128.
Van Fleet, 26.
Van Goden, 62.
Vanison, 44.
Van Lack, 9.
Van Leer, 28.
Van Loom, 42.
Van Martin, 53.
Van Nostrand, 39.
Van Nest, 76.
Vanoute, 102.
Vansel, 6.
Van Steinburg, 79.
Van Vound, 62.
Van Wickle, 42.
Van Wan, 55.
Van Weet, 98.
Varney, 27, 51.
Varlett, 62.
Vashier, 89
Vatang, 33.
Vaughan, 43.
Vauneler, 135.
Veislette, 132.
Venman, 9.
Venerable, 48.
Vernes, 53.
Verill, 74.
Vera, 79.
Vergneray, 103.
Vesne, 153.
Vinal, 33.
Vinegar, 48.
Vincent, 19, 31, 44, 80.
Volk, 33.
Voorhees, 87, 100.

Voyerity, 87, 100.
Vulso, 7.
Vunandeslin, 10.
Vungan, 89.

W.

W——, 123, 123.
Wabbs, 150.
Wade, 19, 74, 90, 98, 157, 158.
Wadleigh, 102.
Wadhams, 150.
Wagenhauser, 12.
Wagner, 58, 70, 73, 86, 111, 113, 120.
Waggle, 25.
Wags, 114.
Waggoner, 124.
Wait, 53.
Waits, 165.
Waitnight, 128.
Walters, 102.
Walston, 50, 71.
Walker, 7, 9, 30, 42, 45, 63, 69, 83, 89, 131, 132, 133, 151, 163.
Waltch, 10.
Wallace, 21, 30, 53, 81, 85, 86, 104, 106, 129, 134, 135, 148, 163, 165.
Wallis, 23.
Walter, 58.
Waldren, 27.
Wales, 28.
Walsh, 61.
Waldrum, 70.
Waltz, 74, 103.
Walmer, 111.
Walls, 115.
Waltons, 122.
Walling, 125.
Wallraven, 126.
Wall, 137, 150.
Walk, 138.
Waldon, 166.
Wambyer, 70.
Wants, 29.
Wanfield, 136.
Ward, 8, 15, 18, 63, 71, 95, 108, 129, 139, 150, 161.
Warren, 12, 29, 37, 48, 95, 150, 163.
Warner, 14, 84, 139, 154.
Warden, 80.
Warren, 12, 29, 37, 48, 95, 150, 163.
Warring, 33.
Wardman, 33.

Wardrad, 76.
Ware, 94, 109.
Warrenco, 116.
Washburn, 7, 26, 37, 38.
Washington, 47, 50, 50, 50, 82.
Wasson, 31.
Wasser, 163.
Watherspoon, 5.
Wattenmyer, 143.
Watson, 48, 51, 51, 60, 68, 75, 105, 126, 151, 164.
Watkins, 50.
Waters, 25, 53.
Wather, 58.
Waterhouse, 83.
Waxwood, 36.
Waycox, 8.
Wayer, 53.
Wayman, 39, 40, 73.
Way, 94.
Weaver, 26, 54, 68, 69, 80, 98, 109, 115, 118, 149.
Weather, 46.
Weatha—, 126.
Weater, 165.
Weber, 7, 91, 137.
Webster, 18, 45, 104, 114, 130, 165.
Webb, 63, 71, 140.
Weddles, 18.
Weeber, 7.
Weeks, 99, 106.
Weed, 125.
Weeker, 164.
Weiser, 114.
Weiler, 131.
Welch, 5, 12, 23, 30, 36, 75, 75, 86, 91, 115, 151.
Wells, 11, 31, 67, 72, 81.
Wellington, 19.
Welsh, 28, 95, 97.
Welling, 36.
Welford, 43.
Welton, 95.
Wellman 107.
Weller, 150.
Wentworth, 61, 88, 118.
Wenkle, 82.
West, 5, 29, 65, 72, 94, 165.
Westle, 27.
Wesley, 30.
Westbrook, 31.
Westcoat, 36, 114.
Wesgate, 36.
Wescott, 41, 90, 116.
Western, 102.
Weston, 83.

Westmoreland, 103.
Wessie, 167.
Wetherill, 59.
Whaley, 35.
Wharton, 37.
Whatford, 57.
Wheeler, 7, 17, 25, 32, 45, 85.
Wheater, 27.
Wheaton, 79.
Whelpley, 148.
Whetzel, 150.
Whittim, 5.
White, 7, 14, 25, 30, 81, 38, 41, 49, 51, 56, 58, 63, 66, 82, 84, 86, 93, 118, 129, 130, 130, 130, 139, 142, 149, 150, 158, 163, 167.
Whiterae, 20.
Whitman, 34, 35, 108, 136.
Whitbeck, 36.
Whitnight, 38.
Whiting, 52, 60, 168.
Whitney, 60, 110, 147.
Whitaker, 68.
Whiteheart, 77.
Whitehall, 91.
Whitecar, 84.
Whitt, 109.
Whole, 112.
Wickert, 20.
Wicliffe, 57.
Widfodt, 99.
Widgell, 107.
Widdigar, 161.
Wieland, 68, 111.
Wigglesworth, 49.
Wiggins, 64, 149.
Willis, 6, 22, 28, 98, 113.
Wilson, 11, 14, 17, 28, 29, 30, 32, 35, 44, 45, 45, 48, 52, 54, 54, 55, 57, 58, 58, 59, 65, 66, 67, 68, 70, 91, 91, 95, 100, 101, 103, 107, 109, 112, 113, 113, 130, 136, 151, 152, 153, 158, 160.
Williams, 16, 19, 21, 23, 24, 25, 26, 28, 29, 33, 35, 44, 46, 47, 48, 50, 51, 51, 56, 56, 57, 57, 58, 62, 72, 76, 76, 78, 82, 82, 84, 90, 98, 99, 101, 102, 105, 106, 110, 117, 126, 127, 148, 149, 150, 154, 161, 167.
Wiley, 18, 101.

Wills, 18, 27.
Williamson, 19, 42, 42, 58, 138.
Wilcox, 20, 33, 69, 110, 111, 140.
Willard, 20.
Willhoit, 23.
Willett, 23, 64.
Willfong, 27.
Willetts, 59.
Willell, 40.
Willey, 64.
Willsie, 73.
Wilding, 123.
Wilday, 85, 108.
Wilkins, 156.
Wilmont, 163.
Wilbert, 165.
Wimberger, 68.
Winckler, 11.
Windson, 53.
Winkworth, 32.
Winters, 51, 89, 131, 147.
Winslow, 37, 52.
Winter, 65, 131.
Wince, 68.
Wines, 77.
Windle, 80.
Wing, 82, 148.
Winons, 87.
Winchester, 90.
Winfield, 91.
Wingrove, 132.
Winck, 139.
Wirth, 109.
Wirtehood, 161.
Wise, 10, 77, 114, 122, 157.
Wishart, 153
Witt, 44.

Witherspoon, 5, 50.
Wittmer, 10.
Witters, 35.
Withal, 35.
Wize, 21.
Wolf, 6, 34, 35, 61, 80, 125, 157.
Wold, 85.
Wolfran, 101.
Wolffer, 122.
Wonderley, 115.
Woodburn, 5.
Woolcott, 8, 148.
Wood, 13, 18, 23, 43, 72, 78, 110, 121, 130, 135,
Woods, 22, 102, 112, 153.
Woodbury, 30.
Woodmanset, 37.
Woosted, 47.
Woodhouse, 51.
Woodson, 52.
Woolheater, 80.
Woodrough, 106.
Woodruff, 106, 119, 129, 155.
Woodman, 121.
Woodcock, 133.
Woodbeck, 135.
Wooley, 151.
Woodward, 152.
Wortz, 44.
Worth, 57.
Works, 104.
Work, 127.
Wouldbridge, 69.
Wraham, 154.
Wreman, 33.
Wright, 9, 24, 29, 34, 38, 43, 45, 47, 51, 54, 59,

69. 72, 81, 85, 118, 118, 119, 139.
Writzland, 41.
Wyatt, 134.
Wyand, 135.
Wyegle, 149.
Wyman, 76.

Y.

Yager, 63.
Yarnall, 126.
Yates, 49. 152.
Yeager, 129.
Yelser, 56.
Yetton, 60.
Yodd, 23.
Yoder, 80.
Yokem, 71.
Yokers, 111.
York, 35.
Yost, 67.
Young, 11, 14, 36, 51, 66, 80, 87, 103, 109, 110, 112, 128, 137.
Yous, 43.
Youno, 109.
Yougher, 155.

Z.

Zalagke, 34.
Zaner, 92.
Zeringer, 14.
Zellhart, 28.
Zeller, 61.
Zeek, 98.
Zimmerman, 9, 45, 113.
Zimmers, 149.

www.ingramcontent.com/pod-product-compliance
Lightning Source LLC
Chambersburg PA
CBHW070915270326
41927CB00011B/2580